CHINESE CULTURE AND CHRISTIANITY

I0124446

Paul K. Chao

University Press of America,® Inc.
Lanham · Boulder · New York · Toronto · Oxford

Library of Congress Control Number: 2006920133
ISBN-13: 978-0-7618-3443-4 (paperback : alk. paper)
ISBN-10: 0-7618-3443-5 (paperback : alk. paper)

To Ms. Patria Anne (Liu) Chao

This book is dedicated to celebrate the
anniversary of William Paterson University
of Paterson 150 Years

The Author

Woman under Communism, General Hall Inc. New York
1967

Chinese Kinship. Kegan Paul; International, London 1983

Changing Geography of China. The Commercial Press Ltd.
Hong Kong 1990

Totemism and Taboo in China. Hsing Hua Publisher Ltd.
New York 1997

Table of Contents

Foreword

Chinese culture for some length has emerged as both a major field of study and of interest to a wider public. Dr. Paul Chao, Professor Emeritus, at William Paterson University has under taken in the present book to trace the origin, the development and growth of Chinese culture in the relationship with Christianity. Professor Chao regards the above study significant and relevant to use to today's world.

Professor Paul Chao has provided us in this book with an outstanding work on Chinese culture done on a people with whom he also shares a cultural heritage. He has the self-observation of a culture seen within rather than from outside.

It is important for the reader to recognize the two roots of his study; the personal experience of Chinese culture on the one hand, and the historical roots for cultural facts on the other.

An examination of the essays in this volume clearly suggests that his writings have been just as influential as his personal contacts. Professor Chao has been engaged in both teaching and research in social anthropology for about thirty years and brings undoubtedly to this project a long-standing interest and experience. Each of the essays is impeccable in conception and expression and at the same time illustrates some of more important changes in the structure and function of Chinese society.

The individual papers are widely spread in time and place, yet more often than not difficult to lay hands on, as they are not easily available in libraries. I feel that in presenting the collection of essays I am not only showing my esteem for Professor Chao, but also am providing a book which will be of great value to students to understanding Chinese culture at length for a long time to come.

William Paterson University

Chapter 1

The Marxist Doctrine and the Recent Development of the Chinese Family in Communist China

The present situation of family organization in Communist China has merited attention and aroused interest in the question of the relationship between the change in the family and its social factors. Engels' ideas on marriage and the family provided the ideal type for its formulation of family policies in Communist China. It would be appropriate to present his ideas on this issue. Engels maintained that in proportion as wealth increased, it made the man's position in the family more important than the woman's. The overthrow of mother-right was the world's historical defeat of the female sex. The man took command in the home; the woman was degraded and reduced to servitude.[1]

Our main purpose in this paper is to present and evaluate the actual development of the Chinese family system, which has demonstrated the unreality of the Marxist prediction of the "withering away" of the family institution in a socialist society.

Several difficulties attach to such a study. Although Communist China is one of the significant "test" cases with reference to Marxist doctrine, the current political situation does not permit of access to first-hand empirical data, and it becomes necessary to confine our scope to the available documents of the Communist regime and current reports of various newspapers, which might shed light on the situation of the family system. Nevertheless, we have fortunately been able to avail ourselves of original Chinese writings and similarly to examine reports in English. This allows for an accurate valuation of Communist sources.

The traditional family system was attacked by Chinese Communists. The low status of women, the traditional maltreatment of wives, daughters-in-law, and domestic maids were branded as vestiges of the evils of this family system. The attempt of the Communist regime to bring about a fundamental, drastic revolution in the family system was implemented by means of the marriage law. Its effect was to implant in the minds of people, especially of youth, new ideas regarding marriage and the family, and to dismiss the Confucian virtues and ethic of the family.

The cardinal principles of the new Marriage Law are:

1. The arbitrary and compulsory feudal marriage system, which is based upon the superiority of man over woman and ignores the children's interests, shall be abolished.
2. The New Democratic marriage system which is based on the free choice of partners, on monogamy, on equal rights for both sexes, and protection of the lawful interests of woman and children, shall be put into effect.[2]

Contained in the Marriage Law are the implications that bigamy, concubinage, child betrothal, and the exaction of marriage gifts are forbidden. Widows were encouraged to remarry. The interference of parents and the intervention of matchmakers were outlawed; husbands and wives were allotted equal rights; each of them could use his and/or her own family name. Infanticide was strictly forbidden. Children, regardless of their legitimacy, had full and equal rights. Divorce was granted when both parties consented. At present, however, in spite of the Marriage Law there has been, in reformulating family policies, a noticeable modification of the Marxist doctrine which laid the foundation of the Marriage Law. The reverse of the original policy on the family has reflected the Communist principle that a revolution always begins with a destructive phase and moves, at an appropriate time, to the constructive stage.

The Restoration of Human Relations in the Family

Filial Piety

With the establishment of the Communist Party came the negation of the value of the old family system. It contended that filial piety, the first of all virtues, made the male the head of each family. [3] However, from 1956 to 1957 the Communists began to revise in some degree their earlier policy with regard to family relationships. They contended that, despite the exploitation of filial piety on the part of the feudal ruling class, this virtue did not have to be eliminated, since it is based on human nature. The magazine *Chinese Youth* criticized young people for their disrespect towards, and non-support of, their parents. With the exception of those cases which were branded as feudal, and those cases in which a man was concerned with his parents to the exclusion of state interests, people were encouraged to show love for, and to support, their parents. [4] Furthermore the Communist effort to accelerate industrial development accounted for the re-emphasis of support for parents. The Communists conceded that the socialist programme was still in its initial stage and not all old parents could work for a living. The state would be compelled therefore to assume the obligations which ordinarily would be the responsibilities of children towards parents.[5] Again, in enforcing the support of parents as enacted in the Marriage Law the Communist Party proclaimed that it was as much an obligation and duty for a daughter-in-law to respect and support her father and mother-in-law, as it was for a son or daughter to do the same to his parents.[6] It is always virtuous to respect the aged and love the young. Sons and daughters-in-law should care for their parents, while society is responsible for supporting those old people who have no sons and daughters-in-law.[7] The Communists emphasize the role and responsibility of parents towards their children. The family is not only the place where children receive proper care in regard to their health and physical development, but also where they obtain their initial education. Since children spend most of their time at home, it is expected that they would regard their parents' behaviour as a model, and thus the parents' words, deeds and attitudes would have a far-reaching influence. Thus in the face of growing juvenile delinquency in the Chinese mainland, parents are often criticized for their negligence towards their children. This led to the re-affirmation of parental authority in relation to children.[8]

The Family Relationship
    The mode of family life at the beginning of the revolution was patterned in accordance with Marxist doctrine. Engles pointed out that private household affair would be transformed into social industry and the upbringing of children would become a public undertaking.[9] In a like manner, Lenin condemned the aspect of 'household slavery', emphasizing that no real emancipation of women was possible while they were oppressed by the 'pettiest, dirtiest, heaviest and dullest toil, that of the kitchen and of the individual family household in general'.[10] The Communists denied that conventional family life was immutable, maintaining that family lift was a product of social development.[11] Some intellectual youths objected that, deprived of the warmth and mutual affection of family life, they would be forced to solitary bachelorhood. The Communists, however, argued that the strength of family ideals became clear when one considers that human feelings are based on natural character in a socialist society.[12] Since the essential elements of family life are

the husband and wife, there still exists the ethical relationship between these two and their children. In fact, in spite of the Communist campaign against the inequality of the sexes, and the Marriage Law enforcing the equality and emancipation of women, it is conceded that the inequality of the sexes still persists.[13]

In theory the old family system has to be abrogated in line with Marxist doctrine; but in practice family relations have not been disrupted as some of the more extreme statements might suggest. It would be interesting to learn the extent to which human relations in the family are gradually being subordinated to the political driving force. Are marital love and relations valued because they are conducive to the stability of the state and thus to greater output by both as workers? Arc they valued because each personality is enriched by them? The grave indictment against a regime which dictates and interferes in people's lives is that it offers an affirmative answer to the first question. We are aware that the Chinese Communists made a considerable effort to destroy the patriarchal family system. [14] Family relations undoubtedly have been altered, but the assumption that family life, particularly between husband and wife, has been completely severed, would be misleading.

The title 'collective living',[15] if it means the disruption of marital private life, might gradually foment resentment. Mere communal eating and communal workshops did not in fact constitute collective living,[16] and hence they are not extremely disruptive of family relations. While priority in new building was given to factories, any new design for communal living remained remote. In recent years Construction Departments have built, on a trial basis, houses which would correspond to the present living standards and habits of peasants. In Miyun and in the suburbs of Peking some 2,170 concrete houses were built in place of the old rural houses built of wood.[17] Again, according to Wickbom's recent report, most of the workers in the new industries are housed in blocks of flats built by the factory concerned. Single workers are given barrack-type lodgings of the simplest possible kind. The family flats with one room or perhaps two, with a kitchen which is often shared between two, even three, families, have increased.[18] In most cases each block is made up of six houses, and hence no attention is given to the preferences of peasants of North China who liked detached houses.

Engels' basic theory in the *Origin of the Family* was that love was proclaimed as a human right, and indeed not only as a 'droit de l'homme', but also as a 'droit de la femme'.[19] Although the leading adherents of Marxist thought showed in their private lives and conduct, no inclination to what is called 'free love', this very thought has exerted a profound influence upon the attitude of youth. [20] The 1956 figure for matrimonial cases handled by the courts made up one third of civil cases, with the ratio of divorce cases particularly high. Of these cases handled by the People's court in the North River District in 1956, 12.6 per cent could be attributed to hasty marriages.[21]

Hasty marriages and the fad of marriage among young people were severely attacked in the mainland press in 1956-57. Firstly, in order to counter this abuse, the government attempted to clarify the concept of 'freedom of love'. Freedom of love should not be interpreted as meaning 'sexual freedom'. Liberation from the past sex tradition and inhibitions should by no means result in a leap into libertinism and promiscuity. In connection with freedom of love, it is interesting to note that for every Chinese woman 'physical love' has been a meaningless, negative phrase. This means that until a woman is entirely freed from past inhibitions she will not be able to adopt a receptive attitude. In other words, instead of feeling gratified with herself for having had no love in the past, she will be free to love as she pleases.[22] Secondly, the Communists endeavoured to implement the Marriage Law as a method of preventing reckless marriages. They saw it as a means towards the establishment of a new family filled with mutual love, respect, and trust. Thirdly, the Communists defined the grounds for divorce; they should be that the bond of affection between the partners had been damaged to such a degree that it could no longer be repaired. It follows that one party's determination to divorce the other party must be valid. Fourthly, a special procedure provided that the party should publish the facts and reasons for divorce in the newspapers and in the notices issued by the courts; and courts were required to collect higher fees in divorce cases. Recently *China Youth* has reported that a good number of women still maintained bourgeois ideas in the selection of a mate and were tempted by material benefits, and their goal in marriage was to be supported by their husbands. It is the belief of youth today that love is founded on money, material comfort and indulgence.[23] There was a story of a woman worker who was enticed by a well-dressed man, with a wool worsted sweater and shiny leather shoes, to be engaged to him secretly. A co-worker recognized the man, and exposed him as having a wife and five children.[24]

With regard to the actual trend of marriage and family system in China Yang Liu said:

> The traditional ideas and customs left behind by the systems of private ownership and of class exploitation do not vanish over-night with the disappearance of these systems. In our socialist society, Communist elements are growing up steadily, and at the same time there are still vestiges, though constantly diminishing ones, of the old society.[25]

The Emancipation of Women

Engels anticipated the emancipation of woman from household chores and her participation in public production. The purpose of his formulation was to specify that in order to establish actual equality between the sexes, the family would have to cease being an economic unit of society, i.e., household duties should not occupy the wife, and she would be free to engage herself in productive labour. There are two ways in which the Communists modified the Marxist doctrine in the reversal of their original policy with reference to woman's status.

Firstly, while women were encouraged before 1952 to participate in industrial labour, in 1955 they were told to wait for a call whenever their work was needed. Because of the spread of unemployment in cities, there was, in the spring of 1957, a proposal for sending employed women back to the rural area so that the number of unemployed men would be reduced. There were, for example, 347 married women workers in the First Maintenance Centre of Peking Municipal Omnibus Corporation.[26] Some of the city inhabitants who still had homes in the countryside and those villagers who had newly arrived in cities were urged to return to the farms and engage in agricultural production.

Secondly, The Democratic Women's League in a rural town near the coast reported that it was extremely difficult to distribute four hundred copies of the Popular Pictorial Edition of the Marriage Law. In contrast to the keen enthusiasm with which the documents were accepted before 1953, this reluctance reflected a lack of interest in the Marriage Law, which was codified on the basis of Marxist doctrine.[27] Furthermore the same report disclosed that since 1953 the Women's Association, the Youth League, the courts, the Communist Party branches and People's Council were all lax in enforcing the Marriage Law unless cases of family conflict involved homicide. Another report in the province of Shensi revealed that most marriages were arranged by the parents. The postponement in launching mass campaigns against family-arranged marriages seemed to reassert the traditional way of marriage.[28] This trend may be illustrated by a case in point. An official of a government department, Chen Hung-ting, fell in love with a co-educational student, named Liu-Mu-hsueh. They intended to be married. Nevertheless Liu's mother strongly objected to this, saying that Chen's income was insufficient. Although Liu knew that her mother's attitude was unjust, she was indebted to her for having brought her up, and was very distressed by her unreasonable attitude to her matrimonial plans. [29] Even now, parental arrangement of marriages has not been ruled out. That parental authority over children on the subject of marriage arrangement has not been expunged can be equally illustrated by a recent report. Ming Yen angered her mother and was deprived of financial help in her schooling because she refused to comply with the marriage arranged by her mother.[30]

In reference to the status of woman and marital relationship it is recently reported that the old ideas still survive. The extent of women's participation in social labour, in terms of the number of persons employed and of the role they have played, still suffers a certain limitation. As a result of this restriction, there still exists, for employed women, in fact though not in law, a falling short of equal rights with men both in society and in the home.[31]

The Marxist Concept of the Commune

Marx and Engels intended to substitute for the bourgeois society some other organizational form, though their writings omitted any explicit statement concerning what it was to be. However, it is indicated in the *Communist Manifesto* that 'in place of the old bourgeois society we shall have an association in which the free development of each is the condition for the free development of all'.[32] The same idea is expressed in the section on political economy in *Anti-During* where Marx says that the colossal productive forces developed within the capitalist system.... are merely waiting to be taken possession of by a society organized for co-operative working on a planned basis.[33] Elsewhere, in the end of the first chapter of *Capital* Marx asserts that the life-process of society, which is based on the process of material production, is not stripped of its mystical veil until it is treated as production by freely associated men, and is consciously regulated by them in accordance with a settled plan.[34] Marx's statement clearly indicates that the means of production will be held in common, and that the 'settled plan' will establish the proper proportion between the different kinds of work in the planned community and the various needs of the community.

The Amendment of the Commune System

The Communist Party introduced in 1958 the system of the commune which, it was claimed, represented a development of the ultimate Communist form of common ownership and equal distribution according to need. In September and October 1958, various Chinese spokesmen looked, not to contemporary Soviet writings, but to the works of Marx and Engels to justify their path to ultimate Communism through the commune. They contended that the Russians had forsaken classic Marxist ideological goals and were interested merely in building a modern, powerful economy. On the other hand, there are traces of Chinese Communists' insistence on incessant struggle, and of experimentation, in Mao's development of the Marxist-Leninist theory of uninterrupted revolution.[35] However, the dysfunction in the commune system indicated the inadequacies of the system and led to its amendment.

Not only once, but three times, the people's communes were amended and readjusted. The first two reorganizations were, to a certain extent, limited to changes in organization and method, whereas the most recent reorganization (August 1960), was accompanied by a political purge. With regard to amending the policy of the commune, Mao Tze-tung convoked a meeting in Cheng-Chow, Hunan province, on November 2, 1958. Again, at the 6th Plenary Session of the Eighth Chinese Communist Party Central Committee, held from November 28 to December 10, four decisions were made:

Firstly, collective ownership still performs its positive function in terms of the development of production in rural areas. The transition from collective ownership to private ownership by the people will be determined by the level of the development of production and the level of the people's political understanding. Even after the transition, the people's communes will retain the differentiated distribution system of 'to each according to his work' instead of 'to each according to his needs'. This system seems to be at variance with the warning by Marx and Engels to workers that they would not receive the full value of the work they create.[36]

Secondly, the Communist Party temporarily discarded its original aim of abolishing private ownership. Ownership of most of the means of production was shifted from the commune to the 'productive teams', that is, the former collectives composed of 20 to 30 families.[37] Small plots of land were returned to individual households for private cultivation. The private plot that a peasant belonging to a commune retained as his own property was limited to one twenty-fourth of an acre. Free markets were permitted to reopen.

A recent letter from a relative of the author in Peking stated:

An equal distribution of lands in our village was accomplished a few years ago. Of 90 acres of our land only 10 acres were allotted us. Because of the agricultural failure and food crisis in 1960, the Communist regime reverted to less rigorous measures in the commune system. They abandoned the communes, while they formed 'productive teams'. At the same time the Communist authorities permitted our family to cultivate our few acres and private gardens after the labour in the collective farms was completed. Your oldest aunt and her husband, your younger aunt and uncle were members of rural co-operatives and engaged in collective farms. Your younger aunt and uncle both live now in our small household. As regards our traditional large household it has been occupied by a few families of our village. At present only I and your younger aunt are confronted by living difficulties due to our advanced age. March 6, 1964

While Communist Party directives continually warned against the spontaneous tendency towards capitalism, this modest liberal economy was permitted. [38] However, Peking's recent uneasiness with the 'capitalist' character of the small agricultural production teams arose from the fact that whereas the production teams helped increase production, they tended to reduce central control and discipline over the peasantry. [39] Tao Chu, a prominent Communist official, has brought home to the public the importance of the commune system which is to be introduced when the level of agricultural productivity is raised. [40]

It is undeniable that it is the state which controls production and distribution according to a common plan, [41] but is equally true that so long as private ownership of certain means of livelihood belongs to individual households, the Marxist insistence on collective ownership must be regarded as partly modified in practice. This was true also in Soviet Russia when in 1933 the balance of functions and benefits between household and collective ownership was frequently readjusted.

Thirdly, to amend various deviations in the communes the Communists decreed that 8 hours for sleep each day and half a day's rest each week had to be guaranteed to peasants. This serves to discard the alleged picture of a commune as a place where regimented 'blue ants' work until they drop, building darns by day and forging steel by night. [42] The Ma Chiao's Commune, about 25 miles northwest of Shanghai is a show case selected for a visit by Western journalists. More than 6,700 families-28,000 individuals live and work in the Ma Chiao Commune which covers an area of 3,224 hectares. [43] Their average working day was said to be nine hours, though it varies with the season. Women have six days' leave a month, and men four days. The average earnings of each employee were about 240 Yuan (some £36) a year. [44] In addition, each worker was entitled to a private plot of land measuring 66 square metres. The crops from these plots could augment the peasant's earnings by about 20 percent. [45]

The Lu Kou Chiao (The Marco Polo Bridge) commune is used by the Communist Party to portray an orderly, contended and successful communal farming. New houses are constructed over the commune; simple structures about 40ft long are divided into two or three rooms. It is said that they are built in five days by the production teams, working under a skilled builder. There are five clinics and about 40 doctors for the 40,000 odd members, 24 primary schools, middle schools, and kindergartens. About 6 per cent of the land is divided into private plots, tiny but enough to grow more for consumption or sale.[46]

The regime, however, is continually endeavouring to brace and purify the commune system, from the seeds of revisionism shown by tendencies to relaxation-the campaign of 'si-chang' translated as 'fur cleanout' in the communes. A recent Chinese pamphlet asks: "Is our society today thoroughly clean?" The answer is: "No, it is not." Classes and class struggle still remain and we can still see speculative activities by old and new bourgeois elements and desperate forays by embezzlers, grafters and degenerates.[47]

The future destiny of the communes remains to be seen. However, despite the amendment of some fundamental features, there is no indication that the present leadership has shown any strong inclination to abandon altogether the commune system. Such a drastic step would vindicate the prediction of the opposition. At present there is some indication that Chinese Communists tend to revive the People's communes. This plan was revealed in an important article published in both Red Flag and *People's Daily*. This official announcement should prove that China is still a great distance from the Communist ideal of a classless society.

Marxist Theory of Communism in Perspective

As a result of the establishment of the communes in China, the Chinese Communists claimed that Mao had discovered a new organizational form leading to full communism. They contended that Marx, Engels, Lenin and Stalin developed almost all of the general principles that foreshadowed the Communist society of the future. Admittedly, Stalin introduced the institution of communes in Russia before Mao elaborated and implemented the idea embodying the Chinese commune system.

One may ask what is the validity of the Communist claim in regard to the communes? Is Mao to be credited for having developed and expanded the Marxist theory of communes? There appears to be no real justification for attributing to him any new significant contribution to the basic philosophy of future communism, except his introduction of the communes. While it is admitted that Mao has introduced some innovations since he gained political power, these have been primarily inspired by practical considerations. One popular Chinese Communist slogan is 'politics takes command' and if the words 'over theory' are added, it fits perfectly into Mao's philosophy. He rationalizes that theory is primarily an implement to be manipulated for the purpose of rationalizing and legitimizing a policy which is based on pragmatic considerations. The same principle is clearly enunciated by Lenin when he said that 'Marxism is not a dogma, but a guide to action'. This indicates that Marxism must not be taken literally, but be adapted to changing social conditions. Given this hypothesis, it is reasonable to assume that Mao, in manipulating theory to achieve political objectives, would have to deviate from the Marxian writings.

The Population Problem in Communist China

Marxist doctrine claims that human labour is the source of wealth, and thus no interference with the natural growth of population is to be tolerated. Marx, Engels, Bebel and Kautsky - the early prophets of Marxism - all disapproved of the Malthusian theory of population.[48] Yet Peking has carried on a campaign against the teeming birth rate. The official version of the present population varies between 'over 60 million'. In point of fact, a grand total of 700 million may be safely assumed, with the annual rate of increase at about 2 per cent.[49]

The recent semi-official estimates of the United Nations Statistical Office place the number of the population of mainland China at between 670 and 680 millions in 1958. It is believed that at present at least 20 per cent of the inhabitants of the world live on the Chinese mainland.[50]

Actually, married couples are being urged in the most strict terms to practice contraception. Sterilization of husband or wife is recommended and, where there are large families, abortion is tolerated. Clinics dispensing birth control information to the public have been established in every city. Shop windows display a complete range of contraceptive devices.[51] A recent tourist in the Chinese mainland reported that family planning was being vigorously urged with lectures and mobile clinics reaching every village. Reliance was placed mainly on rubber goods of which the male variety was on sale in many shops at nominal prices.[52] A report from a recent issue of Women of China stated that the Communist government encourages people to use contraceptives and to practice panned parenthood. The most popular device people resorted to was the diaphragm cap, known as the Dutch cap. Local clinics serve to advise people of the proper way of using it. Since contraceptive methods are advocated under the auspices of the government, the practice of birth control carries no stigma. The birth rate has been limited to three children. Thus any family which has had more than three children is held in derision. Similarly, sterilization was officially sanctioned and accordingly widely performed. A woman named Hsiu fan wrote to her sister that she had been operated upon so as to preclude the possibility of giving further birth.[53]

One may readily ask how this attack on the population problem in Communist China can be consistent with the Marxist doctrine that a large population is viewed as an asset. Peking camouflaged this dilemma on the pretext of the health and welfare aspects. Moreover, the Communist Party has attempted to rationalize and interpret the Marxist stand in terms of the planned limitation of population. T'ien Feng-t'iao maintained that Marxists did not in any way exclude the necessity of the planned limitation of population growth in the future development of society. Thus the Communist rationale in this issue is that limiting population is an effective way of relieving the strain on national resources and so permitting an easier transition to the final stage of Communism. To summarize, what the Chinese Communist Party has attempted to achieve is national self-interest and accordingly its policy on population is quite flexible with no rigid attachment to any specific doctrine.

Conclusion

The present analysis of the case materials extracted from Chinese as well as foreign sources serve to illustrate that the policy of Communist China has not been to adhere consistently to the Marxist doctrine of the family. Economic and political exigencies have prevailed over the dogmatic adoption of the rigidly Marxist position. The Chinese government has found it necessary to modify official policy in opposition to the Marxist point of view. The enactment of the Marriage Law and the subsequent initiation of the communes have had striking repercussions on the traditional family system. Where the trends of 1949-1964 have tended to continue, the newer situation would threaten not so much extended family as nuclear families. The change in the family being still in progress, it seems as yet too early to predict what development may occur.

Chapter 2

Filial Piety and Ancestor Worship in the Chinese Kinship System

Abstract: The paper, mainly based on textual material, deals with the phenomena of ancestor cult and filial piety in Chinese patrilineal kinship system. This is prefaced with a discussion of the notion of soul among both educated and. illiterate Chinese. Ancestor worship is the bond which holds the family members together in terms of morality and decency.

This paper deals with the religious phenomena of ancestor cult in which filial piety plays an. important role. Yet before embarking on a description of ancestral cult it would be proper to discuss the relevant notion of 'soul' as conceived by both educated and illiterate Chinese. Here two questions arise about the nature of the soul. What is the Chinese conception of the dissolution of the person at death, and how do they think of those who have departed? I would say at the outset that the Chinese are not quite explicit about the matter.

Confucius avoided speaking of the fate of the soul and the life after death. When urged to do so, he said that this question was beyond the reach of human intelligence. His silence fits in with his total lack of eschatology, since Confucian religion is worldly, a religion of nature and a harmony of life. However, speaking of the composition of two parts, one of which is aerial substance, the other spermatic, he said that at death the corpse and the inferior soul go into the earth, and decompose there, while the aerial soul rises and is glorified for its merit. The: character "ch'i'', to breath, is employed to describe the substance of the superior, aerial soul and indicates etymologically the "vapour", which steams from boiled rice. In. his study of the soul among Lodagaba, Dr. Goody has made the same point. The Lodagaba hold that a human being consists of two elements, the body (skin) and the soul of double (sic) to which the body acts as a home. To "live" literally mean to "breathe". (Goody, 1962:199)

What underlies Confucius' indifferent attitude towards spirits is his persistent emphasis on the aspect of human affairs and problems. Lu Hsun agreed with this indifferent attitude and said that in spite of spirits being so much as part of the culture in which Confucius lived, he was not interested in discussing them; although Confucius confessed their existence, he refused to speak of them; this marks the shift from deism to atheism in his thinking. Many of the Confucianists boldly deny the existence of a soul when it is separated from the body, since at death the whole man is dissolved and returned to earth, water or air.

In the opinion of Dr. Yang the Chinese do not worship their ancestors in the way gods are worshipped because after death the soul is decomposed into "kuei", the yin (negative) power and into "shen the (positive) yang power. This opinion represents the level of belief of educated Chinese. Thus the belief that the ancestor, if deprived of money and food, will afflict the living with illness does not appeal to educated Chinese. Similarly Addison has pointed out that the only proper attitude towards ancestor cult is an expression of profound devotion and gratitude to the ancestors; while the actual existence of the ancestors has been a matter of doubt. The Greek and Romans honoured the memory of the dead by periodic sacrifices at the graves. The Jews also have a yearly visit to the grave, the so-called "Jahrset" (Boeckh, 1886 : 422). Their service in memory of the death is part of their synagogical liturgy, For Catholic people on All Souls Day the supplications which are made to the souls of the departed faithful have the same symbol and the same significance. On the other hand, there are the masses of peasants who assert that a, man who has died is not altogether finished (Addison, 1925: .14, 35), and accordingly worship their ancestors as gods and believe that "living they are men, when dead, they are gods." It is this form of ancestor cult that the Catholic people were forbidden to perform; it also caused an unyielding controversy and conflict between the emperor K'ang Hsi of Ching dynasty (1962-1723 A.D.) and the popes Alexander VII and Clemens X1.[54]

Buddhism and Taoism on the Concept of Soul

Buddhism exerted considerable influence on Chinese metaphysics. The belief in transmigration which is one of the Buddhist tenets has been professed by a great many Chinese peasants. Nevertheless, the Buddhist assumption of the disappearance of the soul as a result of transmigration complicates the question of posthumous reward or punishment

(Maspero, 1950: 130). The peasant Buddhists believe in the punishment of bad spirits in a, separate state. Assuming this is true, how can the wicked ancestors who are themselves punished help their descendants on earth?

Having been influenced by the Buddhist doctrine Taoism described renewed lives which follow death and admitted the existence of three "hun" (spirits) and seven "po" (material souls). 'These can be grouped into two categories: "shen" (spirit) and "kuei" (ghost). After death they are separated. The group of "po" appears before the posthumous judges, carrying its load of sins and merits. This implies that the concept of spirit and ghost derives and develops from that of the soul. But the soul is a part, of man, whereas spirit and ghosts are parts of man's soul whose fate varies with the ways he will die. The categories of soul can be illustrated by the following diagram:

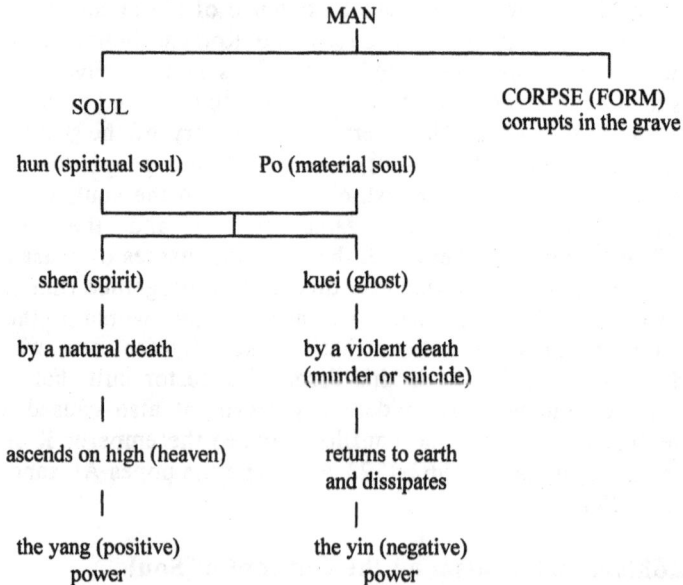

```
                            MAN
         ┌───────────────────┴───────────────────┐
      SOUL                                CORPSE (FORM)
        │                                 corrupts in the grave
  hun (spiritual soul)      Po (material soul)
        └───────────┬───────────┘
           ┌────────┴────────┐
      shen (spirit)        kuei (ghost)
           │                   │
    by a natural death    by a violent death
                          (murder or suicide)
           │                   │
  ascends on high (heaven)  returns to earth
                            and dissipates
           │                   │
    the yang (positive)    the yin (negative)
         power                power
```

Wang Ch'ung, a philosopher of the Sung dynasty (960-1127 A.D.) held a mid-position between Confucianism and Taoism, and was of the opinion that "the dead do not become ghosts -but are unconscious, and that Sleep, a trance, and death are essentially the same." He said that "human death is like an extinction of fire. To assert that a person after death is still conscious is like saying that an extinguished light shines again. The soul of a dead man cannot become a body again" (Forde et al., 1911:346 f).

Tylor argued, however, that the worship of ancestors among Chinese peasants which begins during their life is not interrupted but intensified when death makes them deities. Man's worship is not a rite of mere affection, but a desire for help on the part of the living of the ancestral spirits who reward virtue and punish vice (Tylor, 1913 : 118). But Tylor's explanation fails to attach much importance to the affectionate aspect of the relationship between the dead and the living; in the Chinese religious system.

For Dr. Fei Hsiao-Tung, the living must carefully perform those rites of ancestral cult. Sickness and misfortunes result sometimes from doing damage to the coffin shelter, by selling land or houses (Fei, 1939 : 70). This is a popular belief. In the view of Addison it is the common belief of Chinese peasants that neglect of ancestors will inevitably bring disaster upon the descendants. However, he spoke of the retribution being sent down by heaven by the spirit power other than the ancestors (Addison. 192.1). Freedman maintains that there have been numerous reports of actual cases of misfortune being attributed to the vast pantheon of local gods upon whom the immediate vicissitudes of the family often depend (Freedman, 1965: 86).

In his study of West Town, Yunnan province, Dr. Hsu reckons that when the "kuei" (spirit) of a person leaves the body, it will enter the world of spirits. If the life of the deceased is laudable, the spirit will be received with pomp. If the person was notorious for his wickedness, and condemned to a premature death, the spirit will be put in chains. On the other hand, the fate of the spirit of the dead is thought to be influenced by their living descendants. The majority of West towners seek to acquire spiritual goods by prayers, observance of taboos and offerings, chiefly in expectation of securing certain tangible benefits, such as health, living heirs, proper burial and adequate graveyards.[55]

That the neglect of ancestors will bring down supernatural retribution means that the neglect of rites and norms of solidarity will entail moral decay and the eventual disintegration of the family. For ancestor worship serves as a binding force of stability both within and beyond the family group and overlaps with social relationships. Also it is on the ancestral worship that the greater "corporate" or "we" feeling between ancestors and descendants largely depends. In making sacrifice to their ancestors, the peasant Chinese believe that ancestral spirits live in a world very similar to theirs, and are in part dependent on the contribution of their descendants in the form of periodically burning paper money and making offerings of food and drink.

The Ancestral Tablet

Our next discussion will be concerned with ancestor cult in the context of the location where the cult is held and the paraphernalia of ancestral rites and the established forms of ancestral cult. The ancestral ceremonies are performed in the family, in ancestral halls and at the tombs. Ancestral halls are erected by individuals or several branches of a family of the same surname, and much display is made in ornamentation. Family temples are built by wealthy families and are detached from other dwellings and open to the street for the accommodation of other branches of the family. The ceremony was performed during the four seasons of the year in the temple or the hall and consists of kneeling down and making obeisance to the wooden tablets on which the names of their ancestors are inscribed. As to its origin, it is said that Ting Lan who lived during the Han dynasty (about 25 A.D.) was assumed to be the originator. While he was working in the field, his mother brought him sonic refreshments. Having tripped by accident over the root of a fir tree, she fell to the ground and died. Whereupon Ting Lan took the very root of this tree and carved on it the images of his parents. If what Ting did was the origin of the ancestral tablet, apparently he did it unintentionally. Nevertheless, it is to him that the custom of worshipping deceased parents and ancestors under some visible symbol have been commonly attributed.

At the sacrifice, it is to the tablet that the filial son can attach his feelings of affection for the deceased. The "Hsia" dynasty (1.994-1523 B.C.) used a. tablet made of "pine" wood so as to stimulate themselves; the "Chou" dynasty (1050-256 B. C.) used a tablet made of the "chestnut" wood so as to inspire themselves with awe (Li, 1875: 8b). The tablet is made of wood to symbolize man in his growth and decay.

The ancestral tablet is simply a piece of wood, chestnut being the most orthodox; it varies in its size. Its twelve inches in height represents the twelve months, four inches in width denotes four seasons, and one inch and a half in thickness stands for the twelve hours. The best one is made of fragrant wood, parts of which are elaborately carved. Some of the tablets cost a few pounds a piece. There are three pieces of wood, one being pedestral, and the other two upright pieces. It is on this wooden tablet that the name of the recipient of rites is written with his title, birth and death dates. It consists of a rectangular piece of wood set in a base and covered with a case, which is removed during the ceremony. As a rule, a friend well versed in calligraphy is invited to write the name of the ancestor on the tablet. The top is ranked like heaven, whereas the bottom flat likes earth. In a family temple the tablets are arranged on the shelves in a chronological order, the number gradually increasing downwards, beginning with the founder of the family down to the last generations. On each tablet is inscribed the name of one of the heads of a. family, with the number of the generations, and commonly the dynasty under which the individuals lived.

The spirit tablet is of different sizes for the domestic shrine and the ancestral hall. The tablets in the central hall are at least two or three times larger than those used in domestic shrines. They are placed in niche, which is divided into shelves so that they are not all on the same level. The tablet, being called "shen-wei", the spirit's abode, is preferable to "shen-chu", divine lord. The meaning and purpose of the ancestral tablet is that when the descendants, while offering sacrifices, look on the tablet, they might see their ancestors embodied in it. Ancestor worshippers have attached importance to the tablet in two ways. One, at man's death his bodily form can no longer be seen, but his descendants have a longing for him. For the satisfaction of this longing some visible objects must be used, which, being ever before their eyes, will keep the departed one in constant and vivid remembrance. In the Orient an image is an accepted symbol for worship. At the petition of Jewish people Aaron manufactured an image, a golden bull which, symbolizing Yahweh was an accepted symbol of divinity (Heimisch, 1950 : 93-94). Two, for fear of their departed ancestors bring deprived of any settled abode, the descendants set up tablets in which their spirits may rest. Being aware that. when the tablet is set up, a mere piece of wood as such may not serve as the abode of the spirit, some important person is invited to dot, with red ink in a brush, the character "(wang) which then becomes" +, meaning the dwelling place of the spirit. Before the dotting, the writer breathes upon the brush rising the following form:

The spirit rests in this wooden tablet
And the wooden tablet is spiritualized by its resting,
The Spirit and the wood together dwell

In ages of unending spring.

J. Legge contended that, while the worship is performed, the tablet is supposed to be occupied by the ancestral spirit interested in the service, and at the conclusion the spirit returns to his own place.

The spirits of dead ancestors which are, thought to adhere to the tablet of the domestic shrine include those of the recently deceased, but not those which were removed farther than about four generations from the head of the family. Addison maintains that after the third or sometimes the fifth generation the tablets of ancestors are burned or removed to the ancestral halls of clans (Addison, 1925: 14, 35). At the domestic level, the rites performed to the spirit of ancestors symbolize the rites of kinship solidarity in which ancestors are regarded as the foci for determinate agnatic units, while during the rites of so-called "memorialism" ancestors were attended to simply as forbears and independently of their status as agnatic ancestors of the worshippers. That is to say, when the members of a family performed their own domestic rites as separate units before ancestors many generations distant, they did not connect themselves with all their agnates in other families sharing the same ancestors. In such a. case the ancestors were not taken to be foci for segments in a lineage, and their relations with the living descendants stood outside the hierarchy of agnatic units. It is clear that a man who was worshipped separately in the several households established by his patrilineal grandsons was the object of a devotion which was not directly related to the maintenance of kinship unity beyond the range of one family in a household (Freedman, 1905 : 86), Again the rites of kinship solidarity conducted during ancestor worship appear not to go with the rites of memorialism, which were held when ancestor cult moved from the domestic temple or shrine to the ancestral hall of a lineage or lineage segments. In the hall these rites were performed to represent in ritual the principle of descent in terms of which the lineage is organized.[56]

The Chinese in all parts of China see a close connection between the attending of ancestor and filial piety. They feel it their duty, in return for the gift of life and sustenance, to pay the seniors respect and support them during life. Such a duty does not come to an end along with the death of the elders. They must carry on succouring their ancestors by tending their tablets and providing them with the necessities of the after-life. Thus among the peasants the dead have been thought to be dependent on the living for sustenance and support. It is the assumption of the peasants that if the descendants fail to make offerings to the satisfaction of the ancestors' needs, the latter become hungry ghosts wandering in the world in search of food, and molest both other souls and the living.

Prayers to the Dead

I have expatiated upon the concept the Chinese have of the soul, the ideas and affections they have for it, and some of the actions which they think bring about the intervention of spirit or ghost in human affairs. A brief consideration of some prayers addressed to ancestral spirits will be given because they are used by Chinese only when they make sacrifices to ancestors. Like the North American Indians, the intellectual Greek, war-like Romans, and priest-ridden Egyptians, the ceremonious Chinese are punctilious in rendering religious homages to their departed relatives, and do what they can to pacify: to gratify, and to honour their manes in the world of spirits. Jackson provided us with the examples of prayers uttered to the ancestors at the time of family sacrifice. He maintained that the prayers have, not been derived from books, but supplied to him by scholars who considered the prayers fairly representative of the general practice:
The sacrifice is spread and presented;
Come in peace and partake--
Great are our Ancestors!
The sacrifice is offered at the gate of the ancestral hall.
O ! Our Forefathers,
Send down blessings without limit!
The ceremonies are completed.
Your filial descendants have felicity,
They shall be blessed for ever (Jackson, 1.907 : 11, 16).

Jackson presented another well formulated prayer addressed at the tomb during the Spring Festival:
The spring dews are now distilling their fertility, and my grief cannot be forgotten.
I improve the time to examine and sweep the grave and visit the fir hall (the tomb).

Prostrate I pray your protection to surround and assist your
descendants, that they may be powerful and honoured
Let every son and grandson in the house receive a happy sign,
and become conspicuous over all, their fame rivaling the lustre
of their ancestors.
Looking up, we pray you to descend and accept oar sacrifice
(Jackson, 1907)

We should note that Buddhism exerts influence upon the saying of
prayers in sacrificial offering. Buddhists call in the monks to set up
their altar and pray for the happiness of the dead. Dutiful children
elevating the tablet kneel down in company with the monks and pray to
ancestors for help and protection. The prayers to ancestors shed light on
the significance of the relationships between the living and the dead.
The glory of one party reflects on the other. Like the Nuer (Nath -
living on both sides of the Nile) who emphasize by their public prayer
that in relation to God, all are members of one another, the Chinese,
who, in their prayers to their ancestors, ask to be elevated to an official
status and granted riches and honours, seek to form the total unity of
which they are members. Among Chinese distinguished ancestors are
established in the ancestral hall and their honours reflect on their
descendants, while the celebrity of the living correspondingly enhances
the status of their ancestors. On the other hand, the sins of the living arc
a blot on their ancestors: excutcheon. It is not certain, however, that the
ancestors are capable of bestowing benefits on the living, but to pray to
them helps to strengthen family solidarity. The living who owe a great
deal to their ancestors and regularly offer sacrifice to them will not
infringe without scruple moral codes to incur ancestors' displeasure and
ire.

The Religious Aspect of Ancestor Worship

In China there is not an established Church with well formulated
dogmas; vet in Confucianism there is a body of religio-philosophical
belief; which express the point of view of man in society and of society
in nature. These beliefs lay the foundation of the official religion which
has been practiced in ancestor worship in family temples or ancestral
halls. On the basis of historical evidence ancestor worship has been
regarded as falling into the category of a low type of religion and has
marked the stage developed from earlier nature worship and animism.
Spencer held that the word: "ancestor worship" was the root of every
religion, and the earliest manifestation of man's religious aspirations

from which idol and fetish worship and belief in spirits took their rise (Spencer, 1885 - 20, 26). In the Roman Empire, man-worship in the deification, for instance; of emperors is a great falling off from a simpler faith of earlier times. August is, the son of the deified Julius, was venerated as god; even his name conveys the ideas "consecrated, venerable, majestic, awe-inspiring." As inscription in a stone discovered in Asia Minor is read as follows:

He (Augustus) is the paternal Zeus and. the saviour of the whole race of man, who grants all prayers, even more than we ask. For land and sea• enjoy peace, cities flourish : everywhere are harmony and prosperity and happiness (Botsford, 190.1 ; 214-215).

The ancestor worship existed in China long before Confucius, but he exhibited his sagacity in adapting his teachings to filial feelings of human nature and attempting to introduce a. few simple observances and adopt bloodless ritual. When ancestor worship is practiced, it can be regarded as a. form of religion as well as a• body of moral rules. Like the Jewish Talmud, Mahammedan Korean and Christian Gospel, the religious tenet of "Yu Chiao"; that is, Confucian religion or teaching, is formulated in the ancient writings and in the records of the past. With this in view, Confucius compiled digests of what seems to him most valuable in the sayings of earlier thinkers and in the events of his own and earlier times (Badly, 1951 : 66). It is therefore natural that he attached little importance to metaphysical notions and warns his followers against• any kind of abstract thought.

Worship, a form of religion, may be regarded as a body of moral rules (li), and is supported by law. The teachings of the Confucian school have always attached much importance to "li", moral rules, or propriety of conduct. The word "li" is best expressed as approved patterns of behaviour between individuals standing in a definite relation to each other, and in conformity-with a definite system of values relating to such social relationships (Hu, 1934 : 79). According to the Analects of Confucius (Lung Yü): "If the people be led by laws, and uniformity sought to be given them by punishments, the people will try to avoid punishments, but have no sense of' shame. If they be led by virtue, and uniformity is given them by the rules of propriety "li", they will have the sense of shame, and, moreover, will become good." This statement represents the attitude of the Confucian school in opposition to the application of a rigid code of' laws because it applies sanctions against a crime only after its perpetration.

The Confucianists laid stress upon familiar relationships and urged the proper relationship in the kinship system, for example, the mourning system and the jural rights and obligations. As I have previously explained, filial piety was strongly emphasized by the Confucianists. The "li" urged children to serve and support their parents. This means that not supporting the parents" made children liable to punishment. Again Confucius taught that the father and the son should conceal each other's crime. Such concealment was not, in the light of "li", repugnant to the law which slid not enforce children to bear witness against their parents or bring accusations against them. If the parents and the children report each other's crime to the government, they must be punished in virtue of "li". In the State Ch'u, man who reported to an official that his father had stolen a. goat was punished by death. What justified the capital punishment of the son was that whereas he was loyal to the ruler he was unfilial to his father.

In terms of social function, ancestor worship is thought to be the bond holding the family members together and the main support of morality and decency in family life. Filial piety and its complement, ancestor worship, form the core of the Chinese religion. There are no priests. The emperor, who is the son of Heaven and thus himself divine, acts as mediator between Heaven and earth and, as a part of his duties, performs public rites and offers sacrifice for the welfare of his subjects. Nevertheless those rites which are connected with ancestor cult are conducted by the head of each family. The objects of worship and sacrifice arc the spirits of the dead who are still reckoned as members of the family to which they belonged.

The word "chi", sacrifice in Chinese does not convey the same meaning as the English word. We must not read into it the fullness of meaning which Old and 'New Testaments usage leave conveyed to us. Etymologically- the character "chi" is formed by the combination of the ideas in its three parts, or three ideograms, as it is found in the Shu Wen the earliest Chinese dictionary. In the character "chi" symbolizes a piece of flesh, the sacrificial object. The meaning of this character is that sacrifice is a gift offered to supernatural beings and to the spirits of ancestors with whom the worshippers need to ingratiate themselves; they intend to insure that objects reach the spiritual beings by sacrificial rites. Sacrifice is conceived to be an offering to spiritual beings, whereby communication with them is effected. This is the meaning given in K'ang Hsi Dictionary.

Sacrifices are no doubt taken as gifts conferring on the sacrificers and their participant's rights over their ancestors: the gifts serve to feed them and call upon their blessings. Hsu pointed out that the needs of ancestors in the after-life must be met by the, living for fear they should turn into spiritual vagabonds and cause trouble to the living. However, this is the opinion of peasants, but held in suspicions by intellectuals. Ancestor worship performed by the masses is called "pai", whereas that performed by the intellectuals is designated by the term "chi" (Fung, 1936: 143f). To the educated Chinese, offerings are not connected with any idea of propitiation or supplication but are tributes of duty and gratitude. This in accord with Dr. Yang's view of ancestor worship, which should not be interpreted in a religious way (Yang, 1.948: 90). I suspected that the shortcomings of Yang's point of view consisting in ruling out the entrenched customs of ancestor cult among the Chinese peasants. The matter should not be left without further arguing about the case. Various implications should be laid bare lest one should be misled.

Communion with the dead has always been a chief feature in sacrificial cult not only among the Chinese but also among many other peoples. Among the Semitic and Greek people a communion feast is connected with sacrifice. The Zebah Shelamim is a communion sacrifice.[57] Robertson Smith sees the communion in the practices of the Totemic cult, the origin of sacrifice. He thought of totemism as an essentially social form of worship and the earliest manifestation of man's attempts to get into contact with Unseen. In totemism the totem or the god and its devotees or sacrificers are of the same flesh and blood and, by offering sacrifice, they maintain the communion of life that animates them and the association that binds then together. The communion meal is the simplest means of producing this effect. In the view of Smith, it is the "communion meal" in which the devotees participate and, by eating the totem, they assimilate it to themselves, are assimilated to it, and become allied with each other or with it (Hubert and Mauss, 1964: 2-3).

Legge said that the ancestor cult among the Chinese is not merely commemorative, but a. pretended real intercourse with

the world spirit, supposing that the happiness of the dead
depends on the sacrifices of their descendants (Legge, 1880 : 93-
94). This amounts to Confucian ideas that, at the time of great
offerings, every deceased person ought to have his "shih",
personator. The "shih" is a representative or personator of the
deceased ancestor to whom sacrifice is offered. The dead,
existing in a spirit-state are of course not visible so that ore of
the sacrificer's relatives is selected to be taken possession of the
ancestor for the time of sacrifice. It is written in Li Chih (The
Book of Rites)[58] that the "shih" means "shen hsiang", the visible
image of the spirit. Also the "shih" personator is addressed in
such a way as to make him the living image of the vanished
reality, the person thus selected for this part is necessarily
inferior in kinship system to the principal sacrificer, but for the
time being he is superior to him, occupying the place of departed
ancestor. As soon as the personator appears in the domestic
temple, the sacrificer under instructions from the master of
ceremonies asks the personator to be seated, to eat and accept the
homage paid to the ancestor. In one of the Odes the response of
the ancestors through their personator "shih" reads as follows:

> The offerings in your dishes or vessels of Bamboo and
> wood are clean and fine.

> Your friends assisting at the service,
> Have done their part with reverent demeanour.

> What will the blessings be?
> That along the passages of your palace

> You shall move for ten thousand years, and there will be
> granted to you for ever dignity arid posterity.

In the context of the social function sacrifice serves to fulfill
human relations. Honouring ancestors is a way to fulfill these
relationships, which have been interrupted but not terminated by
death. In the past, the educated performed ceremonies before
ancestral altars, not to entreat for blessings or to provide
deceased parents with material needs, but to demonstrate the
affectionate feelings of filial piety and respect (Chan, 1953 :
245). I am of the opinion that in Chinese ancestor rites there are
the individual Status as a social person, rank, lineage,

ceremonies, and ritual with which social structure and culture correspond. As ritual is a symbol, it makes the social structure real; the rite has a symbolic function for the sacrificer as political religious, educational, and moral leader of a group. The meaning of these rites corresponds to that of the rites which have been described by Dr. Goody (1961). Dr. Leach considers ritual to be a "Pattern of symbols", referring to the system of socially approved proper relations between individuals and group. Durkheim views religious rites as mechanisms for expressing and reinforcing the sentiments most essential to the integration of society. Tseng Tzu, one of the disciples of Confucius, said: "If people are careful about funeral rites and remember their ancestors in sacrifices, the morals of the people will resume their proper excellence." (Mei, 1929: 236),

The term "chiao" conveys the ideas "religious system", "teach" and "filial piety". This interpretation suggests itself to the ancient saying that the ancient sages established teaching on the ways of the gods. The Confucian school does not believe in the existence of supernatural beings, but stresses the performance of sacrifices in order to give emotional satisfaction. Mohist utilitarianism, however, regards the performance, of sacrifices as meaningless. Mo Tzu said: "To hold that there are no spirits and learn sacrificial ceremonies is like learning the ceremonials of hospitality when there is no guest or making fish nets when there are no fishes" (Hu, 1933 : 79). Dr. Hu Shih seized the same idea that teaching a moral life is the essential thing, and worship of the gods and religious observance merely provide one of the possible means of sanctioning the teaching. That is in substance the Chinese concept of religion (Loisy, 1920 : 1).

This study has made it clear that ancestor worship, the quintessence of Confucianism is an important part of the social control, part of the complex system by which the Chinese people are enabled to live together in an orderly network of social relations. The ancestor cult involves certain ideas or beliefs on the one hand, and certain observances on the other. These observances are spoken of as rites-the results of beliefs. Loisy said that "rites are in all religions the most stable and lasting elements and consequently that in which we can best discover the spirit of ancient cults" (Loisy, 1920:1).

In Chinese ancestor worship the simplest form of sacrifice consists of daily burning of incense in the front of a wooden tablet in the family temple. This constitutes the channel of communication with the invisible spirits of ancestors and serves as a memento of the existence and guardianship) of the dead among the living. Sacrificial rites were performed on the anniversary of the deceased members, during the Chinese New Year in the spring and autumn festivals. The head of the family conducted the rises and the rest off the family members followed in order of their status within the kinship system. The head of the family is a senior member both in terms of his advanced age and of his genealogical order, and his status in sacrificial rites is equivalent to that of a priest in Christian churches. The arrangement of the position of each family member during a sacrifice is based on kinship system. The family representing a collective life was periodically reaffirmed by dint of ancestor worship.

Like in many other cultures, the offering of food and drink to the ancestors were methods of communion with the ancestral spirits. The following commensal of the entire family group was an occasion when a great many members were gathered and renewed their group cohesion. Sacrificial rites are seen to be the regulated symbolic expressions of certain sentiments and to have for their effects to regulate, maintain and transmit from one generation to another sentiment on which the structure of society depends. If the ancestral tablet is a symbol, the essential quality of that which it symbolizes is the very entity which would command moral respect and lend itself to group solidarity. Here again these rites serve to perpetuate the memory of ancestors, sustain the moral beliefs of living descendants and refresh group consciousness. They are also an expression of dependence on a power outside the worshippers themselves, a power which may be spoken of as a spiritual and moral power. This can be exemplified by the work "li" which Chinese scholars have substituted for the word "chiao" (religion). The character "li" is composed of three parts: 'spirit'; two pieces of jade 'offering' and 'vessel'. This character is translated to account for ceremonial, customary morality, rites, rule and propriety.

In the Chinese society religious rites are thought to be efficacious in the sense that they are apt to avert evils and bring blessings. What was considered to be important was the social function of the rites that is their effects in bringing about and maintaining an orderly human society. In a text earlier than Confucius it is read Chat "sacrifice is that through which one can show one's filial piety and give peace to the people, pacify the country and make the people settled." It is through the sacrifices that the unity of the people is achieved. One of the important points of the teachings of Confucius was the importance of the, proper performance of rites. In the Book of Rites (Li Chih) we read that "ceremonies are the bond that holds the multitudes together, and if the bond is broken, those multitudes fall into confusion." With regard to the mourning rites Hsün Tzu said: "Funeral rites are for the living to give beautified ceremonial to the dead: to send off the dead is if they were living; to render the same service to the dead as to the living; to the absent as to the present; and to make the end the same as the beginning."

Apart from expressing grief at a kinsman's death which had the significance of reaffirming the cohesion and solidarity of the family group as has been put forward by both Durkheim and Malinowski, funeral rites have attached importance to the essence of filial piety. The dutiful son only discharged filial devotion to his parent while living but also performed funeral rites upon their death. This performance serves two purposes. It mitigates son's great grief over the death and bereavement of his parents. From the point of view of social group, the expression of filial sentiments through funeral rites bespeaks filial piety a basic value in the function of the kinship system.

In ancestor worship we can easily see and demonstrate its social function to reaffirm, renew and strengthen those sentiments on which the social stability rests. The cult group consists of persons related to one another by descent in one line from the same ancestor and only the members of the group take part in the cult. Ancestor worship then consists of rites carried out by the members of a larger and smaller lineage with regard to the deceased members of the lineage. But what makes the social structure stable is the solidarity and continuity of the lineage.

With the multiplication of the members of a lineage over several generations the kinship group grew large and the contact between the members became infrequent. The gathering in the ancestor cult helps reminding the kin group of their common origin and keeping alive the social obligations between the members. The primary duties due to one's lineage include duties and obligations to the members of now living and also to those who have died and to those who are not yet born. In point of fact kinship relations amount to moral obligations that are involved in the categories of values and behaviour which may be summed up in such concepts as rights, duties, respect, virtue and sin. In discharging those duties the object on which individual's sentiments are expressed is the lineage itself, pasts, present and future. Likewise the gist of Chinese kinship system lies in it function as a mechanism through which the basic morality is translated into the concrete social life. These are the basic features common to all patrilineal societies.

Again in the ancestor worship the Chinese feels that he depends on his ancestors in that he has received his life and livelihood that are his inestimable inheritance. If he is remised in his duties to live up to the expectation of his ancestors, he will not only be deprived of their blessings but will be visited with some misfortune. Moreover an idea of commemoralism is that the participants in ancestor worship are disposed to express their gratitude towards their ancestors for whatever has been bestowed, and their dependence upon them. The sense of dependence has two aspects. On the one hand, Chinese people can stand up to the difficulties and adversity of life when they know that there are powers and forces of ancestors to which they can turn for help. On the other hand, they ought to control their conduct by rules which have been laid down. Jackson said that our care should be to live worthily of ancestors, and also through our lives we should be careful not to disgrace them. The idea of the continuity of the family and the thought of what is clue to one's ancestors can hardly fail to have some lingering influence for good upon those who cherish such ideas. To the mind of Jackson, the ancestor worship is reckoned as the bond which brings about group cohesion and collective consciousness. The descendants have a strong repugnance against a bolt on their ancestors' escutcheon.

Chapter 3

Socialism in Confucianism

Confucius (551-479 B.C.) was born into a China when it was torn by political upheaval and cultural anarchy. It was an age when a subjective or arbitrary sophistry akin to that in the Greek tradition infringed upon the traditions of China and plunged her into a welter of civil strife. Political contenders were buttressed by preachers of new ideas and panaceas. It was then that Confucius made a defense against these sophistic innovations by reasserting and reviving, older principles and practices. The teachings of Confucius, the master, were carried on at least by three schools, but the teachings of all three were written down in their collective works: Motzu, Meng tzu and Hsün tzu. Among these three only Meng tzu-Mencius (372-289 B.C.) was regarded as Confucian orthodox and listed as the thirteenth and last item in the Confucianist canon around 1100 A.D. Meng tzu records chiefly the travels and verbose teachings of Confucius and provides evidence of the polemical ideas among the various schools of Confucius' adherents.

Confucius was recognized as the first ancestor of the religious and literary tradition of China. He had no counterpart in the Western as well as in other oriental traditions. However, the Chinese have never worshipped Confucius nor prayed to him as a god. China has always been a class society where the upper classes arc conscious of a natural obligation towards their social inferiors, and the inferiors look up to their superiors for exemplary conduct and right action. Thus by imitation and by a societal osmosis the high moral standards of Confucianism were transmitted down to China's masses. Though China has been a class society socialism abounds in Confucian teachings. Again, though modern socialism originated in Europe, it also germinated in ancient China. We need not take pains in pointing out socialism in the teachings of Confucius and Mencius. These teachings inspired a great number of modern reformers with utopian thought. It stands to reason that social conditions and circumstances in Europe gave rise to the prominence of socialism; nevertheless with the help of Western missionaries Europe soon came to know more about China and Confucianism. The waves of humanism and rationalism which swept Europe in the seventeenth and eighteenth centuries seem to have been derived to a certain extent from this new knowledge and have paved the way for socialism.

I shall endeavour in this paper to investigate the extent to which socialism has been preached in Confucianism and to compare Confucianism with Platonism on .socialism.. I am aware that for those who are well-versed in Chinese classics, such as Lun yü - The Analects of Confucius and Meng tzu-Mencius, there may be dispute on this subject, particularly with respect to socialism found in "Ching-tien", the Well-Field System. I shall attempt to point out the presence of socialism in Confucian teachings and restrict the sources of my investigation chiefly to Lun-yü and Meng tzu.

First let us define what is meant by the term "socialism". The term "socialism" was first adopted in 1872 in the Owenite Co-operative Magazine to designate tendencies opposed to liberal individualism. George Bernard Shaw understands "socialism" to mean "the complete discarding of the institution of private property . . . and the division of the resultant public income equally and indiscriminately among the entire population." The "sum unique" of Platonic socialism is its regulative principle. It is socialism which disregards the selfish interests of individuals and endeavours to establish Justice by organizing society in variegated groups. Othmar Spann, who views popular socialism as an inconsistent medley of collectivism and liberalism has attempted to refurbish such aristocratic socialism in a system called "universalism".

Communistic socialism purports to be the ideal of absolute equality and seeks to express the volonté de tons. Its ideal can be couched in the maxim, probably of stoic origin: "from each according to his capacities, to each according to his needs." However, the ideal of Socialism is not a mechanical equality of all members of society but rather a potential equality - in the maxim of Saint Sknon's followers: "from each according to his capacity, to each according to his merit", has as its quintessence not common ownership but the elimination of all unearned increment or profit. We now enter into investigation to what extent Confucianism has a bearing on socialism.

Equal Educational Opportunity

In the Chinese hierarchical society, as Confucius suggested, members of the ruling class were to be selected on the basis of individual merit. For it was Confucius' belief that political and social disorder arose from the top stratum of society. As it is read in the Lun Yü, the ruler and his officials arc likened to the wind and the commoners to the grass. When the wind blows, the grass bends. When "chün-tzu", the morally and intellectually superior man serves in government, peace and social order will ensue. But how should we distinguish the intellectually and morally superior man from the mediocre? Confucius took for granted that men are not born equal in intelligence and capacity. However, Confucius proposed equal opportunity of education to both the high and the low. He said: "In education there should be no class distinctions.[59] The Confucian idea purports that education is based on a Grand Union without distinction of the rich and the poor, the high and the low or the wise and the stupid. Whoever is disposed to learn will always be welcome. Here again, Confucius sought to make education universal and popular. Mencius, the foremost exponent of Confucius' orthodox doctrine, argued that it is incumbent on the state to provide schools at various levels for the education of the people. We must remember that in his life-time when education had been a prerogative of the hereditary feudal nobility, Confucius who made every effort to implement his doctrine by offering equal instruction to all his disciples regardless of their social origin, should indeed receive credit for his initiative with regard to intellectual emancipation and common education. Thus when Confucius and his followers sought to uphold the feudal system they actually heralded a new social order, based not on hereditary status, but on individual merit. In other words, while lending support to a hierarchical society, they procured means to deal a blow at its inherent injustice and bring about social equity chiefly through education. Confucianism on education can therefore be thought of as a precursor of modern socialism.

Likewise, in conformity with Confucian doctrine Mo-tzu offered similar teachings. He said:

> In administering the government, the ancient sage-kings ranked the morally excellent high and exalted the virtuous. If capable, even a farmer or artisan would he employed-commissioned with high rank, remunerated with liberal emoluments, trusted with important charges, and empowered to issue final orders . . . Ranks should be standardized according to virtue, tasks assignedaccording to office, and rewards given according to labour spent. When emoluments are distributed in proportion to achievements, officials cannot be in constant honour, and people in eternal humility.[60]

This clearly shows that the existence of a hierarchical society, with its discrimination between the ruling and ruled, can be justified by the principle that status and emoluments should be based on achievement and virtue.

In contrast with Confucianism Plato's view of human nature is in opposition to egalitarianism. Men are innately unequal and thus must be classified in a hierarchy of innate ability and merit. This being true, men must all be equally subject to the control of a complex and authoritarian constitution. With regard to education Plato insisted that reason, the noblest part of man, should be the ruling faculty, and that only by intensive training through education can man attain the higher levels of experience to the benefit of a state or society. This group of citizens on a par with Confucius' "chün-tzu" arc rulers and guardians of the welfare of all.[61] They are lovers of wisdom and philosophy and regard flabbiness of character and selfishness as unbecoming to them.[62] They show utter repugnance to whatever runs counter to the best interests of the state.[63] On the other hand, in opposition to Confucius' universal education Plato subscribed to the opinion that the common people have no access to the advantage of a special education. For in accordance with the aristocratic strain in Plato's social philosophy it is of no avail to offer a higher education to that proportion of the people who are mentally incapable of profiting by education.

Division of Labour

Although Confucius proposed that in education there should be no class distinctions, the Confucian school believed that human beings were different in intelligence and ability. Thus people in a society could not all be assigned the same roles and bear the same responsibilities. Social organization requires a division of labour and the assignment of different kinds of work to people according to their capacity. There are two types of work, the mental and the physical. Farmers, artisans, and merchants are engaged in the second type. It was incumbent upon them to produce goods and render services. Another group included scholars and officials whose function was to study and to acquire virtue. This class is characterized as the "great man", in contrast to another class, the "small man". The former class not only was superior but was entitled to be served and supported by the latter. This shows a relationship of subordination and superordination. It is read in Kuo Yü: "The commoners., the artisans and merchants, each attend to their profession to support the superiors."[64] Moreover, the division of labour was also politically oriented. Mental labour was concerned with governing, whereas physical labour is manual. The point has been emphatically described in Ch'un-ch'iu Tso chuan: "It is a rule of the former kings that superior men should labour with their minds and smaller men labour with their strength."[65] In like manner Mencius said:

Some labour with their minds, and some labour with their strength. Those who labour with their minds govern others; those who labour with their strength are governed by others. Those who are governed by others support them: those who govern others are supported by them. This is a principle universally recognized.[66]

Since the work of chün-tzu was considered to contribute more to society and to accept greater responsibility than a member of another class, he deserve more rewards and better material comforts.

In the Republic Plato explained that the division of labour was essential to the existence of a society. Increasing size of a community requires division of labour. The fundamental division involves three classes, the rulers-guardians, tantamount to Confucius' "chün-tzu", the soldiers and the farmersartisans (Confucius' small men).[67] Justice lies in the harmonious co-operation of these three groups, each performing its proper role. Nevertheless, the guardians, the ruling class or "best men" seek righteousness and must prove that the ruling interest of their lives is to be the highest interest of the state. For it was Plato's insistence that only the guardians, presumably the true philosophers, are fit to rule. Only the man who gains an insight into the nature and function of a state and who strives to bring the actual state into conformity with the ideal, can be entrusted with civil power.

Confucian Ideal Grand Union

Confucian socialism amounts to Grand Union. Such a society has been clearly described in Li Ki as follows:

When the Grand Union was pursued, a public and common spirit ruled all under the sky; they chose men of talents, virtue and ability; their word:, were sincere, and what they cultivated was harmony. Thus men did not love their parents only and treated as children only their own sons. A competent provision was secured for the aged till their death, employment for the able-bodied, and the means of growing up to the young. They showed kindness, compassion to the widows, orphans. childless men, and those who were disabled by disease so that they were all sufficiently maintained. Males had their proper works, and females had their homes... (They laboured) with their strength, disliking

that it should not be exerted, but not exerting it (only) with a
view to their own advantage. In this way (selfish) schemings
were repressed and found no development. Robber, filchers
and rebellious traitors did not show themselves, and hence
the outdoors remained open, and were not shut. This was
(the period of) what we call the Grand Union.[68]

These texts lay bare socialism in Confucianism. The statement
"they chose men of talents, virtue and ability" implies the democratic
foundation. Sincere words and the cultivated harmony put much
emphasis upon sincerity and peace. That men did not love their parents
only nor cherished as children only their own sons has lucidly reflected
universal love. The idea that the aged were provided with necessities of
life until death, employment was procured for the able-bodied and the -
means secured for bringing up the young amounts to the realization of
social security and welfare, and shows kindness and compassion to
widows, orphans and childless men. The equality of the sexes has been
urged by what is said in Li Ki "Males had their proper works and
females their homes." In such a social order selfishness can be
abolished, and robbers, filchers and rebellious traitors will not develop
to the effect that outdoors remain open. This is a society of Grand
Union. In fact, what Confucius called the Grand Union is equivalent to
democracy and socialism, and a counterpart of what Plato taught about
the discarding of the selfish interests of individuals and the
establishment of justice in a state.

Confucian Foreign Policy

Confucian foreign policy is also imbued with socialism. In Lun-Yü
he said:

Rulers of states and chiefs of families are not troubled lest
their people should he few*, but are troubled lest they should
not keep their several places; that they are not troubled with
fears of poverty, but are troubled with fears of a want of
contented repose among the people in their several places. For
when the people keep their several places, there will be no
poverty; when harmony prevails, there will he no scarcity of
people; and when there is such a contented repose. there will
be no rebellious upsettings.[69]

This Confucian equalization of rich and poor is what socialist states have nowadays predicated on equal distribution. Socialists have considered an unequal distribution to be the gravest evil, whence all social turbulent phenomena have taken root. Confucius foresaw in ancient times such social ills and did not spare himself to urge upon the states the need of an equal distribution. As for those people who were unsubmissive, Confucius insisted that all the influence of civil virtue shall be cultivated to attract them; and when they have been so attracted, they must be made contented and tranquil.

Confucius' theory of equalizing poor and rich has reflected what modern socialism has emphasized on the question of distribution. Socialism has conceded an unequal distribution to be the most serious flaw in modern world and to entail social disorder, which was foreseen by Confucius in ancient times. As for his foreign policy, Confucius, in dealing with unsubmissive remote people, advocated the cultivation of civil culture and virtue. Such a point of view is obviously in opposition to jingoism and colonialism, but in accord with orthodox socialism and peaceful foreign policy. It seems that although the Confucius' thought is trite in the modern world, it was workable in the ancient and feudalistic society two thousand years ago.

Mencius' Doctrine on Socialism

Mencius, the staunch follower of Confucius carried further the latter's socialistic ideas. Mencius was almost contemporaneous with Plato. Both of them put forward similar ideas of socialism though they appeared in two different words. Mencius' thought is more progressive than Confucius', and was not simply an advocate of the greater importance of people than that of rulers. His economic thought is rife with ideas of socialism. He said:

I would ask you, in the remoter districts, observing the nine-squares division, to reserve one division to be cultivated on the system of mutual aid, and, in the more central parts of kingdom, to make the people pay for themselves a tenth part. of their produce... A square "li" covers nine squares of land, which nine squares contain nine hundred "mow". The central square is the public field, and eight families, each having its private hundred "mow", cultivate in common the public field. And not till public work is finished, may they presume to attend to their private affairs.[70]

The well-field system or "ching-t'ien" of Mencius was laid out like the character "#" or well for his eight families' fields and a ninth, the common field. In the Choir-li (Book of Chou) nine "fu"-cultivators comprise a "ching" or well and "kou", drains, four feet wide and deep marked off one "ching", well from another; a square often "ching" by ten was a "ch'eng" and between "ch'eng" there were "hsu", ditches, eight feet wide and deep.[71] For some the well-field system was the basis for socialism; for others, it became a form of which the content was a trans-national universal stage. However, on the basis of a modern translation of Mencius' text, the well-field system has been thought of as the socialistic goal of men or feudalism.

Among Confucius' followers one group adhered to socialist outer commitment to strive for perfect government, a commitment concurrent with the monarch's interest in restraining private aggrandizement in land, and the other group subscribed to the inner commitment to morality in an egalitarian spirit from such hierarchically ordered possessors as the bureaucrats themselves.[72] In Shih-ching (Book of Poems) the well-field system is described as follows: "Rain (was petitioned) on our public field and then on our private field.[73] We see this as a symbol of the relation of the empire to the family. Ku Yen-wu said: "The Sage-kings knowing the primacy of the empire, yet knew, too, that man's original nature had a private impulse."[74] The kings sympathized with conferred lands in the well-field system and so joined communal and private in the empire. Around the turn of the twentieth century (1858-1927) K'ang Yu-wei, in his preface tribute to Confucius, held that Confucius had devised the well-field system in which land was allotted to every man and thus slavery in ancient China was abolished.[75] Likewise in 1899 Liang Ch'i-ch'ao (1873-1928) said: "China's ancient well-field system stands on the same plane as modern socialism." Tang Ssu-t'ung was of the same opinion and wrote: "With the well-field system or chingt'ien the government of the world can be made one, that is, "ching-t'ien" makes the rich and the poor equals."[76]

The well-field system of Mencius excels the well-field system described in Chou-li on the ground that land was owned by the kingdom and was apportioned to every man to cultivate. This is unlike the private ownership of land by the state or aristocrat in which people were allotted land, yet they were rendered slave peasant.

The Economic System of Husbandry

In presenting further description of socialism Mencius stated:

Let mulberry trees be planted about the homesteads with their five mow, and persons of fifty years may be clothed with silk.

In keeping fowls, pigs, dogs and swine, let not their times of breeding be neglected, and persons of seventy years may eat flesh. Let there not be taken away the time that is proper for the cultivation of the farm with its hundred mow, and the family of several mouths that is supported by it shall not suffer from hunger.... It never has been that the ruler of a state, where such results were seen-persons or seventy wearing silk and eating flesh, and the black-haired people suffering neither from hunger nor cold,-did not attain to the imperial dignity.[77]

This passage laid bare the higher principles which completed royal government. After the due regulation of husbandry and provision for the certain livelihood of other people, there must come the business of education. The schools aimed at the practice of archery, as a trial of virtue and skill. It refers to the inculcation of human relations by the institution of schools. Thus Confucius said: "The means of education should be provided for all, the poor as well as the rich."[78] When this principle was put into practice, one is bound to become a regnant emperor. Such a description of the social and economic system has brought out socialism in clear relief.

Likewise, Plato was convinced that the good state is a rational state, and that the good ruler (wise princes called by Mencius) is the man who knows precisely the plan of life which will bring about happiness to his people. Like a doctor looking after our bodily health and attending us when we are ill, the ruler must direct our whole life, plan our existence, and order' our thoughts and emotions. He must not be beguiled by our complaints or tempted by our bribes. He must care so much about the plan which he knows to be our welfare that he can overlook the distress and pain we shall suffer, just as the doctor must neglect our suffering if he is to save our life.[79]

Elsewhere Mencius wrote: "There must be in the territory of Tang men of a superior grade, and there must be in it countrymen. If there were not men of a superior grade, there would be none to rule the countrymen. If there were no countrymen, there would be none to support the "men of superior grade."[80] Plato expounded similar ideas, when he held that the civilians and the vast majority of the population, the peasants and artisans arc engaged in the production and distribution of. wealth. Their function is to provide the material foundation of social welfare and their happiness is to enjoy the just fruits of their labours under a stable government. The gentlemen, on the other hand, unsullied by trade and menial labours of agriculture and craftsmanship, serve as public administrators and must rule in Plato's state.[81] Here again, in the

Republic Plato drew a blueprint of a Utopia and had convinced himself of a possible enjoyment of a blissful life here. From this motive he embarked on describing how to apply rational principles to social organization so that an ideal society would come true. He insisted that the public admininistration shall be committed to philosophers on the ground that by dint. competence which the higher education brought about they were capable of leading society to reach its happy goal. In this state work is to be distributed to each according to his ability; education and support of children must be provided by the state. Women and men should work abreast and bear responsibility towards the state. However, unlike Mencius, Plato upheld communism: "From each according to his ability and to each according to his needs", and the community of wives and children. In this state there is neither dictator or tyranny nor a noticeable hiatus of poor and rich. Apart from Plato's fallacious communistic ideas, what is defective is the existence of slavery.

As for the division of labour Mencius has succinctly expressed the same ideas as Confucius' and said: "Greater men have their proper business, and little men have their proper business.. . . In the case of any single individual, whatever articles he can acquire are ready to his hand, being produced by the various handicraftsmen."[82] In like manner, Plato recognized the need for correlating the different types of occupation.[83] The common people are engaged in the occupations as skilled artisans, industrial and agricultural workers. The soldiers are bound to maintain order at home and repel invaders, and the guardians rule the state.[84] This principle of division of labour and co-operation has laid the foundation of socialism and has been equally adopted by both Confucius and Plato. Whereas Plato built an ideal commonwealth, Confucius established the Grand Union.

One, may be eager to know what has became actually of Confucianism in Communist China. Confucius asserted a "benevolent government" using moral virtues and the dictates of propriety as the criteria for judging people. The practice of the dictates of propriety redounds to respect for others and the treatment of people on an equal footing. On the other hand, the more the countries are on an unequal footing, the more there will be the hostility towards one another. In fact, what Confucius meant by "benevolence" had all the people in mind, that is to say, "benevolence" means "love of people"-a recognition of man's right to survive. Whereas Confucius' "love of people" subjectively imparts loving the ruling classes, objectively it means love of the masses and benevolence with all the people. In the People's Daily-Jen Min Jih Pao-we read that "Forum on Confucius" was held and assailed Confucius and Confucian scholars whose crimes included "fanatical exaltation of Confucius as a scholar and teacher", "acclamation of the Confucian principles of "benevolent government" and "rule of moral virtues." [85] According to the declaration of the Communist Party in the Forum, for more than two, thousand years China's reactionary ruling class adored Confucius as a "holy man" and took advantage of Confucian concepts to subject labouring people under the yoke. Confucian ideas therefore became heavy spiritual fetters imposed on the working people. Today in the socialist new China, the people have made a clean sweep of Confucian concepts and capitalist and revisionist ideas which serve to exploit the proletariat. As the vanguard for destroying Confucian ideas Red Guard has made the following comments:

1. Those people who have worshipped Confucius as a paragon of virtue had glorified him to the point of hysterical frenzy want to establish the absolute authority of Confucius in the hope of unifying the thought, language and feelings of 700 million people under the auspices of Confucian ideas. They use every conceivable means of disparaging and attacking Mao Tze-tung's thought. Under no circumstances should this be tolerated. We will certainly shatter Confucian thought and establish instead the absolute authority of Mao Tze-tung's thought.

2. It is only the dictatorship of the proletariat that can offer democracy to the people and impose dictatorship over all reactionaries. The reactionaries denounce us as not being "benevolent". That they want a "benevolent" government from us means doing away with proletarian dictatorship. If their schemes and plots are met with success. our Party and our country will be brought to ruin and the revolution will be a failure.

3. The relationships between slave-owners and slaves, between landlords and peasants and between capitalists and workers are those of exploiters and the exploited. The struggle between them is a life-and-death and implacable struggle devoid of the idea of "loving one another". In a Socialist society in which class struggle still exists, the principal reason why these monsters and demons have publicly propagated the idea of "loving one another" is to blur the class boundary and disown class struggle.

These comments have made it clear that in the great proletarian cultural revolution nowadays one of the Communist paramount tasks is to putrefy the rigid feudal corpse of Confucius and obliterate all of the reactionary Confucian ideas and tenets.

Conclusion

The multifarious social and political ideas of Confucius and his followers appear in the Book of Odes, the Book of History, the Book of Change and the Book of Rites which became the "Old Testament" of Confucianism. [86] The Analects of Confucius or the Sayings of Confucius, the Book of Mencius, the Book of Filial Piety, the Doctrine of the Mean and the Great Learning. [87] which formed the "New Testament" contain the verbose Confucian tenets. In their political thought Confucius and Mencius were socialistically inclined. Both laid down principles of humanitarianism and benevolent rule by the wisest members of society. Mencius stressed the importance of taking heed of the voices of the people. He devoted much attention to the problem of land distribution, conservation and of hunting through closed seasons in terms of economic life. He maintained that poverty entails crime and that responsibility for such crime rests with the ruler. Confucius, on the other hand, was in favour of government granaries, aid to transportation and state relief for orphans and the aged, widows and widowers, apart from private charities.

The government should make as its objective not the pleasure of the rulers but the happiness of its subjects. To this end Confucius advocated such measures as reduction of taxation, mitigation of severe punishment and abstention from needless wars. It is Confucius' belief that the state should be a wholly cooperative enterprise. The right to govern depended upon the ability to make the government well-organized and the people contented. This in turn depends upon the possession of virtue and ability which can develop by dint of education. Like Plato, Confucius did not advocate advanced education for all but believed that some education must be offered even to the humblest citizens for two reasons: (1) Since ability does not depend on birth, only a greater opportunity of education can enable the most capable to develop themselves for their own good as well as that of society. (2) Since the state is a co-operative enterprise, it is in dire need of enlightened citizens to serve it effectively.

The administration was conducted by ministers regardless of rank; they were selected not because of their ancestry but of their personal qualities so that a man of very humble origin could be elevated to wield the foremost power over the entire empire. However, considering that men have by nature been endowed with different degrees of intelligence and capacities, there ought to be social classes: scholars and officials labouring with their minds rightly deserve the service of those who are engaged in manual labour. This constitutes the division of labour and the principle of subordination and superordination in society. Confucius was of the belief that in case the rulers and their subjects discharge consciously their duty towards one another and enjoy bliss, the Grand Union would take shape in action.

Chapter 4

Discourse on the Main Stream Chinese Ideas of Ultimate Reality and Meaning

Introduction: Though there is a good number of general studies on Chinese religions (Wieger, 1927; Hughes, 1948; Smith, 1968; Eichhorn. 1973) and philosophies (Forke, 1927-1938; Needham, 1956; Fang, 1957; Fung, 1966) our knowledge of the Chinese ideas of ultimate reality and meaning is piecemeal, and every attempt to be systematic in this research involves us in a scramble for bits of documents to fit together. Well-documented, China could, indeed, provide an admirable framework for a better understanding of the ultimate reality and meaning of human existence. To gain a full understanding of Chinese ideas of ultimate reality and meaning we should scrutinize Tibetans, Turkus, Maio and Yi who had been regarded as ethnic groups and each of them may have their own ideas on ultimate reality and meaning. Even limiting ourselves to the main stream Chinese tradition as opposed to Tibetans, Turkus, Maio etc, there is still a vast field to research e.g.. that of the pre-Confucian ancient Chinese tradition, Confucianism. Taoism, Buddhism, Neo-Confucianism, modern China and Chinese Communism. Within each system there are many and varied views and schools of thought listed as separate topics for articles to be published in the present journal (see Ultimate Reality and Meaning 1:45ff). Researches on Old Chinese Haruspical bones with inscriptions from 16 B.C., Annals of China's history from 11 cent B.C., Confucius, Mo-Tzu, Mencius, Ch'an. Chu Hsi, Mao Tse-tung etc., are challenging tasks for the Sinologists and it might take many years before they can be presented to the scholarly world. But they are all indispensable for an adequate appraisal of what the Chinese mind has contributed to a better and deeper understanding of the ultimate reality and meaning of human experience.

    The purpose of the present essay is to introduce this research and call the attention of the Sinologists as well as that of all the readers of the present journal to the great wealth of the Chinese ideas of ultimate reality and meaning and to the complexity of grasping it. We plan to achieve this by presenting all the basic concepts which might come to a Chinese mind when the idea of ultimate reality and meaning is mentioned in the general context of his tradition. Evidently the various key words carry different meanings in the different epochs and cultures they involve. For this reason we will begin with a short historical description of Confucianism, Taoism, Buddhism and Neo-Confucianism fully developed by the end of 13th century A.D., the end of the Sung dynasty. But it seems that in spite of a wide range of differing meanings there is a certain sense which these terms provoke in the mind of an autochthonous Chinese to whom at once it becomes quite clear that Chinese ideas of ultimate reality and meaning differ profoundly from Western thought and that they are unlike Christian ideas to say the least. To bring this into better relief I will limit my discourse to the main stream tradition which, after having reached a certain completion in the 13th century, remains a dominating influence in the life of Chinese people and can be called 'Chinese' in the most authentic sense of that word.

From Pre-Confucianism to Neo-Confucianism

A number of the elements of Confucianism were reckoned as elaborations of the ancient Chinese tradition and owed their authority to the exemplary character of the sage kings such as Yao and Shun. Confucius himself showed due deference to the Duke of Chou, son of King Wen, as his inspiration. The Duke of Chou was also considered by Chinese tradition to be a source of Confucian ideas and even the founder of Confucianism, which developed in the Wu Ching 'Five Classics.' I Ching 'Book of Changes' and Shih Ching 'Book of Poetry' anteceded Confucius by several hundred years and constituted Confucian teachings. The theory 'never too much' in I Ching provided the principle argument for the Doctrine of the Golden Mean which was favored by Confucianist as well as by Taoist. Again, Confucius derived his moral value from the Book of Poetry and he said that the essence of three hundred poems can be expressed succinctly in one sentence 'Have no depraved thoughts.' One of the inserted chapters of the Shu Ching 'Book of History.' Goodness itself has no constant resting place, but accords with perfect sincerity, corresponds to what Confucius treated at length on the concept of Jen in Lun Yü 'The Analects of Confucius.'

Confucianism did not become the official philosophy until early in the reign of the emperor Wu (140-86 B.C.) and it was Tung Chung-shu (177-104 B.C.) who was instrumental in making Confucianism a state cult of the Han dynasty. Before the Fall of the Western or Former Han dynasty (A.D. 8), a favorable attitude towards rationalistic and moralistic Confucianism set in. Towards the end of the Han dynasty both Taoism and Buddhism gained ascendancy but they did not in any way supersede Confucianism; Confucian classics continued to be the corner-stone of all literate culture. It was the later unification of the Sui and T'ang dynasties that gave momentum to Confucianism simply because there was a craving for a restoration of Confucianism. Nevertheless, Taoism had a special appeal to the T'ang emperors. To understand why this was so, it is necessary to know that the emperor claimed to be the descendant of Lao Tzu.

Likewise the general ideas of Taoism existed at the beginning of the 5th century B.C. or even before; but Taoism Tao Chia was not used until the first century B.C. Lieh Tzu emphasized pessimism, fatalism and self-interest, while Yang Chu (c 440-c366 B.C.) held that the Taoist spirit was simplicity and harmony. In Lü-shih Ch'un-ch'iu (A Compendium of various Schools of Philosophy written by Lu Pu-wei in the third century B.C.) we can see the root and source of the two main trends of Chinese thought, Taoism and Confucianism. Both in the sphere of nature (Taoism) and in that of man (Confucianism), when anything developed to its extreme, a reversal to the other extreme occurred. This is one of the main theses of Lao Tzu's philosophy and that of the Book of Changes as interpreted by the Confucianists.

Buddhism was introduced into China from India in the first century A.D. Simply akin to Tao, the ultimate reality of the Buddhists was thought of as something that cannot be spoken. But the Buddhists began to use Taoist terms, such as Yu 'being.' Wu 'non-being,' Yu-Wei 'action' and Wu-Wei 'non-action' to express Buddhist ideas. There was consequently a considerable overlap between Buddhism and Taoism, and here the spirit of Ch'an (Zen, Meditation), came on the scene. Tao Shen's theory of sudden awakening by reverting to the inmost nature of the mind heralded the philosophy and school of Ch'an which was, on the one hand, a branch of Chinese Buddhism and, on the other, a combination of both the Buddhist and Taoist ideas. Tao Shen's concept of the importance of reason helped to gain an insight into ultimate reality and, in relation to the problem under consideration, anticipated Neo-Confucianism of the Sung dynasty. In effect, Neo-Confucianism is the continuation of the idealistic wing of ancient Confucianism, and especially of the mystic tendency of Mencius (Fung 1966, p. 268).

We see here three lines of thought that mark the main sources of NeoConfucianism. The first is Confucianism; the second is Taoism along with Buddhism through the medium of Ch'anism; the third is the Taoist religion, of which the cosmological views of Yin and Yang school, according as they bear on ultimate reality and meaning, are of great significance and interest. In expounding Chin Ssu lu 'Reflections on Things at Hand,' Chu Hsi expressed the point of view of the Sung philosophers who, in challenging Buddhism. embarked on formulating a new Confucian metaphysics. Nevertheless, inspired by Buddhist Hua Yen's philosophy of perfect harmony and Ch'an Buddhism, the NeoConfucians set off, under the leadership of Chou Tun-i (1013-73), Ch'eng Hao (1032-851), his brother Ch'eng 1(1033-1107), Chang Tsai (1020-77) and Chu Hsi (1130-1200) in the Sung dynasty, to revive the teachings of Confucius and Mencius, and to enrich their doctrine with more metaphysical and rational aspects.

There were three main doctrines in Neo-Confucianism which arose from Confucianism. The first is the principle Li underlying all truth and values. Although both Mencius and Hsün Tzu spoke of the principle Li, they did not in any way bring home the importance of the principle. Second, to know and live up to the principle Li, the Neo-Confucians investigated things in a rational way. The wisdom and calmness of the Ch'an school comes from this emphasis on extending knowledge and cultivating seriousness. The third point consists of anew look at the Confucian classics; the Neo-Confucians interpreted them in terms of rationalism, and, like Chou Tun-i, took them as an outlook on the universe, or, like Ch'eng 1, as an explanation of the principle of daily human affairs.

Within Neo-Confucianism there were three rival schools of thought, that is, the rationalistic school of Chu Hsi, the idealistic school of Lu Hsiang-shan (1139-93), and the empirical school represented by Tai Tung-yüan. Lu Hsiang-shan undertook to investigate the mind. The an empirical school aimed at practical results and the application of Confucian thought to social life and returned to what is called the central harmony of Confucius and Mencius.

All along this trend certain deep-rooted beliefs developed which distinguish Chinese thoughts from others in regard to the ideas of ultimate reality and meaning. Indian thought is characterized by profound metaphysical speculation and asceticism; Hebrew-Christian thought by a theocentric emphasis; early Greek thought by semi-materialistic speculation concerning the essence and origin of the universe. Chinese thought is characterized by an ethical realism that imports the deep-rooted beliefs; (1) both the universe and man's life are real, and running through the universe and life is a pervading ethical principle, i.e., man's duty is to follow the natural order of the universe; (2) the ultimate reality of the world must transform itself into an ideal pattern and axiomatic unity of supreme perfection, which consists of first developing one's own 'Nature' and ultimately culminating in well-ordered state; the word Jen simply means human perfection; (3) Tao or the observed order of the universe in Taoism and the Great Ultimate in

Neo-Confucianism are to Han scholars ultimate reality and meaning of life; (4) the Neo-Confucianism on which Buddhist Hwa Yen's concept 'One-in-All' and 'All-in-One' exercised influence held that 'Many' is subordinate to the 'One' on which 'Many' depends for its ultimate reality and meaning; the 'One' reality is called the Great Ultimate; (5) in Confucianism there is the relation of the self to the universe; (6) the perspective which recognizes no other than the present, i.e., selfishness, attachment and worldliness is not in accord with the ultimate reality; (7) the universe is a macro-cosmos and man a micro-cosmos - a world in miniature, so that Sheng Jen 'the sage or saint' who helps the transforming and nourishing power of Heaven and Earth forms a triad with Heaven and Earth; (8) in Taoism all forms of change are due to the interaction of two opposite forces - Yin and Yang. As in nature. the vicissitudes of Yin and Yang account for the regular succession of day and night and the alternate waxing and waning of the four seasons so man has his days and nights and the prime of life and its decline. Nevertheless, accounts of ultimate reality and meaning can barely become luminous without dwelling on the cosmic order, law, harmony, love and Tai Chi, the Great Ultimate, etc.

Li "Ultimate Principle"

There is a certain similarity of ideas in Confucianism, Taoism and Neo-Confucianism in term of Li. It means ceremony, ritual, decorum and rules of propriety. It is equivalent to the natural law, or reason and means also ultimate principle. It is the ultimate principle of harmony of man and nature, and each man with all men and with all things. On account of Li natural order and social order are two parts of a single cosmic order, and well-being for the individual or society depends on the continuance of this harmonious order free from serious disturbances. This is the purpose of the ancestral rites which remain uninterrupted in Chinese society and are part of the mechanisms by which an orderly and harmonious society maintains itself in existence, serving as they do to bring about certain fundamental social values. When the rites, symbolic actions, and beliefs of an ancestor worship are carried out by the one head of the large family, they achieve a greater degree of rationalization and common sentiments within that family than otherwise. Again, to render service to the living is embellishing their beginning; to send off the dead is beautifying their end. When both the beginning and the end are attained, the service of the dutiful son is well rendered and the way of the Sage is completed, and the principle Li has been reached.

The Neo-Confucian philosophy of One-in-All and All-in-One was based on Li. The Ch'eng Brothers said that all things are one reality, because all things have the same Li 'reason' in them (Ch'eng Shih I shu, ch. 2, 15a). Li or reason alone cannot operate without an agency or substantiating principle; this is Ch'i 'vital force' which, working by means of the Five Agents and in the form of Yin and Yang principles, differentiates the 'One' into 'Many' so that each of the 'Many' has its own determinate nature. T'ai Chi, 'the Great Ultimate' is also Li, reason, while activity as well as tranquility are a vital force. Although reason and vital force function differently, they co-exist. It is due to the co-ordinating function of reason and the vital force that the universe is made a cosmos, and a central harmony takes shape in action. Much the same could be said of the universe which in all its manifestations is a harmonious system. The order of the universe is central. and harmony is its immutable law, and thus it stands for cosmos, a moral order. This is the reason that Chu Hsi said: 'The Great Ultimate is nothing but the reason of ultimate goodness' (Chu Hsi Yü lei, vol, 1, lb).

All the characteristics of the universe are accounted for in reason. Therefore man must understand this reason to appreciate fully the meaning of his existence. We must investigate things also; a thing is an event. When we comprehend the reason for things, we will be persuaded that all people are our brothers and sisters, and our companions are all things. Moreover, reason is the moral law dominating the vital force; neverthless moral law refers to the operation of the vital force and to its unceasing transformation. So man's reason is his highest means of conscious self-control, conceived as true and just.

Since the mind is a full embodiment of the Li, a fully developed mind will embrace the whole universe. In support of the Li, Lu. Hsiang-shan (A.D. 11391193) said that the universe is identical with mind, and my mind is identical with the universe (Ch'üang-chi, 'Yü Lu', vol 35. 14a), simply because the mind and the universe are thought of as expressions of the moral law or principle. There is no moral law beyond the universe, nor are there events beyond the moral law. For any event within the universe is my affair, and any affair of mine is an event in the universe. Thus my mind, my friend's mind, the mind of the sages generations ago, and the mind of the sages of the future generations are all one. So all people have this mind and all minds contain this moral principle Li in full. The mind and the principle are one and only one. In Ch'ung Hsi Lu 'Record of Instructions.' Wang Shou-jen asked one of his disciples what the mind of Heaven and Earth was, the disciple replied. I have often heard that man is the mind of

Heaven and Earth or it is simply consciousness of them; if Heaven, Earth and things exist, it is due to my consciousness of them; when Heaven, Earth, spirits and the many worldly things are separated from my consciousness, there are no longer, Heaven, Earth, spirits and a multitude of things.

The moral principle Li corresponds with the ethical nature of law, which is inherent in the mind (Chu Tzu Ch'üan shu, book 53, 22a), the organ of its function. Now the Divine Being is law as ruler and his mind functions in the universe. Like Taoists the Neo-Confucianists also hold that the word Te 'virtue' may also imply a property of the mind in the same sense as humidity is a property of water and heat is one of fire. The four virtues of the mind, love, righteousness, reverence and wisdom are component elements of Li 'law.' Since the word 'law' involves a ruler, the ruler here is law without which there is no mind. Mind and ruler connote the idea of personality in the Divine Being and its attributes consist of love, righteousness, reverence and wisdom that are also the attributes of man's mind.

Wang Yang-ming held that the mind and reason are one and the same thing, because no event or reason in the universe can exist independently of the mind (Ch'üan shu, book 2, 73a-74b). The Chinese philosophy is spoken of as being idealistic, in view of the importance of mind, Li, both in rationalistic Neo-Confucianism and also in naturalistic Taoism. For the naturalistic Taoists, its realization depends on mind, mental activity, insight and enlightenment. At the same time, the mind constitutes the starting point in the realization of reason, since reason takes its form in the mind, though it is manifest in all things. The principle of filial piety, for instance, lies not in one's parents, but in one's own mind. Wang Yang-ming wrote. 'If I seek the reason of filial piety in my parents, is it in my own mind or in the person of my parents? If it is in the person of my parents, is it true that after my parents pass away my mind in consequence lacks the reason of filial piety? What is true for filial piety holds equally true with regard to the reason of all things: in short, reality' (Ch'üan shu, book 2, 73a-74b). Further, the controlling power of the body rests in the mind which gives rise to the idea, and the nature of the idea is knowledge; yet wherever there is the idea, there is a thing - a reality. Thus the idea rests on serving one's parents; serving parents is of course a thing.

Some Chinese thinkers, such as Chou Tun-yi, Chang Tsai and Ch'eng Hao endeavored to identify human nature with cosmic reason, but laid the blame on the part of human nature that has obviously been contaminated by selfish desires. Other thinkers like Ch'eng-I and Chu Hsi identified the quintessence of human nature with the cosmic reason.

Some Confucians have divided the universe into the supra-physical Tao 'spirit' and physical matter, and human nature into what is intrinsically good (Muncius) and what is extrinsically evil (Kao Tzu). They expounded the theories of harmony between man and the universe, which have been fitted with metaphysical and ethical dualities. Accordingly their emphasis lies chiefly upon transcendental reason at the cost of human nature.

CH'i "Instrument, Substantiating Principle"

Ch'i means first thing or object in contrast to Tao which lacks spatial limitation and physical form. Secondly it refers to material force. Before the idea Li developed in the Neo-Confucian doctrine, it denoted a power associated with blood and breath so that it is rendered as vital force or vital power. In contrast to Li it means instrument, substantiating principle. Since Li cannot operate without an agency, it is Ch'i which is working by means of Wu Hsing 'the Five Agents' in the form of Yin and Yang 'polarity principles' and differentiates the 'one' into 'Many' so that each of the 'Many' has its own determinate nature. When the five vital forces are distributed in harmonious order, the four seasons run their course. Ch'i is the instrument of Li and the foundation of the harmony of man and nature and each man with all men and with all things.

T'ai Chi "The Great Ultimate"

The term 'Great Ultimate' is rendered in Chinese T'ai Chi 'Great Terminus and pivot.' The wooden pivot is substituted for hinges in a Chinese door. Therefore the Great Ultimate seems to be the final cause of the universe, the controlling pivot on which all things turn and depend. Again, the word Chi together with a negative prefix forms two words Wu Chi 'without limit' which are translated as 'Infinite.' It is read from Ching Yi that the T'ai Chi is the great pivot of the universe, the source of all things whether visible or invisible, material or moral. In a word the Great Ultimate is the ultimate reality in the cosmos, the extreme limit in the vast chain of causes and the final cause of all things (Chu Tzu, Hsing li Ching yi, part 1.3a). The Great Ultimate or T'ai Ho, 'Great Harmony' is related to the concept of Ch'eng in man which serves as the stepping-stone to understanding and achieving the ultimate and the total (Cheng, 1973, p. 51). That the Great Ultimate is the immaterial element is expressed by the word 'law' (Chu Tzu Ch'üan shu, book 44, 8b). It is the source of all laws and all things, and thus is called the highest law. The law corresponds to ethical perfection and is termed by Chu Tzu 'Good' in Heaven and Earth, man and all things. Hence the Great Ultimate is not only in every individual but also is external and comprehensive. There is only one Great Ultimate which is received by each individual in its entirety and undivided, like the moon shining in the heavens. When it is reflected on river and lake and is thus visible everywhere, we should not say that it is divided (Chu Tzu Yü lei. vol 1, 10b). 'As for the entire universe there is in it one Great Ultimate; as to its parts there is a Great Ultimate in each of them' (Chu Tzu Yü lei, vol 1, tab). It resembles very much what Plato called the idea of 'Good' or what Aristotle called God. C. Chang expatiated upon the comparison between Chu Hsi and Aristotle. 'While Chu Hsi, Chang said, is an Aristotelian in the field of nature, he is a Platonist in the field of moral values; recognizing that there exists an eternal unchanging truth' (Chang, 1957, pp. 255-256).

The Great Ultimate moves and generates the active principle Yang. When activity reaches its limit, it becomes tranquil, producing the passive principle Yin. Yang's union with Yin, the Five Agents of water, fire, wood, metal and earth ensue. The two principles Yin and Yang are in fact two aspects of the one reality. The Five Agents constitute one Great Ultimate, which is basically Wu Chi, 'the Non-Ultimate.' The term Wu Chi has a double meaning of 'no limit' and 'nonbeing to the highest degree.' Chu Hsi said that the Great Ultimate goes in all directions without limit and goes above and below without limit. The reality of the ultimate 'Non-Being' and the essence of Yin and Yang and the Five Agents are mysteriously united. Ch'ien 'Heaven' and K'un 'Earth' are one great system of Yin (female) and Yang (male). The interaction of these two material forces engenders and transforms the myriad things, which produce and reproduce in an unending transformation. The successive movement of Yin and Yang constitutes the 'Way.' And here the Great Ultimate in Neo-Confucianism can be on a par with the concept of Tao as the way of self-transformation.

Yin and Yang "Polarity Principles"

Yin and Yang polarity constitutes Chinese metaphysics. They are not opposed to each other, but are two essential forces in the ceaseless activity of an impersonal universe or cosmos, which runs its course through the interplay of light and darkness, heat and cold, male and female. As a result the 'Many' is ultimately 'One' and 'One' is differentiated in the 'Many.' The two principles are co-eternal and inseparable. They appear in all directions and in all degrees with a perfect order. Reality is a continuous process of production and reproduction. This is the foundation of Neo-Confucianism. Now this continuous process of production and reproduction is possible because of the alternation of action and inaction including Yin as decrease and Yang as increase. It is the interaction of 'being' and 'non-being' that makes reality possible. In terms of change in the universe, Buddhists compare the universe with a sea wave, and make considerable efforts to cross the sea of waves to arrive at the other shore where the perpetual becoming will cease (Chan Wing-tsit, 1957, p. 135). In comparing the universe with a galloping horse, Taoists view this drama with detachment, and a spirit of indifference. Confucius conceived the universe as a great current which plays a leading role in the drama with pleasure. One of Confucius's disciples, Tseng Hsi felt like going swimming, adults and children together enjoying the breeze and returning home singing. Confucius was delighted and said: 'You are one after my own heart' (Lun Yü, Hsien chin, 7a).

Yin and Yang account for the fact that some men are sages and some are criminals. In some men, the Yang principle predominates, in others the Yin principle does. In the former there have been sages and the great men or Sheng Jen 'Sage or Saint.' The latter includes the wicked man and the criminal. However, since man produces evil, he can hate and combat it. Chinese philosophers on the whole agreed that it is within the power of man to wipe out evil himself. This is understandable since in the universe man forms a center of creation and participates as a generating power of creation. In the form of likeness of the original creator, individual human beings stand in a relation to universal love and mutual aid to Heaven and among themselves. However, if the human beings have perverted their ultimate reality of life so as to do violence to, and harm others for selfish gain, they will be labeled as the differentiated men, not sages, going to their doom and destruction (Fang, 1957, p. 140). This being so, it may be clearly seen that the idea of original sin and its atonement is lacking in Chinese philosophy. Man perpetrates wicked action which entails his own downfall. He must end this wicked action and can with grim determination restore the perfect state of life.

Wu Chi "Ultimate of Non-Being"

The term has a double meaning of 'non-limit' and 'non-being to the highest degree.' Neo-Taoist Wang Pi (226-247 A.D.) observed: 'Ultimate reality is Pen Wu "the original non-being" transcending all distinctions and descriptions; it is the "One" which underlies and combines all worldly things.' What underlies the extension of 'Many' is that their ruling principle returns constantly to the 'One' and all activities can be carried on because they are derived from the same source. The original Pên Wu is the mind of Heaven and Earth, which can only he revealed and seen in a state of tranquility and with cessation of activities within Earth. What seems to be unreal is the unnaturalness of certain man-made things and deeds that run counter to Tao. The Taoists were anxious that the ideal of 'nothingness' should come to the rescue of everything relevant to the realm of Being and a simple and harmonious life of the most sincere man should come from following nature. And the Neo-Confucians were anxious to teach men to achieve Confucian sagehood and a state of Wu-Yu 'having no desires.' The famous injunction Wu Wei, however, does not mean 'inaction,' but 'non-action' that is contrary to nature. Thus when Chinese scholars said that only in a state of tranquility can the mind of Heaven and. Earth be seen, they apparently failed to see that the mind of Heaven and Earth is rightly found in the beginning of activity.

Wu Hsing "Five Agents"

Water, Fire, Wood, Metal and Earth are the five agents or elements arising from the active principles Yin and Yang. The Five Agents are diffused in harmonious order. The nature of water is to moisten and descend; of fire, to flame and ascend; of wood, to be crooked and straighten; of metal, to yield and be modified; of earth, to provide for sowing and reaping. When the Five Agents influenced by the eternal world become activated, there follows the distinction between good and evil, and the myriad phenomena of conduct appear. Thus they not only influence the four seasons to proceed in their natural order, i.e. rain ought to fall in its proper season, plants should grow fruitful etc, but they can amount to irregularities in human society and in nature on account of Hsing 'Nature' and the existing Ho "Harmony."

Hsing "Nature"

The Chinese word Hsing is composed of two parts: the Hsin 'heart' denoting mind or mental activity; and Sheng 'birth' denoting the continuation of life. Chuang Tzu said: 'Hsing is the essence of life; the movement of Hsing is action' (Chuang Tzu, Kêng Sang ch'u', 9b). To Neo-Confucians the nature of a thing or man consists in production and reproduction. The concept of Hsing evolved from Sheng, life, a blessing received from Heaven. The Tao of Man with a status at the center of the universe is in connection with the creative and procreative power of Heaven and Earth and becomes a co-creator in the perpetual continuation of life. The Tao of Earth is the power of procreation, a construction and extension of the creative origin, involving all forms of existence. And finally the Tao of Heaven, a primordial creative power, makes all creatures and molds them into a cosmic order of dynamic transformation leading to a complete harmony and to an attainment of the ultimate good. Things exist and transform according to 'Nature,' because each and every thing has its own nature. The gigantic roc can soar high and the quail can fly low not because they take any action, but because Nature fashions them that way. The word 'Nature' means that things come into being spontaneously. Whatever deviates from nature is contrary to the philosophy of Tao. The question of whether promoting longevity is contrary to nature arises. The answer is rather negative, in that nature's time-scales are variable. As the slow growth of minerals could be accelerated by the alchemist, so man's short life could be slowed down and be unending. A man might defer death without going outside 'Nature' if only he could find out certain natural processes (Needham, 1974, p. 83). We cannot command 'Nature' except by obeying it. Hence Tao abhors competition, or any effort to expand oneself beyond the natural bounds of one's nature. To the Western thinkers, naturalism implies competition and control, but the Taoist mode of thought views nature as a harmony. But whereas Taoism insists that long life can only be preserved by following Nature, Confucianism holds that sagehood and the moral order can be achieved by living up to the .]en, the Golden Mean within this world. The actual world should be completely transformed into an ideal pattern embellished with the axiomatic unity of supreme perfection. This is the reason why Confucians have longed for the continually creative potency of the heavenly Tao in the forms of cosmic order. And it is in the universe that man found his own level.

To gain a full understanding of the word 'Nature' one must scrutinize Confucianism, Taoism and Neo-Confucianism each on its own. One of the difficulties involved in understanding the word 'Nature' has been the different senses this word may convey. This difficulty does not simply lie in definitions. but involves the culture in which one happened to be born and raised.

Yü Chou "Cosmos"

The universe or the world is thought of as embracing within itself a physical and a spiritual world. It is conceived as a comprehensive realm wherein matter and spirit have become completely unified so as to form a coalescence of life which continues with creation unlimited by space and time. The word Yü is a constellation of a three-dimensional series of changes in succession: the past continuing itself into the present and the present into the future. The two words Yü Chou symbolize the primordial unity of the system of space with the system of time. The universe is conceived as characterized by the regularity which Western philosophy has called 'law.' but it lacks the idea of God or a lawgiver. This regularity involves three features: (1) the cyclical processes, such as the succession of day and night; the rotation of the seasons; (2) the process of growth and decline, such as the waxing and waning of the moon; (3) the polarity of nature, i.e.. everything has its opposite, and opposites are complementary to each other.

In Needham's view, Neo-Confucianism arrived at essentially an organic view of the universe which, though neither created nor governed by any personal deity, was entirely real (Needham, 1956, p. 412). All things exist in relations. Needham saw a striking similarity between Chinese organism and that of Whitehead; nonetheless, there is in Neo-Confucianism an absence of Whitehead's God, who as the principle of coalescence is ultimate irrationality. As for the change in the universe. Buddhists subscribe to the opinion that, as events are illusory, time is illusory, and it moves on but will come to an end in Nirvana. Buddhists speak of the true state of reality as the state without a specific nature. This state is 'Nirvana,' the state of perfect freedom from bondage and is the ultimate principle of life, when all earthly conditions have been blown out. To Taoists time travels in a circle, and since a thing comes from 'non-being,' it will return to non-being. For example, ancestors exist in the changeless dream time of the past, and wherever our ancestors are now, it is there that we are going too. The eternal changeless past and future time tend to coalesce (Leach, 1964, p. 5). In the process of production and reproduction, Confucians counted that time never comes to an end or repeats itself. Neo-Confucians, however, have savored a metaphysical flavor and have decidedly agreed that the universe is good because there are the greater acts of love, and in the oscillation of Yin and Yang there is harmony which is to be achieved here and now in this world-reality. The universe embraces all things, and what moral act can be better than identification with everything?

Ch'ien and K'un "Heaven and Earth"

Heaven or male, Earth or female result from the interaction of the two principles yin and yang and from the movements of the Five Agents. All things are produced spontaneously by the fusion of the vital force of Heaven and Earth. If Heaven had produced all things on purpose, it taught them to love each other and not to prey upon and destroy one another. 'Reality is the way of Heaven; yet making oneself real is the way of man. That which Heaven entrusts to man is to be called his human nature and the pursuit of this nature is to be called the Way' (Chung Yung, Ia). In fact it is only man who, owing to his reality in the world has the capacity to develop his human nature fully, in line with all natural species, and to help transform and nourish the work of Heaven and Earth in himself. In man's life body corresponds to different parts of Heaven and Earth. Man and the universe can be reduced to the same reality, Tao, the beginning of Heaven and Earth (Giles. 1972, p. 19). The mind of Heaven and Earth also refers to the Supreme Being designated by the term Tien "Heaven".

Tien and Shang-Ti "Heaven and Supreme Personal God"

The Confucian concept of Tien is the source and ultimate control of man's destiny. Hsü Tzu's concept of Tien is purely 'Nature.' We approach the meaning of the term Tien if we mean by it both 'Nature' and the divinity which presides over nature, with emphasis sometimes on the one, sometimes on the other. The concept of Tien 'Heaven' and 'Shang-ti' as represented in the Songs and Hymns of the Book of Odes is that of knowing, feeling, loving and hating supreme ruler of men and the universe. But instead of such an anthropomorphic deity, a new philosophic concept of Tien is Tao, the 'Way' or all-pervading and everlasting process. Lao Tzu spoke of Ti 'Lord.' Nevertheless if the idea of God is insinuated in Taoism, it is completely overshadowed by the cardinal Taoist doctrine of self-transformation. Christians believe that all things save God are imperfect, Taoists hold that men can become perfect through selftransformation. Since Taoism lays emphasis on a simple and harmonious life, we are able to see why this naturalistic and atheistic philosophy should have a relationship with a superstitious religion geared to the 'here' rather than the 'hereafter.' A religion which lends support to the practice of alchemy and believes in immortality in this world, has a search for the elixir of life. This Taoist religion led men to a negative philosophy to the loss of self confidence and a progressive social order. In Confucianism, Heaven is of anthropomorphic character and is identified with Shang-ti who not being the personal God as held by Christians implies the great mystery in the process of. production and reproduction. The Confucian attitude towards the metaphysical and transcendental question tended to widen the distance between Shang-ti 'God' and men, particularly when the terms 'Heaven' and 'Earth' came to the fore. Chu Tzu relegated God to a position of infinite remoteness, though he admitted the existence of an ultimate ruling power.

Ho "Harmony"

The theory of harmony Tai Ho 'great harmony' between man and the universe has played an important role in Chinese philosophy. Confucius maintained that to find Chung 'the central clue' of our moral being and to be Yung 'harmonious' with the universe is the ultimate goal of our moral life. This doctrine is the essence of Chinese philosophy. Chinese philosophers have conceived the universe as a plane of the confluence of universal life. The earthly primordial life, in conjunction with Heaven makes up the cosmos within which all men come to be in harmony with Heaven and Earth, in sympathetic unity with one another and in perfect equilibrium with all things. In the Han dynasty, it was the people's belief that there was a unity between Heaven, Earth and man and that the activities of any one of them tallied with those of the others. Disturbances in the heavens or earth were closely related to human actions and acted as a warning of impending catastrophe. The hui-hsing or nova which was seen for 70 days from the second month of 5 B.C. was linked, perhaps retrospectively, with an important and potentially treasonable suggestion put forward in the sixth month (Loewe, 1977, p. 13). On earth, in 4 B.C. seven 80-foot long monsters were cast up on the shore of East China. The Chinese people imputed the disturbances of the natural order to the social disarray. Hence to make every form of life congruent with comprehensive harmony is the prospect of the universe. The Chinese people by respecting nature strive to the best of their ability for the attainment of the supreme good in imitation of cosmic order, radiance and splendor. The harmony of self and society in Jen is expressed by Chung 'conscientiousness' and Shu 'altruism,' which is essentially the Golden Mean or the Golden Rule. There exists a harmonious relation between the universe and man, an identity of attributes under the form of reciprocity, and the principle of creativity, that is, the universe and man are equipotent in creation (Fang, 1957, p. 135).

Ch'an "Meditation" and the Undifferentiated Continuum: One in All and All in One

Ch'an is a method of direct intuition into the heart to find Buddha-nature. Together with its 'abrupt enlightenment' it provided the Chinese mind with a way of ready and complete release. The fundamental beliefs or the ch'an meditation such as salvation for all and salvation by faith are based on the principle of 'One in all and all in One,' that is. Nirvana has neither space nor time. neither life nor death. This is interpreted as the land of the Buddha of Infinite Light and Infinite Life, i.e. the Pure Land.

S.C. Northrop said that the theory of the 'undifferentiated continuum' represents the metaphysical or more mystical truth of Taoism (Northrop, 1946, pp. 186-187). Taoism is identical with monism, for Tan the only real, is one, and it produces many, although they are but appearances. The subject of the 'One' and 'Many' was broached in a Buddhist essay The Golden Lion by Fa-tsung (643-712 A.D.). In the Golden Lion the gold and lion are one substance, the lion being inlaid with gold, every part of the lion penetrates the gold and vice versa. In a word, the 'One' is the 'Many,' and the 'Many' is the 'One.' But Buddhists argued that the 'One' was the true form or the true mind. Since Tao is the moral law, it is the universal principle of all things, the essence of reality. Here Tao is conceived as bearing a resemblance to Brahman, but Tao is the Way, the principle of reality. It stands for 'One,' while Te 'virtue' for 'Many.' Although the many are formed by the 'One' they are most real in proportion as they are in conformity with Tao. the Way of things. The 'One' and the 'Many' each has its determinate nature. This is the question of the relationship between the undifferentiated continuum and the particular individual differentiated units (Chou Lien-hsi, I T'ung shu. vol 6, 2a). It is read in Chu Tzu Pu chu 'Supplementary Annotations to the Elegies of Ch'u State.': 'Thus, transcending inaction, I attained to the Great Clarity and entered the principle of the Great Beginning; the undifferentiated continuum is virtually the final abode where one's reality is identical with oneness; of great interest is that this identity amounts to the loss of individual reality in the universe; in the same way water flows down to the ocean.'

The Great One or Great Unit has always been emphasized and has resulted in the Taoist doctrine of equality of things. In Confucian doctrine Li is one of many manifestations. Neo-Confucians would be in accord with both Buddhists and Taoists on the point that reality is one. In fact, Chinese philosophy has been in want of pluralism, for it has thought of the one in preference to the many. Nevertheless, this thinking in no way indicates that Chinese metaphysics tends to be monistic. The Neo-Confucians's synthesis is that both the 'One' and the 'Many' are real. Chou Tun-i said that the 'Many' and the 'One' are complementary and they have each its own correct state of being; the great and the small each has its definite function (Chou Lien-hsi, I T'ung shu, 2a). We have mentioned that the Neo-Confucian philosophy of One-in-All and All-in-One was based on Li. The undifferentiated continuum serves as the ultimate solution to the problems of Ti Hsien and Tien Hsien earthly (material) or heavenly immortality.

Ti and Tien Hsien "Earthly and Heavenly Immortality"

To become a hsien means succeeding in becoming an immortal. Man is aged but not dying. He has removed his habitation into the mountain and has all gone into the world of light. Tien Hsien are those who departed from the flux of changes and vanished from men's sight; they escaped unafraid from all life's troubles, and no one could tell whither they had gone.

Immortality as conceived in the Confucian tradition and eternal life in the sense of Christianity are two separate things. Most Chinese people crave for something which is immortality, not beyond the present world, but in this natural world. In no Chinese philosophy, be it Taoism or Confucianism, is there the Western conception of personal immortality. True, there is the realm of immortals in the Taoist cult. but this belief which I think we call 'secular' or 'mundane' is a conception of man's place in the universe, namely, salvation in this world or long life and lasting vision. In Confucian doctrine, the sage or sainthood and the moral order which are bound up with the cosmic order do not transcend this world.

A question may be raised: can temporal or this-worldly immortality last forever'? The simple answer is to produce a male heir. What constitutes the raison d'être is that the continuation of a line for individual families and for the society at large depends on a male heir. For a male heirdom has symbolic meaning for Chinese people beside what is meant for them as a family continuous link, that it is a projection of the self and its identification with the large self. Although Chinese people lack formal religion, and this worldly immortality is aptly achieved by an heir, they do entertain the idea of religion in a more anthropomorphic way than they speak of God; these ancestors are spoken of as spirits and stand for the collective strength of the lineage to which the person belongs. The Confucians insist that a religion like ancestor worship can be rationalized as immortality in the minds of men. In the rite commemorating the ancestors the participants should express their respectful gratitude to those from whom they have received their life, and their sense of duty towards those who have not yet been born and to whom they in due course will stand in the position of revered ancestors.

Although both Taoism and Neo-Confucianism are interested in life, the former argued that unless nature is followed, the goal of life will by no means be reached, whereas the latter contends that life can only achieve its ultimate reality by the full development of man. Taoists have as their main goal the nourishment of our original nature and the preservation of life by letting it run its natural course. What really matters to Taoism is the Taoist immortal's freedom and durability within the world of Nature. The Taoist aspires to be incorporated into the ranks of the invisible hierarchy of the universe as Tien Hsien 'heavenly immortal' or else seeks for transformation into Ti Hsien, 'earthly immortal' purified, ethereal and able to spend the rest of eternity wandering as a kind of wraith through the mountains and forests, enjoying the company of similar enlightened spirits and the cycle of the seasons ever repeated yet with glory ever renewed.

In the belief of Chinese philosophers, at death man's soul returns to the heavenly paradise from which it comes, and his spirit returns to the earthly or passive universal principle from which it originates. It is taken for granted that people have some sort of existence after death, though the Chinese do not presume to know where and what kind of life it is that they have. But when people die, one thing is certain that they have departed for good (Needham, 1974, p. 78). Influenced by Buddhism the Chinese masses had no doubt that the individual continues to live after death. Yet the Chinese intellectuals speak of their belief in individual immortality, namely, social immortality or immortality of influence. At death, our bodies dissolve, but blood-flesh in our children, our interests, our words and contributions to society persist unbroken. H.H. Dubs rejects the Chinese idea of immortality, but insists that Lao Tzu meant an immortality of influence, and he did not believe in earthly immortals (Dubs, 1954, pp. 149-161). Mo Tzu believed in spiritual beings and founded a religion in ancient China (Hu Shih, 1928, p. 57). Confucius, however, neither denied the existence of spiritual beings nor ignored ancestors, but he was very keen on substituting moral principles and social decorum for barbaric customs, such as burial of living persons and wooden images. He urged his pupils to serve parents when alive, according to propriety; bury them, when dead, according to propriety; and sacrifice to them after death according to propriety (Lun Yü, Wei Cheng, 8a). Hence to all intents and purposes Confucius weakened, if he did not destroy. the belief in personal and spiritual survival after death. Man's soul and spirit do not depart immediately after death, in that he retains his identity for some time and, in the course of time, his active and passive principles are gradually dissipated. Confucius was a holy man and lives still within our memory as a spiritual being, while his descendants have fallen into oblivion; this is simply Chinese belief in world fame.

Tao "Way of the Way"

Tao means a road, or path. As 'Way of the Way' it refers to ethical, religious truth, and in terms of conduct it amounts to the normative standard. It is the actual moral law not away from the daily human life. Further Tao is the reality within appearances, the ultimate metaphysical truth, like the God of the Western Philosophers and 'Nirvana' of Buddhism. In short, Tao is likened to the laws of 'Nature' or better still 'Nature' itself but is in no way conceived as deity (Chung Yung 1a).

Conformity with Tao is the summum bonum, or self-realization above the material level. It opens the way to peace and happiness. C.S. Medhurst is of the opinion that benevolence, righteousness, filial duty, paternalism, loyalty and devotion dwindled when Tao, the Great Ideal, the One Life, receded from view (Medhurst, 1972, p. 30). Tao is in fact Jen, love and righteousness and is not something enigmatic, a vague and incomprehensible ideal, but it matters to everyday life and daily relationships. Arguing against a false mysticism in regard to Tao, Chu Hsi said that Tao, a mystical love of paradox is still more conspicuous. 'The Tao which can be expressed in words, said Lao Tzu, is not the eternal nameless Tao, but is the beginning of Heaven and Earth; and with a name, it is the mother of all things' (Giles, 1972, p. 19). Medhurst wrote glosses on this passage: 'That aspect of God which is hidden in eternity, without bonds, without limits, without beginning, must be distinguished from that which is expressed in nature and man, the one apparently subjective, certainly unknowable; the other, selfmanifestation, or the commencement of our knowledge as of our being' (Medhurst, 1972, p. 1). Chu Hsi insisted that Tao should have a real existence and not be so transcendental as to lack any connection with men. Tao in itself is diffused in such an infinite variety that its substance is invisible; yet it is only when we see Tao in our own nature that we perceive what constitutes its reality here and nowhere else (Chu Tzu, book 42, 2 lb and 22a). Tao has a real illimitable substance, and, though transcendental, it is the moral law written upon the heart of man.

The Confucians have aspired to the continually creative power of the Heavenly Tao to mold the whole cosmic order.

Jen "Human Perfection, Manhood"

Jen '人' means man '二'means 'two', i.e. only two persons can contract a human relationship. As moral perfection it is translated as benevolence, perfect virtue, goodness, human heartedness, love and altruism. But none of them expresses all the meanings of the term Jen. In the book of Mencius, Jen is man's mind. In the Han dynasty, Confucians conceived Jen as love of men living together (cf also Chu Tzu Ch'üan shu, book 47, 4b-6b). Neo-Confucians interpreted it as the character of production and reproduction, seeds that generate, the will to grow, one which forms body with Heaven and Earth. Thus Jen is rendered 'humanity.' Humanity surely possesses the characteristics of life-giving and the like, and it is man who forms one body with Heaven and Earth.

Jen is called Man because loving comes from Nature, and is the allcomprehensive attribute of Mind so that it constitutes the source of all virtues: righteousness, propriety and wisdom. It is thought of as a source of cosmic creation, conceived as the vital impulse which is rendered Shing-yi. The word Shing 'life' and Yi 'purpose' are combined to imply the principle of life, such as exists in the grain of wheat, in peach and apricot kernels, although to all appearances they are dead (Chu Tzu Ch'üan shu, book 47, 3a). Moreover, the expression Shing-yi conveys more meaning than the principle of life. The principle of vitality latent in the seed or kernel will under auspicious conditions burst full-blown; this can clearly be seen in the budding life of spring when all nature is surging. This impulse, whether in man or in the universe is Jen. In the creator it is the delight in giving birth to things. In the creatures it is Jen, the impulse to preserve it. This Jen is the gentle mind which loves mankind and is kind to other creatures. It extends from observation and feeling and experience to man and animals as well because when Man hears the pitiful cry of an animal that is to be slaughtered, he instinctively has compassion. Chu Tzu even was loath to let anyone cut the grass in front of his window (Chu Tzu Ch'üan shu, book 48, 8b). This 'feeling' and 'experience' bear witness of the innateness of the heavenly nature within man. For the creative power of ultimate reality and meaning found as it is in Heaven and Earth proves to be evidence in confirmation of Jen inherent in man (Cheng, 1973, p. 53). Jen the true manhood involves self-realization and the creation of social order. To he a true man is to love all men. He renders to no man evil for evil. Instead he meets wrongdoing with love, shows filial piety to his parents.

Te "Virtue"

Te means moral character and excellence, but in relation to Tao it means Tao particularized in a thing. It includes Ching Hsin 'seriousness, calmness of mind.' Ching means reverence which implies an object. and bears resemblance to 'calmness' in Buddhism and in ancient classics it signifies composure, yet Neo-Confucians lay emphasis upon making effort in handling affairs. Chung Shu means consciousness and altruism. Chung indicates the full development of one's original nature, whereas Shu implies the extension of that nature to others. In relation to the Confucian Golden Rule, Jen, Chung refers to the self, while Shu to others. Ch'eng 'sincerity' is described as perfection. When there is perfection, there is enlightenment and vice versa.

Sheng Jen "Sage or Saint"

In both Confucianism and Neo-Confucian philosophy man is enabled, by striving, to aspire to ultimate perfection whether he is called Sage, saint or a perfect. It means that perfection can come to man without being what is thought to be transcended and other-worldly. Here we speak of the pragmatism of self-cultivation, or edification which is in an anthropomorphic way a substitute for the worship of, and dependence upon God. In Confucianism man depends upon other men for self-cultivation and perfection. In Taoism Man relates to all things and interacts with. and participates in the activities of Tao in pursuit of goodness and perfection.

Men should strive for inner sagehood or sainthood. This, however, can by no means be achieved unless men participate in the universal law, live in accord with the general pattern of the universe and foster moral life, namely, benevolence. righteousness, wisdom and propriety. These four virtues are the manifestation and moral fulfilment of the ultimate reality and meaning of human existence in this world. This is simply what Mencius said: 'To dwell in the spacious habitation of the universe (to practice benevolence), to stand in the right place of the universe (to conform to propriety or moral rules of correct conduct) and to walk on the grand path of the universe (to observe righteousness). (Mencius 'Li Lou,' Pt. 1. 7a-7b). These are the marks of a great man.

Conclusion

The purpose of this essay was to list the basic concepts which one has to analyze and research in order to see what Chinese ideas on ultimate reality and meaning of human existence can possibly be. To study these key words in their proper historical and cultural context as well as in their continuous development is the great task of the scholarly world. After having read this essay it must be very clear that the Chinese ideas of ultimate reality and meaning differ profoundly from Western ideas on the same subject.

Chapter 5

Totemism in China

Abstract : The paper deals with the nature and content of totemic beliefs in China and has examined the existence of a boud of mutual dependence and friendship between man, animals and plants. Often such beliefs are strengthened with the conception of fertility and growth, weal and woe, bad omen or good omen. The author has also drawn a distinction between a natural order and social order contrasting nature and man. The process of personification of certain species of animals has been seen to be significant. The nucleus of the animistic system is based on the concept of soul in animals and plants. Here is again the concept of external soul whereby it is beheved that the totem is a safe place where a soul can be deposited. Though totemism is not an ubiquitous phenomenon, available in every society, its presence among the Chinese has equated the Chinese totemic beliefs with those present elsewhere.

Introduction

The purpose of this paper is to investigate a class of phenomena which bear on totemism. There has been some disagreement as to the definition of totemism. The term "totemism" serves this purpose in so far as it brings together for our study a number of phenomena which are in reality related to one another and have formed the general relation between man and natural species in mythology and ritual. The primary basis of totemism lies in the 'feeling' of a connection with a given species of animals and plants conditioned by the material production and, in the end, in a feeling of a bond of a human group with the occupied territory.

The belief in supernatural conception was at first part of totemic complex, and betokened an uncertain paternity and thus vague ideas as to the role of man in the coneeption of a child. Chinese legend abounded with tales of supernatural births of certain eminent persons who are said to have been conceived by women with a deity or, by its command, with animals. Such stories give to all intents and purposes an impression of the innate superiority of certain heroes. The Christian doctrine 'conception immaculate' of Christ by the virgin represents the evolution of the ancient idea.

Totemic creatures in China, such as bird:,, animals and plants are in the nature of legends of the marvellous, concerned with the birth of heroes, but do not suggest the descent of human groups from natural species. The creatures are not themselves of paramount importance, but the designs of the creatures are symbols of an impersonal force distributed in images, animals, and men. They were selected because they are fitting models for pictorial representation.

Many primitive tribes are divided into clans. A clan consists of a group of lineages all of which claim to have been descended from a remote and common ancestor, who may be a totemic ancestor. The clan namo may originate from an animal, plant or natural objects. The clansmen exhibit special attitude towards these creatures which are thought of in this sense by anthropologists as totems. The word 'totem' originates in the Ojibwa, an Alonquin language of the region. The expression of the following parts -0-, the third person prefix ; -t-, epenthosis, separating the vowels ; -m-, possessive; -an-, the third person suffix; and -ote- expressing the relationship between 'Ego' and a male or female relative, and thus defining the exogamous group at the level of the generation of the subject Ego'.[88] The Ojibwa conceive the totem as assuming the shape of some beast or other, and hence they never kill, hunt, or eat the animal whose form they think this totem bears.[89] A man respects his totem by refraining from harming it in any way, yet the respect is mutual and the totem should refrain from harming those who respect it. A totem is an animal, and more rarely plant or a natural phenomenon, which stands in a peculiar relation to the whole elan, that is, the totem is the common ancestor of the clan and is also their guardian spirit which sends them oracles, and, if dangerous to others, recognizes and spares its own children. It is in these ideas that it behoves the Ojibwa Indians not to kill, hunt or eat their respective totem.

The system which involves the clans, their totems and beliefs, customs and rituals is called totemism. The sum total of totemic phenomena, such as tribal groups, a clan, or a family, the natural species of animals or plants as well as inanimate objects is reckoned as a totemic system, It should be borne in mind that, however widely or narrowly totemism may be defined, we can scarcely gain a better understanding of the phenomena in question unless we study the general relation between man and natural species or objects in the context of legends, myths and tales. One may readily ask if totemism has not outlived its usefulness. To this question we may quote what old King Arkel said : -history does not produce useless events'.[90]

The Origin of Totemism

The subject has gradually awakened great interest and has brought about an abundant literature, such as Frazer's four volumes Totemism and Exogamy, Andrew Lang's The Secret of the Totem, Sigmund Freud's Totem and Taboo, and Levi-Strauss' Totemn.ism. But it was John McLennan who brought home the importance of totemism to human prehistory. In agreement with McLennan, Lang said that the, origin of totemism lies far beyond our powers of historical examination of experiments. Certain vestigial remains bear evidence of the existenee of totemism at one time among the Chinese. How did it come that primitive people adopted totems ? How did they call themselves or their clans after animals, plants or inanimate objects ? How did they believe that they were descended from one animal or another ? Lang held that

All theories as to how totemism arose must be mainly guesswork as regards the original character of man. Nowhere do we see absolutely primitive man, and a totemic system in the making.[91]

The origin of totemisrn in China can be sought in an animal name or a sacred name ; and where wo find totems we find the institution 'exogamy'.[92] Totemism in China can be explained satisfactorily from nominalist and psychological point of view. The origin of what we know of totemic phenomena has been attributed to the need felt by clans to distinguish themselves from one another by use of names. A totem is akin to a clan name, and a group emblem; then the name of the ancestor or a clan, and lastly the name of an animal is worshipped by a clan. The swallow is the dynastic bird or a totem of the Shang dynasty. A tablet in the form of a tiger was placed in the emperor's coffin on the right ; this symbol represented protection. A passage in the Li Chi accounts for a sacrifice of the tiger, performed daring the Great 'Ka' sacrifice to earth.[93]

The core of totemism. nomenclature takes root in the primitivc technique of writing ; totem is hence like an easy drawn pictograph. When ancient Chinese bore, the name of an animal, they proceeded to form the idea of kinship with it and thought that the clansmen are under sacred obligation to help one another; the giving of names was regarded as the decisive factor in the origin of totemism. If we strive to explain animal worship, we must keep in mind how human names reflected the qualities of animals, and how the former were borrowed from the latter.

Thence it occurred that the animal itself has come to be looked upon first with interest, then with respect and at length with a sort of awe. Chinese people consider names to be of considerable value and significance, for a man's name is transmitted from his ancestor and is to be treated with deference. Whoever stains his clan name, he will cringe to his ancestor and be visited with misfortune as Chinese give the impression of so believing. The Fu Hsi's surname (about 2852 B.C.) is said to have been 'feng' (wind). which is connected with the bird 'fang' (phoenix), a herald of peace and prosperity. It stands to reason among the Chinese that a dynasty or an emperor bearing the same name as animal must lead him to the exist-ence of a mysterious bond between himself and that particular animal. The similarity of names would involve all the totemic ordinances, including exogamy, that is, the custom of a man marrying outside his own clan group. In China a rule of exogamy relating to family names is observed, since no Chinese is allowed to marry a woman who bears his own family or clan name. Exogamy in itself showed a trace of totemism, but the Chinese exogamy is of modified form. Externally, they are endogamous, i.e., they refuse marriage with any surrounding tribe ; internally, they are exogamous, i.e., they are forbidden to marry any one whose surname shows him to be of the same stock; which is not necessarily of one blood.

The Chinese practise endogamy regards any surrounding tribes, since it was only one tribe, that is, the whole Chinese race, so that they should be descended as endogamous.[94] Among Yi group, an aboriginal race of southern China, the custom forbids intermarriage between the people having the same surname. Children take their patronymic name from their father, and no persons who bear the same patronymic are permitted to marry each. other. Further a social system which bears some resemblance to totemism has been found to exist among the Lolos. an aboriginal race of southern China. Henry has studied the Lolos at Szemao, a Custom post in the south of Yunnan province. He wrote:

It is interesting then to know that Lolo surnames always signify the name of a tree or animal. or both tree and animal, and that these are concidered to be the ancestors of the family bearing the name.... . Thus the surname Bu-luh-beh is said to be an ancient name of the citron; which is known as Sa-lu, The common way of asking a person what his surname is to inquire what is it you don't touch; the person of this surname would reply : 'we do not touch the Sa-lu or citron.[95]

Lolo people cannot eat or touch in any way the plant or animal or both which enter into their surnames, though they do not worship the plant or animal on any account. People of the same surname may marry if there is no obvious relationship. There are, on the one hand, groups of two or three surnames among whom intermarriage is forbidden ; there are, on the other, groups of two or three surnames who are called comrades and among whom intermarriage is preferred.

There are also some hints of totemism existing among the aborigines. of Formosa. The inhabitants of mountains and forests in the northern part of the island are reported to be divided into tribes, each of which has its own name and possessor; an animal under whose special protection the inhabitants believe to live and they keep and feed it in a cage. The animal may be a serpent or snake or a. leopard. Presumably these guardian animals are reckoned as totems. According to the testimony of Chinese history, Chili people, that is, of Hopei province, sprang front at wolf and a beautiful Hun princess, who married a wolf. Likewise the Tungus professed to derive their origin from a 'she wolf' : the Chincse assert that Balachi, the hereditary chief of the Mongol Khans, was the son of a blue wolf and a white hind.[96]

When an animal or plant is made the totem of a social group, a man of this group would refuse to eat this animal or plant because to do so would amount to eating himself. Again the origin of totemism is allied with the institution that grew out of the animal, which has a mystical significance in national strength and might, and thus it deserves cult. Tiger in China, for instance, deems to be guardian spirit against evil spirits and to protect the living and the spirits of the dead. In the Shang or Yin dynasty (about 1500-1100 B.C.), if the shooting of the Prince sallied forth in the provinces, the tally-holder was tiger-shaped.[97] The king gave the Marquis of Han the leaning-board with leather, and a tiger's skin to cover it.[98] On the same dynasty bronzes the tiger's head appeared more often in a composite than in a natural form., conveying the original tiger-god and tiger-guardian of the souls of the Shang ancestors. When the emperor made sacrifice to four objects in mountains and near rivers he put on wool clothing on which an emblem of tiger and monkey was embroidered.[99] The ancient wise men met and sacrificed to the tigers because they devoured the bears that destroy the fruits of the fields. Throughout the agricultural connection the tiger protected the living and the spirits of the dead : this was one reason for the persistence of the tiger symbol throughout the ages. The tiger quality is something added in thought to the human attributes, and does not detract from them.

The Chinese theory, as we may call it, of the origin of totemism flows very naturally -from the Chinese social structure. Whereas the Egyptians had a mystic affinity with animals, the affinity of the Chinese was with natural phenomena and charm they appreciated perhaps more than any other people do. The Chinese may not have totemism with the same import as that of Australians or American Indians. It is principally the primitive animal-worship, the animal-god and the animal ancestor that must betoken totemism. The images on the vessels, the marbled sculpture, the white pottery and the carved bones bear evidence to the animal gods.

Totemism and Name

On the totemism Professor de Groot wrote:

A strong belief in animal progenitors of men, families, and tribes may, in any country where the worship of ancestors is prevalent, readily lead to methodic veneration of such beasts.[100]

In fact, in perusing the long list of Chinese tribal names we find a few names of animals, such as bear (hsiung), dragon (lung) (Pl. I), horse (ma), cow (niu), crow (ou), deer (lu), fish (yü), camel (lo t'o), fox (hu), wolf (lang), and swallow (yen) among others, but they do not point to any alleged descent of the tribes they denote from an animal ancestor. The bear and dragon tribal names are said to have originated in the individual name ;the children of the man who was called 'bear' or dragon naturally turn his name into a clan name: it invariably became the badge of a group, no longer of an individual. The relationships between clan and totem and name can easily be documented. When the Son of Heaven would ennoble the virtuous he gives them surnames from their birth-places of their ancestors. The princes also confer the clan-names from the designation of the grandfather.[101] Elsewhere Shih ching says that the noble grandsons of our princes, Ah! they are the lin! benevolent and generous like the Duke's sons.[102]

The word 'sing' surname is used for grandson because the gransdon's descendants became a new clan, with the designation of the grandfather for a clan name. The words 'Kung-tsu' mean all who could trace their lineage to the same high ancestor as the duke. The word 'shêng' also conveys the idea "birth' which is tantamount to what was conceived by many primitive people as totem. The turtle clans of the American Iroquois are descended from a fat turtle ; the bear and wolf clans of the Iroquois are descended from bears and wolves respectively.[103] The osages are said to be descended from a male snail and a female beaver. When the snail burst his shell, it developed arms, feet, and legs, and became a tall man ; hereafter he married the beaver maid.[104]

To further our understanding of the relations between clan name and totem, there is an evidence in Chinese society of the name in association with the mysterious birth of ancient ancestors. According to

Shih ching, Heaven commissioned the swallow to descend and give birth to the father of our dynasty Shang. The dark bird is a name for a swallow (P1. II). Chien-Ti was bathing in some open place, when a swallow suddenly appeared and dropped an egg, which she took and swallowed; then came the birth of Hsieh. It appears that the birth of Hsieh was specially ordered by Heaven and became the Lord of Shang. [105] The mysterious birth has likewise been described among American Indians. The Haidas of Queen Charlotte Island believe that. long ago the raven took a cockle from the beach and married it ; the cockle bore a female child whom the raven took to wife, and from their union the Indians were brought to life. [106]

Another mysterious birth of tin ancestress evokes even keener interest ; it was concerned with the birth of Hou Tsi, which was recorded in Shih Ching. The first birth of our people Ku was from Kiang Yuan. She had presented a pure offering and sacrificed so that her childlessness might be weeded out. She then trod on a toe-print made by God and was moved, and became pregnant ; later she gave birth to a son who was Hou Tsi. She was accepted as the founder to whom the princess of the House of Chou traced their lineage. The accounts of the supernatural conception and birth. may be compared with the Roman legend about the she-wolf who reared Romules and Remus. As for the myth of Hsia dynasty (about 2200-1766 B.C.) the Sage held that the mother of Yü gave birth to him because she ate Pearl barley or Job's Teats; thus Hsia dynasty was named after Sze. All these myths indicate that the founders of the dynasties of Hsia, Shang and Chou (about: 1134-256 B.C.) were born without the father. and had a mysterious birth. A passage in Shih Ching illustrates this. Sublime and lofty are the mountains whence was sent down a spirit, who produced the princes Fu and Shen. [107]

The viscount of T'an traced his lineage up to China Tien, the dynasty title of Shao Hao, the oldest son of Huang Ti. Chao Tzu asked the viscount what was the reason that Shao Mao named his offices after birds. The viscount replied:

Huang Ti came to his rule with the omen of a cloud, and so he had cloud offices, naming them after clouds ; Yen Ti, Sheang Nung (about 2737 B.C.) carne to his with the omen of fire ....T'ai Hao came to his with omen of a dragon, and so he had dragon offices, naming them after dragons. When my ancestor Shao Hao succeeded to the kingdom, there appeared at that time a phoenix, and so he arranged his government under the mendature of birds, making bird officers, naming them after birds. There were so and so phoenix bird, minister of the calendar.... [108]

Birds as totems are humanly constructed, and only acquire significance when they are believed to possess propitious augur. The surname 'feng' (wind) represents the most ancient people and is one of the totems. Fu Hsi's (about 2852 B.C.) surname is said to be feng and his mother's surname Hwa Hsu, but his father is not mentioned. The 'feng' surname is a synonym of the phoenix, so that the surname feng and the phoenix are cognate. The K'ang Hsi Dictionary provides descriptions regarding the bird phoenix - Feng Huang, male and female (Pl. III). The bird is the very essence of the red spirit and has the body of a cock and a red tail ; its plumage is variegated with five colours; it is a bird of soul. Primitive people have all the belief that this bird totem is endowed with enormous power. In the Hsia dynasty the phoenix signified peace and prosperity, and it originally symbolized the ruler. The emperor set about diffusing, on a grand scale the virtuous influence of peace; with shields and feathers the phoenixes danced between the two staircases in his courtyard.[109]

That the phoenix can fly a very long distance In a short moment proved its flying velocity, This capacity resembles the, power of fêng (wind) and points out clearly the affinity of the phoenix and the fêng. The phoenix is the totem of feng surname or clan, and Shao Hao was a hero of the sub-clan of 'fêng' totem ; he had also assigned an officer after the name of this bird. This leaves no doubt that the phoenix totem is a counterpart of 'fêng' (wind) clan.

The Surname of Kiang and Chi

The prince Shao Tien has two sons, Yen-ti and Huang-Ti (fig. 1)

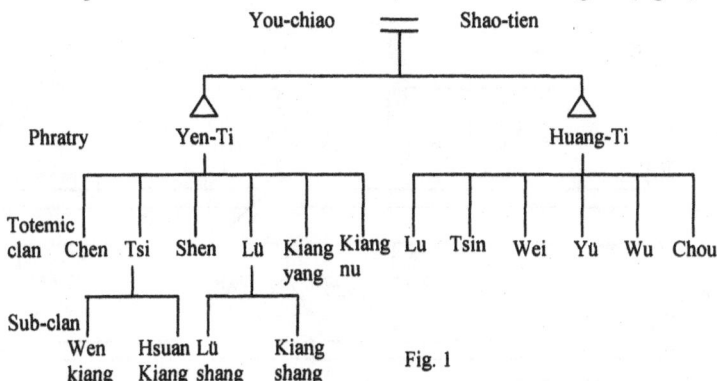

Fig. 1

The eldest son of Shao Tien, the Yen-Ti was brought up near the Kiang river and was so named after Kiang. Ruling under the element of fire he was called Yen-Ti. His brother Huang-Ti grew up by the Chi river and was thus named after Chi. Ruling under the element of earth which has the yellow colour he was conferred the title of Huang-Ti (Yellow emperor). The surname Kiang has. a sheep as its totem and symbol, whereas the surname Chi is a synonym of Chen and refers to the plant as its totem. Likewise among the Australian aborigines individual men and women appear to be symbolized by semi-circular lines and to be subordinate to the animal or plant in the design. It is difficult to interpret exactly the design of any particular 'churinga' except by one. of the old men within the totemic group to which it belongs ; only the old men continuously see and examine the 'churinga' of their group. For knowledge of their ancestors the 'churinga' hand down from generation to generation.[110]

The two clans Kiang and Chi frequently exchanged women, that is, it was the practice of men from Kiang phratry to exchange sisters (fig. 2) of the children of Kiang to marry the children of Chi phratry. The tribe, Shao Tien as a whole was divided into two phratries which exchanged women. Within the phratries there were smaller divisions, such as clans, lineages of local groups, which arranged the exchange of women. Phratries are often named; like clans, after places of origin. The phratry includes clans in the same way as in the feudal system; one surname branched out into many clan names, and one clan name branched out Into many families. The phratry had its surname, but clans were distinguished by clan names. The kinship system is similar to what was the legend among Kwakiutl. Kwakiutl had two phratries, Guelela and Gomouone ; they are said to be

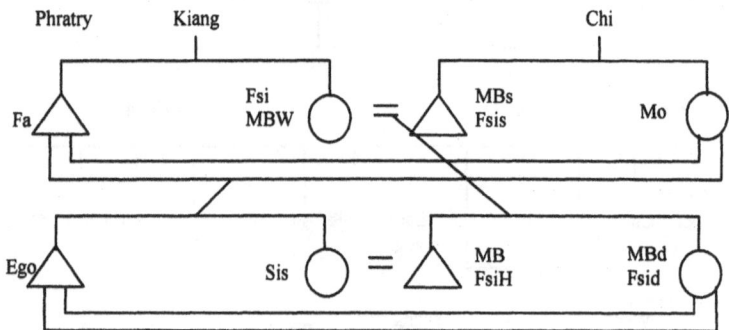

Fig. 2 The Model of sister exchange between Kiang and Chi phatries.

twin brothers, the one being fed by his mother's right :breast, and the other by her left breast. This legend attests the close relationship .between the phratries.[111]

Plate I   Walking Dragon stone plate, Cultural objects.

Plate II   CHIO, Ritual wine Vessel with cover in the form of a swallow, Bird-ancestor of the Shang Kings, shang Dynasty.

Plate III Double Phoenixes pot, Cultural objects.

Plate IV Chinese tomb figures showing a bird with two heads.

The Surname Tzu

The surname Tzu was associated with birth. 'shing'. It was. God's command that the line of Shang dynasty : was. established through the medium of the swallow. There was an allusion to the legend about the connection. of the swallow with the birth of Hsieh.[112] As I mentioned previously, the mother of Hsieh, Chien-ti was a daughter of the House of the ancient state of Sung and a concubine of the ancient ruler Khu (2335 B.C.). She accompanied Khu at the time of vernal equinox when the swallow first appeared, to sacrifice and pray to the first-match maker. The lady was bathing in the open air, when swallow appeared and dropped an egg which she took and swallowed, and then she bore Hsieh. The association of the Shang dynasty with the swallow was an accepted part of the culture. The reason for the preference for this bird was that the behaviour of the. totem is usually held to indicate the action or intentions of the supernatural being or Heavens. This leads to consider what is the most significant factor in Chinese totemism, namely that the natural species, the animal or plant, are believed to be linked with their respective social groups not by their own virtue, but because they are the vehicle of manifestation of supernatural beings. The system of totemism is dependent on the belief in supernatural beings, not separate from it.

The above legend brings home to us the existence of mother without mentioning father. This is in line with what Tylor held that the. maternal system preceded the paternal in primitive society on the grounds that the maternal system consisted of the mother and her children, and the mother group bequeathed its territorial rights, property, and title to her children. Since a child must belong to the family of his mother and adopt her totem, the mother's clan name. was passed to her daughter and her grand-daughter. By contrast, in a patrilineal system son and daughter assume their father's clan name and his totem.[113] There appeared a patrilineal system when the originator and totem ancestor were emphasized. Furthermore in ancient tines it was found that at a. fixed time woman and... her totem were united to give birth to children. The swallow must be united with a woman, so that the Son of Heaven sacrificed to the first match-maker in person, with his queen and helpmates, attended by his nine ladies of honour.[114] Considering that no children were born without union with the swallow, it follows that Ti Khu was at least a necessary match-maker. Since many primitive people had no knowledge of the physiology of paternity, they understand the term 'union' not to mean the sexual intercourse of man and woman ; nevertheless, they sustained the shibboleths that merely by contact with, or staring at, totem, a birth will ensue.

With regard to the swallow the sacrifice yin corresponds to 'spirit and swallow on her nest'.[115] Nearby everywhere yin means 'wall in' ; the 'bird' suggests that the swallow is the typical 'wall-bird', that is, it makes her nest always under the roof. The idea 'bird-swallow' on her nest holds out a hope that the bird will come back and with its return is associated the idea of fecundity and of nature's revival. Chiang yuan, ancestress of the Chou, offered the yin sacrifice to procure her own fecundity.[116] The child of Chiang yuan was Hou tsi, prince of millet, the genius of vegetation: it thus fully marks the seasonable character of the yin sacrifice.[117]

In ancient times there was totem which was given due respect by the whole group. For instance, the dynasty Shang regarded the swallow as its totem and Chien-ti as its ancestress. But the dynasty of Chou reckoned Chi as its totem and Chiang yuan as ancestress. We should bear in mind that there was no account of a 'male' ancestor due to a matrilineal system then prevalent in Chinese society. In other words, there was no husband for the ancestress. As for how it came about that a woman became pregnant remains unclear. When a patrilineal system superseded the matrilineal one, the 'ancestor' loomed large, while the 'ancestress' became inevitably attenuated. Then all children were descended from this ancestor and had but indirect relationship with the totem-swallow, indirect because this ancestor was surmised to have been born directly from the swallow. In a patrilineal system all men began to have their father recognized. As a result, the hypothesis that all ancestors were descended from a totem, once the idea was held true, was no longer convincing. When the ancestress finds a husband. the totem will be laid aside. Here again. in a matrilineal society it was only the surname of the ancestress that was transmitted to, and accepted by, her descendants. The male being of no importance, his surname remained unknown until a patrilineal system was established.

Contemporary anthropologists and sociologists are confronted with welters of questions in respect of the original ancestor and totem ancestor, both being called ancestors ; the term 'totem-ancestor' is restricted to the fictitious progenitor of our ancestor. To combine these two ancestors there appeared a 'heavenly-born' emperor. In the antecedent stage of development there was only totem and ancestress, then emerged an ancestor in the second stage, and finally this ancestor and 'heavenly-born' emperor came into co-existence. This development can be illustrated (figs. 3 and 4):

The mother of Hsieh, the ancestress of Shang was Chien-ti, who was a concubine of the emperor Ti-khu. In theory the people of Shang dynasty were the descendants of Chien-ti ; she bore the child Hsieh who became the father and, centuries later, the founder of Shang dynasty. Thus later the people of Shang made sacrifice to both Chien-ti and Hsieh.

The Two Principles of Yin and Yang and Totemism

What are yin and yang principles ? They are like male and female. These two principles have time and again been rejected out of hand as having no bearing on totemism in China. We must note, however, that an understanding of these principles will afford us an important insight into totemism. I present here some myths in Chinese legend that shed light on totemism. Totemism can raise the general problem of how an opposition can produce an integration rather than obstruct it. The division of eagle, hawk and crow among the Darling River tribes is seen to be no more than one particular example of a widespread type of applying a structural principle consisting of the union of opposites.[118] In China the model is to be found with opposition and union of these two principles yin and yang and results in an ordered whole, for instance, the unity of a married couple. According to Lěvi-Strauss, the mental structure underlies human behaviour and takes the form of binary contrasts or oppositions ; and moieties or other forms of dual organization are associated with contrasting or opposing qualities, such as left and right, low and high, cold and warm,

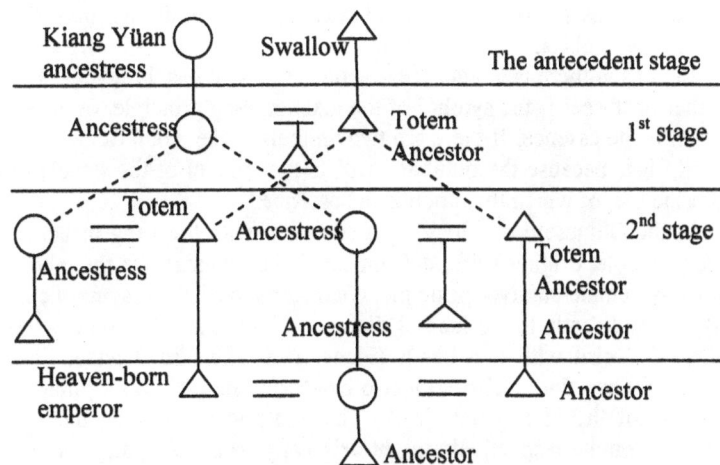

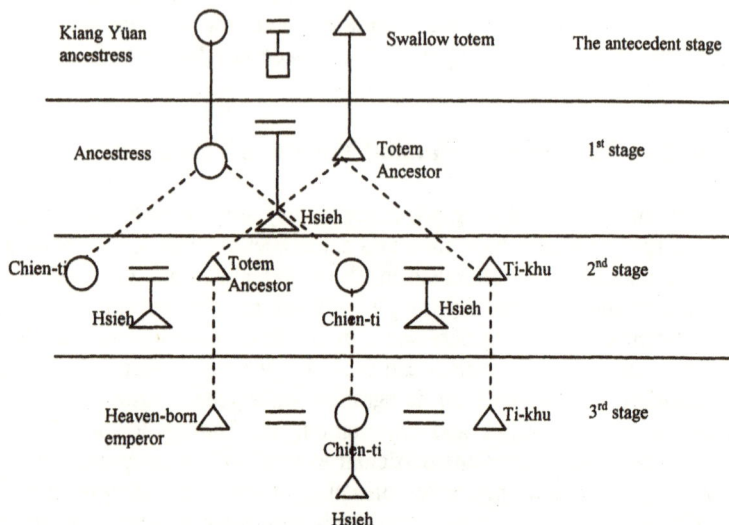

earth and sky, north and south, white and black and so forth.[119] The Australian aborigines have the idea that where there is a quarrel between two persons or two groups which is likely to smoulder, the thing to do for them is to fight out and then make friends.[120]

To gain a better understanding of the relationship between yin and yang principles as well as their relationship with birds, we may put forward the explanations of Huai Nan-tzu (died 122 B.C.) who wrote:

In the sun there is a lame crow, lame because it has three legs. The number of 'three' is the symbol of the male or yang principle, of which the sun is the essence. If there are two animals in the moon (a hare and a toad), it is because the number 'two' is the symbol of the female or yin principle, of which the moon is the essence.[121]

In the Chinese cosmology, in association with the yang or active male principle, origin of life, the sun stands in opposition to the moon, the yin or female passive- principle, characteristic of night, symbolic of darkness and death. In the funeral chamber of Wu Liang-tzu there is the figure of a bird with two heads (Place ,IV). The bird depicted is a phoenix for we find it also with two heads on one body on a pillar of the tomb of the Shen (Plate V).[122] The two phoenixes, feng huan, a male and female respectively might originally be simply yang and yin phoenixes, alternately representing the increasing activity of the stuff, yang or male and its decrease yin or female. The union of two heads on one body symbolizes a perfect balance between the two principles that rule the sun's power with equal strength.

It is well known that the emperor's virtue interfered with the cosmologic balance, for he vouched for excessive rain, drought and calamity. Such a balance could never be more perfect than at the equinox, and the image of two phoenix heads, male and female on the same body, comports perfectly with the favourable moment among all, the equinox being in the center of the corresponding celestial palace, and the two heads symbolizing absolute balance between the two principles, yin and yang. The union of the male and female phoenix is also a symbol of good understanding between man and wife ; ideally marriages are celebrated at the equinox because of the balance between the male and female principles. When Yi's wife sought the meaning of the indication in the tortoise-shell about marrying his daughter to Ching-chung, she said:

It is fortune because the male and female phoenixes fly together, singing harmoniously with gem-like sounds.[123]

The phoenix serves also as totem of all virtuous rulers and is said to have been appeared at the time of Huang-ti and during the reign of the emperors Shao Hao and Yao (2597-2514 B.C.)

As for inanimate objects associated with totems there was a well-known legend of the Fu Sang tree upon which three legged solar crows perched.

This legend is borrowed front Shan Hai ching as follows:

There stands a large tree, the Fu Sang tree over the Yang Ku valley ; its trunk is 300 li (00 miles) in height and its leaves are a little larger than mustard seed. Of nine suns which perch on the lower branches, one sun is an the highest bough ; and each of the suns rests on the back of one crow totem. There are ten suns which appear in turn, one for each day of the cycle. One day ten suns appeared together and scorched everything on earth, so that I Shang shie, the expert archer had to bring nine of them down with his arrows. As a result, people overjoyed at peace. Nine of the suns lived under the Great Mulberry Tree, but the tenth lived above it in the Heavens. (Pl. VI, VII) [124]

The nine suns and nine crows with three legs were emblems of the cyclical suns. Whether I Shang shie be a legendary hero or an officer of the state, the archer showed human interference to restore order in nature and to shed all disturbances that make inroads upon the regular succession of natural phenomena. The legend clearly alludes the appearance of a totem in nature. Human interference is necessary when the yin, the weaker principle invades the yang principle at a time when it should be entirely under the sway of the yang principle. The yin principle, over running the yang trammels the cosmic order and .accordingly infringes the natural rules that govern the succession of the seasons.

It is commonly held that when the conduct of the- totem is not all that its clansmen could expect, they bring pressure on it to bear. When the birds eat the corn in harvest time, the small bird clan of the Omahas take some corn they chew and split over the field. This is deemed to keep the birds from the crops.[125] The structural principle of totemism consists in the fusion of the contrary polarities, friendship and animosity : the contrasts in nature serve to create the solidarity and unity of a totemic society. If natural, species and inanimate objects fall short of expectations of people, they must bear the punishment.

Nature and Mana

The conception of 'soul substance' has been described in Indonesia and Polynesia. Human beings, animals, plants; and even inanimate objects are believed to be imbued with this substance : portions of the substance can be acquired from the body, particularly the head. The conception resembles to some extent what is called the Polynesian 'mana', which is thought to be powerful and supernatural power possessed by spirits and certain persons, and may be passed to inanimate objects. The 'soul substance' is associated with the practice of head-hunting among the Naga tribes of northeastern India. They had a belief in a power called 'aren' equivalent to mana, which is conceived to be stored up more in a person's head than in any other parts of the body. The Melanesians believed that all success and advance of a chief in life is believed to be due to 'mama' supernatural influence. In Lepers' island and in Arago, the real ground on which the power of a chief rests is in the mana he possesses.[126]

Mana maybe dangerous as well as beneficial, and thus it is linked to to idea 'taboo' in Polynesia.. The word 'taboo' is thought of implying what is respected and forbidden and so it refers to totem. The Melanesians believe that totem pervades not only the whole body, but parts detached from the body, such as hair, nail, sputum and excreta which are saturated with it. Kiwai Papuans hold that wherever an enemy's foottracks are shot by an arrow he will be hurt.[127] In ancient China the essential element of a totem is 'nature', which is bound up with birth. In origin nature is on par with birth and a clan name, and the members of each totem bear the same clan name. The philosopher Kao tzu said that life is what is to be understood by 'nature'. Associated with nature is virtue, the meaning of which can be fully understood if we quote some passages from Tso Chuan:

Even the royal house has been small and the descendants of Chou are daily losing their patrimonies......... Heaven is manifesting its dissatisfaction with the 'virtue of Chou. Though the 'virtue of Chou is decayed, the decree of Heaven is not yet changed. The weight of the Tripods may not yet be inquired about.[128]

Virtue is the strong stem of man's nature. Although names are different, one group reckoning nature with its totem, and another group regarding birth as its totem or virtue, their meaning is the same. The word 'virtue' is analogous to what Melanesians call 'mana'. For virtue may be high and low and it thus entails a different social status. Tso Chuan says:

If any one transgresses his convenant, may the intelligent spirits destroy him so that he shall lose his people and not be able to possess his state, and, to the remotest posterity (descendants), let him have no descendants, old and young.[129]

Virtue imports regulating power, authority and mana, and is identical with the 'li', which is translated as customary morality, rules and propriety. Most noteworthy is the belief' that the cosmic phenomena, the seasons would not follow one another in harmonious order unless the emperor, the Son of Heaven, performed virtue. If he lost virtue he would be deprived of mana and be unable to govern. Importance was attached to the social functions of the virtue, i.e., its

PAUL CHAO   J. Indian anthrop. Soc., 11 : 55-81 (1976)

Plate V. Chinese tomb figures.

Plate VI. Chinese tomb figures.

Plate VII   Chinese tomb figure.

effects in producing and maintaining an orderly human society and achieving social integrity. The ancient kings felt concerned at not being remiss in striving for virtue by which the mind was affected. They instituted laws to force upon virtue, and punishments to guard against mens' propensities to evil and their recalcitrance against rules. The end to which laws and punishments lead is one ; they serve as the cudgel by which the mind of people is conducted.[130]

Totem and Soul

Primitive men incline to the view that the ideas of a soul constitute the original nucleus of the animistic system, and. that the souls of animals, plants, and inanimate objects are constructed on the analogy of human souls. These souls have made themselves independent of their bodies. This leads to a belief in an 'external soul'. Given this view, the totem stands for a safe place of refuge in which the soul could be deposited. When the primitive man had his soul deposited in his totem, he himself was invulnerable, and lie naturally abhorred any injury to the receptacle of his soul. Although the soul resides in the whole body, it may also be lodged in different parts of the body, such as the head, the eye, the breath, the blood and the liver. The Kai of New Guinea thinks of his shadow as his soul ; hence people should not tread on a man's shadow for fear of injuring his soul. The soul is assumed to dwell in a man's heart, in the eye, in the foot as much as in the head ; it lurks even in the saliva and the other bodily excretions. The soul pervades the body just as warmth does ; the mysterious entity exists in the very sound of his voice.

There are two kinds of souls; one is the soul which survives the body at death ; in every respect it is akin to the man himself as he lived on earth attenuated by death. The second kind of soul is a spiritual essence which pervades the body as sap pervades the tree, and which is diffused like corporeal warmth over everything -with which the body is brought into contact.[131] The Chinese admit of the existence of two souls : the inferior soul 'p'o' is produced at conception and known as 'kuei' after death, and the superior soul 'hun' is of slow growth after birth. The 'hun' and 'p'o' are equivalent to the two kinds of souls of Kai, New Guinea ; the word 'p'o' conceived as a shadow or shade is tantamount to what Kai believe in the soul material. Furthermore the word 'kuei' is cognate with ancestors.[132] The word 'shen' indicates the function of the superior soul of the dead ancestor, which dwells on the wooden tablet, that is, the clan totem because it is spiritualized by the ancestor's resting. The living descendants offer regular sacrifices to their ancestors to pacify, to gratify and to honour the spirits of the dead who are still reckoned as members of the family to which they belong. The character 'chi' is composed to three parts ; one standing for a piece of flesh, the other for the hand, and the third for the spirit. Altogether the character represents a communion with the dead. The sacrifice and totemism are thought of as an essentially social form of worship. In Chinese ancestor worship the totem symbolized by the wooden tablet and his sacrificers are of the same flesh and blood ; and, by offering sacrifice, they maintain the communion of life that animates them and the association that binds them together.

Totem and Personal Name

The essence 'wu' represents an emblem. The banner, for instance, is a badge of commandment and stands for the coat of arms ; the red raven appearing on the banner of Chou dynasty was the principle of its authority and an emblem of its virtue. By contrast, members of sea-weed clan in Samoa, when they sailed out against the enemy at sea. took with them some sea-weed, which, when thrown into the sea would hinder, the flight of the enemy.[133] When an individual has his totem, his life must be bound up with it, the death of either, of which would entail his own. The Indians of Central America had their guardian spirits known as Năguals. They appear in the form of a lion, or a tiger, or in the forma of an alligator, a, snake, or bird. When they died. the Indian who was in league with them died also.[134] In the first battles with the Spaniards on the 'fable-Lands of Quertzalternango the Năguals of the Indian chief fought in the shape of serpents. The Năguals of the head chief had as his totem a great bird resplendent in green plumage on his banner. The Spanish general, Pedro de Alvarado killed the bird with his lance, and the chief fell dead to the ground at. once.[135]

In Chinese history, the personal totem of Duke Mu, 'lan', the orchid was his personal name and soul and symbolized the guarantee of life- the title of power, and maternal prestation, Duke Wen, the father of Duke Mu had a concubine of mean position called Yen chi ; she dreamt that a messenger from Heaven presented her with 'lan', the orchid, saving : 'I am Po Yü, the founder of the House and I am your ancestor. 'lan' shall be the emblem of your child. Since the 'lan' had a royal fragrance, he would be recognized as prince and be loved. Thereupon Duke Wen paid her a visit and gave her an orchid and lay with her'. She, pleading said : 'I am but a poor abject concubine ; should I be fortunate enough to have a son, I shall not be believed. Dare I take the orchid as evidence? The Duke agreed and she bore a son who became Duke Mu and named him 'lan', the orchid. When Duke Mu was ill, he said: 'When the 'lan' withers, I will die ; it is by it I live. When the lan was cut, he died'.[136] Among the M'Bengas in West Africa, about the Baboon, when two ehildren are born on the sane day, two trees as totems of the same kind are planted. The life of each of the children is, to their belief, bound up with the life of one of the trees ; if the tree dies, the child will soon die.[137] The story of Duke Mu has some bearing on a ritual practice. In the ritual as well as in the history, the 'lan', the orchid served as matrilineal prestation; from a historical point of view the 'lan' served as, and stood for the gift of the maternal ancestress, while in the ritual it was used in the holy place during a person's name-day.

With regard to the essence 'wu', it is associated with a totem. In terms of its etymology the character 'wu' is cognate with 'cow' ; the essence 'wu', in Wang Kuo-wei's word, implies that the colours of a cow are variegated ; its essence comprehends not only colours, but all that pertinent to a totem. This point is what has been read in the Tso Chuan : 'Shuh Sun's buffcoats have their own marks ; we do not dare to take them with us'.[138] Elsewhere this point has even more clearly been made. When Hsia was distinguished for its virtue the distant regions sent pictures of the remarkable objects in them, the nine pastors sent in the metal of their provinces, and the tripods were cast with representations on them of those objects ; all these objects were represented, and the instructions were given of the preparations to be made for them, so that the people might know the spirit and evil things. The objects represented on the tripods amount to totems. The essence 'wu' symbolizes moreover ethical rule. The practice of what should be observed is called the ethical rule; and the acquisition of the material supplies which serve as an ornament for the various requirements of the state is the guiding principle to show what creatures should be pursued. For lack of such measurements and such materials, the government is in disorder ; the frequent indulgence in a government of disorder paves the way for ruin, and failure to abide by the ethical rule dooms to destruction. The rule implies what is written in Shin Ching:

Heaven in producing mankind gave them their various faculties and relations with their specific laws. There are the invariable rules of nature for all to hold, and all love this admirable virtue.[139]

The various faculties stand for totems, whereas the specific laws for all ethical rules. In other words, Heaven, in producing mankind, gave their nature the pictorial representations of the objects, which are benevolence, righteousness, propriety, knowledge, and sincerity. The

Chinese conceive of these objects inherent in nature, which is equivalent to the totem symbols in an abstract form.

Finally, that essence 'wu' is a totem is based on what is written in 1 Li:

For a banner each uses the material proper to his rank.[140] If there be no material proper to his rank then combination of white and red features is adopted, the pole being three jen long (24 feet), and and sheathed for the upper two hsin (16 feet) with swans-down.[141]

The word 'material' means totem paint on the banner. The material proper to one's rank suggests that each individual possesses his own totem, and varies with colours, banners, and whatever pictorial objects are paint or carved on weapons and buffcoats. The special marks, for instance, embroidered on Shu Sun's buffcoats betray the totemic trace. A passage in Tso Chuan corroborates this point:

Every kind of creatures must have its own officers, who carefully attend to the laws of its nature, morning and evening, thinking of them, and who, if for a single day, are remiss in their duties, should be liable to death, lose their offices, and muster up no support. When the officers rest in the performance of their appointed duties, the creatures come to them of their own accord. If they neglect and abandon duties, the creatures cease to appear, and lie concealed ; then production is restrained and stopped.[142]

Likewise Dr. Haddon gave an account of a story among Kiwai. At Iasa in Kiwai, ceremonies are performed to ensure good crops of yams, sweet potatoes, bananas, and sago. In order to ensure these crops the novices are taken into the bush, and a wooden image of a naked woman is shown to them. Dr. Haddon was told that the wooden figures representing nude women look after sago as the bull-roarers look after yams, sweet potatoes and bananas.[143]

The totem must benefit the men who put their faith in it; it gives also them important information by means of omen. The Samoan totems gave omen to their clansmen. If an owl flew before. the owl clan, as they marched to war, it was a signal to go on ; but if then flew across their path, or backward, it was a sign of retreat.[144] In his study of totemism in Polynesia Firth wrote that when the animal was seen preceding in front of the war party, it was usually regarded as a token of suceess ; when it retired, or went behind them, then coming failure was foreboded.[145] Accoroding to Shih Yi-chi, the use of designs representing birds increases a prodigy which the founder of Chou dynasty favoured when he was waging war against Yin. When the army was crossing the Yellow River a bee as big as a red bird (Pls. VIII,IX,) was flying above and landing or perching on the barque of King Wu.

He designed then the bird on his banner, and next morning he won the war. The red bird, crow, the emblem ,animal is regarded as the escutcheon of the Chou family and the name of one of Chou's branches. The crow augurs the triumph of choir. When King Wu gained the victory, he beheaded the enemy and hanged him as a triumphal and sacrificial object to the banner which bears the escutcheon of the red crow. The essence 'wu' of an individual is determined by a symbol which is allied to an animal-totem this is no doubt illustrated by a coat of arms symbolically represented in the banner. The banner deseribed chiefly the virtue proper to each individual, and his totem is representative of his personalities, seeing that it lays down his rank.

We are wont to draw a distinction between the social order and the natural order ; contrasting between man and nature. The Seasonal changes that influence the rhythm of social life, and the animal and plants that provide for food or other ritual purposes enter into the essential part of the social life. A study of totemism has illuminated this. One of the examples is the personification of natural phenomena and of natural species. When a species of animal is personified it is treated as if it were a human being, and, in terms of mythology, such personified species are thought of as ancestors. This process of personification permits nature to be conceived of as it were a society of persons, so that nature is imbued with a social or moral order.

Among the Chinese we have found the ritual value they contribute to objects of different kinds. For certain dynasties the myths and rites that are associated with the natural species have a specific social value for the clan. The common interest in the totem brings the individuals together into a firm and enduring associations. And the avowed purpose of the totemic rites is to renew the relations with nature, such as species of animal or plant, rain, mountains, rivers, land and grain In China ritual value was attributed to the phoenix and the dragon, not because they arc believed to be the progenitors of mankind, but because they represent growth and fertility in nature to which much importance is attached. The phoenix and swallow are the symbolic representations of seasonal changes and of harmonious, happy marriages. Moreover, when the cosmology of the sun and the moon transgresses the natural order or course, a virtuous emperor, the Son of Heaven will bring pressure to bear on them and restore the cosmological order for the publie weal.

On the whole, totemism that is embedded in natural species, animals, plants and so forth has done much to strengthen the social ties and thereby enrich civilization which makes progress possible by virtue of the co-operation of men and their mutual trust and good-will. The totemism is also described as a mechanism, that may have worked out in different ways and societies, but, wherever it exists, it possesses this character. The function of totemism is to knit men together in social groups. This is laid bare by legends and myths. Ample evidence of totemism all over the world has led to my analogies. But totemism has not been found in every human society as yet. People appear to need certain other things with totemism.

Nevertheless, this paper has tried to parallel Chinese totems with those elsewhere, and it seems reasonable to suggest that while the moment for a final verdict is not yet reached, the parallels are closer than merely random chance data : so we feel justified in concluding simply that we are looking at phenomena of a universal kind and significance.

Plate VIII   Inlaid bronze bird deity.   Plate IX   Bronze figure with wings,
                Middle Chou   bird-deity. Late Chou

Chapter 6

Human Nature and the Concept of Sin in Confucianism and Christianity

The aim of this paper is to analyze the Chinese concept of human nature in relation to moral evil and sin. Since Christianity has formed the basis of moral religious denominations in Western society and Chinese moral principles are pervaded by a spirit of common humanity similar to that found in Christianity, Christian ideas will be propounded briefly so as to throw some light on Chinese thought.

A study of the Chinese concept of sin is a study of what Chinese thinkers consider to be a violation of human nature and man's responsibility to it. I have spent a good deal of time in reading Chinese classics and have attempted to elucidate the word "sin" in Chinese thought. I feel that I can gain a full understanding of the meaning of this word in comparison with what is thought to be its meaning in Christianity. One of the difficulties of presentation has been the different meanings the word "sin" may convey. This difficulty is not merely a matter of definition, but it also involves personal value judgment. The Chinese who do not embrace Christianity conceive of sin differently from those who are Christians. I thus find it helpful, in trying to understand Chinese thought, to take notice of this difference. In using the word "sin" we have to be on guard against reading into Chinese thought what may be in fact Christian teaching. A large part of Christian doctrine is built on the notion of sin--the fall of man, atonement, sacrifice, conversion and salvation-the ethical content of what Christians regard as grave sins may be altogether absent in the Chinese mind.

In the Western thought the word "sin" is conceived as a violation of rules amounting to a moral code set up and guarded by the supernatural, i.e., by personal deities or supernatural powers. All crimes are sin, but not vice versa. In the Chinese thought the word "sin" refers to crime, punishment or a crime. It also means a criminal act and sin which have been unintentionally committed. The term 'tsui' can be combined to form a double word as in 'tsui-o', 'tsui-kuo'. Other terms, such as 'fan' (offence), 'nieh' (ill) and 'ch'ien' (error) are used generally in combination with 'tsui', for example, 'tsui-nieh', 'tsui-ch'ien' or 'tsui-fan'. None of these terms conveys exactly the idea of sin. The nearest to the idea of sin is the word 'tsui', which may also import a crime and penalty imposed on a criminal, or violation of order, a wrong, fault or iniquity or even a breach of decorum and etiquette; such as is the case when young men use invective language. A breach of decorum entails to a greater or lesser extent social sanction and failure to be a 'Chun-Tze', a gentleman. A gentleman is supposed to have the virtue, education and good manners (rite) that are highly esteemed. All crimes "tsui" and "kuo" are sin, but not all violations of the moral code set up by deities are crimes and punished by the laws of Chinese society. Thus although sin is conceived in Western thought as a moral and spiritual depravity and would call down divine retribution, the idea of sin among the Chinese is ambiguous. In the Judeo-Christian tradition, while the sin against the First and sixth commandment when it is committed deliberately, is a grave sin, it is not thought by the Chinese as a fault at all.[146] For example, whereas concubinage has been condemned as sin in Christian teachings, it has not been branded as such by the Chinese. The Sage Confucius who was venerated as a holy man in China was born of a concubine,[147] and he himself later on took a concubine who bore him a son Li.[148] The Chinese may wonder why the above act is considered to be a sin, since the law of the Empire had not been infringed.

The Chinese possess a laudable moral code entrenched in and sustained by divine sanction. As a result, they have a sense of sin and recognize its consequences which, however, are often not clearly discriminated. Calamity, misfortune, sickness or death arc not differentiated from their cause, but are thought of as punishment, probably from some unknown fault. They are frequently unaware of any cause of misfortune, yet they confess that there must be something wrong somewhere or there would not be misfortune. Evil is thought to be the outward manifestation of the sin which is supposed to exist in man. The Chinese think of sin more as a calamity or misfortune than as a moral evil. Moreover, sickness and the destruction of family wealth, and the loss of life among others which have resulted from sin are spoken of by the name of sin. Not much light has been thrown on the subject "sin" in the sayings of Confucius, since he made no effort to examine its nature. He said, however, that there are three thousand offences against which the five punishments are directed and there is not one of them greater than being unfilial. This is the sin of sins.[149] On the other hand, Confucius conceived "virtue as consisting in a happy "mean" between two vicious extremes." That is to say, he held that there is a due medium between the vice of excess on the one hand, and that of defect on the other. All sin and its bad consequences arise from the neglect of the golden rule, the due medium. The term "Mean" or consistent Mean is called in Chinese "Chung-Yung" (literally, central or middle) means "without excess or deficiency" and "the Right Path" that should be pursued by all within the universe. Generosity, for example, is a virtue,[150] yet one who is more generous to his friends than "just" to his creditors cannot be reckoned as practising virtue. The mean would be just to your creditors and generous to your friends. The Right Path may not be departed from for any movement. What may be departed from is not the Right Path. The "Jiun Tze", i.e., Noble man is vigilant over what is known to himself alone, that is, his thoughts and conduct that are known only to himself, lest he might in these deviate from the Right Path.

The sage is disposed to the sin of excess, while the foolish and wicked men succumb to the sin of defect. Moreover, the concept of "shame" often appears in Confucian texts. Nevertheless the element of shame was felt only when the sinful act became public knowledge. It is recorded in Chinese history that Feng Tao in the tenth century served twelve emperors. In effect, to serve more than one ruler was neither a sin in the religious sense nor a crime in the legal sense; but as a trusted and staunch minister, a member of the elite, Feng was bound to remain loyal, since loyalty was one of the cardinal Confucian virtues.

In contrast to such Confucian ethics is the idea of sin in the Old Testament. The word "sin" means to miss the mark, and morally to fall short of the goal. It also refers to human relations, the goal being a person whom the sin is failing to reach. In reference to God, sin amounts to a failing of him, that is, it is the falling short of the mark God sets for mankind. Furthermore, Confucius and his disciples were concerned with the inculcation of virtue for happiness in this life rather than with the character and consequences of sin. He warned men that sin against Heaven leaves them in a woefully hopeless position and said that "if a man sins against heaven, he has nowhere left for prayers." But Mencius buttressing this point said that "even though a man be evil, if he fasts and bathes, he, too, may serve God." [151] By fasting and bathing Mencius did not mean a mere physical act, for both he and Confucius lay great stress upon the spirit which lies behind formal sacrifice and worship. This is in accord with the idea of the Nuer who regards sin as something which brings about an unclean condition of the person; the uncleanness is not simply a physical impurity which can be purged away. Sin is also for the Nuer a spiritual state, which can only be changed by sacrifice, which carries with it the will and desire of the sinner. [152]

The term "sin" (kuo), transgression, or error, is often mentioned. Confucius said that "to err and yet not reform, this may indeed be called error." [153] What becomes of the sinful, unrepentant transgressor is not discussed. It is implied that he will come to an unhappy end, but in what way it is not clear. Likewise Mencius stated that weal and woe are of men's own making, and quoted the Ode in The Book of Poetry (Shih King) as follows: "Constantly strive to be in harmony with the will of Heaven, and thereby you will get for yourself much happiness." [154] Similarly, in the Old Testament "pesa" denotes transgression, the violation of the rights of others and sets sinners against God. David's sin is a case in point. He was ungrateful to God, flouted his words and even despised God himself. As a result, David was duly punished.

The law of cause and effect in sin and its consequences is the recognized rule of Chinese moral life, at least in so far as this life is concerned. Sin against filial devotion is conceived by the Confucianists as an infraction of the general law of nature. In the State of Ch'u a man reported to an official that his father had stolen a goat. The official Yin killed the son on the grounds that, while he was loyal to his ruler, lie defied his father. [155] The Confucian concept or notion of filial piety may serve to shed light on what is taught in Christianity on this subject. The fourth of the Ten Commandments stipulates that a person should honour his father and mother, but Christian love based on the idea of personality would rule out blind obedience to despotic and evil parents. The Christian idea of father and son is based on God's abiding love lavished on his children. For centuries the Christian concept has been in conformity with the Confucian principle that the young should sacrifice their own comfort for the well-being of the old. Proverbs says: "He that curseth his father and mother, his lamp shall be put out in the midst of darkness." [156] St.

Matthew[157] wrote: "... Honour thy father and thy mother; and let him who curses father or mother be put to death." The English philosopher John Locke, however, was convinced that the act of begetting did not endow a man with absolute power over his children. But Confucius and Mencius went even further in commanding obedience to despotic and wicked parents as in the case of Shun. Confucius spoke of filial piety which is based on the virtue of benevolence and is inherent in human nature. Here Confucianism and Christianity condemn with one accord the disrespect shown by children for their parents. Hsu reported a story to this point. A father-in-law committed incest with his daughter-in-law. When this ignominious sin was committed, the son uttered the most abusive language against his father.[158] This incestuous union caused an irretrievable disharmony in the household because the daughter-in-law had a jealous spouse, and so did the father. The sin exposed the existence of a psychologically disruptive force, i.e., jealousy. Dr. Fortes says that among the Tallensi sexual prohibitions (family engendered norms) and marriage prohibitions (legal rules) cannot be extensions of each other, and a social equivalence cannot be attributed to the two types of phenomena.[159] The above sin would, in the view of the Chinese, arouse the wrath of Heaven which causes family misfortune, sickness and poverty for the descendants. Needless to say, Christians regard incest as a most abominable sin

Confucius expressed no opinion as to a future state of rewards and punishments after this life. What underlies the Confucian ideas is that man is endowed by nature with a virtuous disposition. As a consequence, the followers of Confucius, while admitting of the continued existence of the departed through ancestor worship, are no doubt loth to think of any of their own ancestors as existing in hell. Such an idea would be intolerable to a filial son. If a son has a wicked parent, he should still respect him and perform his filial duties at his best. Mencius recollected that though Koo-Sow, the evil, blind father often wanted to kill his son Shun, the sage emperor, he was none the less well treated by his son Shun.[160] The Christian view runs counter to that of Confucianists. Christianity preaches that every sin indicates contempt of the authority of the lawgiver; whoever commits sin transgresses the law. For the non-Christian Chinese such a concept does not exist. Even the term "Heaven" in the passage "if a man sins against Heaven, he has nowhere left for prayer" is vague. As we have noted previously, the Chinese moral code, filial duty, is based on nature according to Confucianists, and the sin of filial impiety poisons the spring of nature.

Shame also is felt when social obligations, even custom or decorum, are violated, but we would be led astray were we to attempt to put sin on a par with breach of convention and custom. The Chinese not only express indignation at sins, such as the five capital sins: "Beside theft or robbery, malignity, perverseness, mendacity, vindictiveness, and vacillating weakness", but they frown also on the infraction of convention and decorum, such as joking between an older brother and his sister-in-law, or the overt expression of intimate feeling of husband and wife in the public,[161] or the re-marriage of a widow. We see that the ethical significance of sin against convention does not lie only in violation of something which involves intrinsic evil; the prohibition itself may have no ethical import in the view of outsiders, but it involves some trifling injunction for the Chinese. If people do not live in conformity with proper behaviour, they lose honour, that is, the loss of honour and accordingly gentlemanly state was a serious matter in Confucian thought and practice. To Confucius sin was, more than anything else, the improper performance of rites, traditions and government duties, or the distortion of human nature. By contrast, Christianity conceives sin as a result of self-will, excessive pride and revolt against God.

Sin is also thought of as violation of the cosmic order which is consistent with the social order. Cosmic order refers here to Heaven. Nevertheless, the latter is not based on the whims of a deity or a pantheon. A true Confucianist is not afraid of deities, but of disarraying the cosmic or social order. Like a religious person, a Confucianist has internalized his social code which has a moral import. Along with the feelings of sin, feelings of guilt are associated with transgressions in the field of social relations social role behaviour. These were punishable by human laws and, according to popular religion, led to punishment in the hereafter. Similarly, tabu consciousness is present in the Old Testament. When Oza put forth his hand on the Ark of God, he was struck down for his rashness and died at once before the Ark of God.[162]

As I have mentioned previously, the doctrine of a future state has not been discussed by the Confucianists. Now the question remains: what is the view of the Chinese in the matter of salvation? The Confucian attitude is that the way of salvation is to lead a virtuous life. Heaven blesses virtuous men. If a man does wrong and lives a wicked life, let him reform himself. If he dies in his sins, Heaven will cause him to perish. Yet the hereafter is not mentioned. Thus the Confucian attitude towards sin is that sin is an offence against the majesty of Heaven, a departure from law; it is constantly spoken of as error, deflection, something to be grown out of by self-culture. If we conceive sin as a violation of a divine code, Chinese folk religion before the Han dynasty (206 B.C.) appears not to have had the concept of sin, though it recognized a great number of supernatural beings. Philosophers before the Han dynasty were reticent about the supernatural; and they set up an ethical system which was based not on relations to the supernatural, but on "human nature" or a system of social ethics serving to achieve a peaceful co-existence of individuals.

With the introduction of Buddhism into China from the first century A.D. the doctrine of the punishment of sin committed in this life took root in Chinese religious thought. However, there appeared to be no strong conviction about the future life nor had sin any connection with it. The absence of this conviction was attributed no doubt to the negative view of virtue which Buddhism has preached. Sin is conceived as more a calamity or a misfortune than a moral evil. In Buddhism one finds no Creator, no God, so that Buddhism is atheistic. It starts with the recognition of sin and evil as the heirloom of mortal man, but it does not elaborate this point so as to bring home to men the idea of sin, nor does it appeal to his own inner sense of moral goodness. It enjoins men to cease from doing evil and demands the total extinction of all desire, but stops short of urging men to do good. This moral system, while it begins with the idea of the total renunciation of self-interest is universally altruism. For the consciousness of self is often described as the source of all evil or suffering.

Although Buddhist ideas of sin and retribution in a future life were vague, they were instilled into Taoist and Confucian doctrine. The influence of Buddhism on Taoism was particularly felt in its doctrine of future rewards and punishments for sins. Taoist founders anticipated a state of happiness which is incompatible with the flesh, that is, a state resulting from a moral and spiritual sublimation of moral wickedness. This belief can be seen in the ceremonies performed by Taoist priests over the dead. One of the Taoist keynotes is: "Woe and weal have not gates, i.e., are not predestined, but men call them on themselves. In heaven above and earth below there are spirits who take account of men's transgression, and, according to the gravity of offences, curtail their allotted span of life." Despite this tenet the Taoist laid emphasis on longing to see virtue rewarded by material benefits, such as a long life, wealth, health, official rank and prolific offspring.

The Doctrine of Confucius's Disciples on Human Nature and Sin

The ancient period of Chinese thought may well be compared with the classic period of Greek philosophy with which it coincided in time. In the context of human nature, Confucius (551-478 B.C.) attested the ethical development of human beings, -while Socrates (469-399 B.C.) held that the acquisition of knowledge is no guarantee of overcoming or redirecting instinctive tendencies. Mencius (398-314 B.C.) subscribed to the opinion that all men are alike in their original capacity and that human nature is good. To Plato (427-348 B.C.), however, virtue is a kind of health, beauty, and good habit of the soul, whereas vice is the disease and deformity and sickness of it. Aristotle (381-322 B.C.) adhered to the middle way-the mean being the thesis of his ethical philosophy. Likewise Hsun Tzu (320-233 B.C.) supported the infinite improvability of human nature.

Mencius advocated the doctrine of the goodness of human nature, maintaining that every man possesses within himself a principle of benevolence, which moves him to pity and sympathy; a principle of justice, which makes him feel remorse for what is shameful; a principle of propriety, which induces him to show respect and reverence to those to whom respect and reverence are rendered; and a principle of wisdom, which points what is right and approvable and what is wrong and reprehensible. To develop our nature is to realize the four fundamentals. Benevolence refers to man's mind, while righteousness to man's path. The term "benevolence" (jen) imports true manhood. The moral man does nothing that runs counter to true manhood. The path of true manhood consists in loyalty to parents, which to Mencius was the greatest of all virtues. Of all the virtues a filial son can practice there is nothing greater than honouring his parents.

It is interesting to note that Bishop Joseph Buttler preaches the same doctrine as Mencius and maintains that the benevolent affections are disinterested. Lie said: "It is from considering the relations which the several appetites and passions in the inward frame have to each other, and above all, the supremacy of reflection or conscience, that we get the idea of the system of constitution of human nature. Thus nothing can possibly be more contrary to nature than vice; meaning by "nature" not only the several parts of our internal frame, but also the constitution of it."[163] He continued: "The nature of man, considered in his public and social capacity, leads him to a right behaviour in society to that course of life which we call virtue. Men follow or obey their nature in both these capacities and respects to a certain degree, but not entirely; their actions do not come up to the whole of what their nature leads there to in either of these capacities or respects, and they often violate their nature in both, i.e., as they neglect the duties they owe to their fellow creatures, to which their nature leads them and are injurious, to which their nature is abhorrent...."[164]

In contrast with Judaism and Christianity which teach that the character of man, and the divine institution dealing with his merits and sins, have been unchangeable from the beginning of the world to the last day, folk religion, ultimately based on the doctrine of 'kalpa' (era, world period) in philosophical Buddhism, contended that human beings were originally good, but became bad as time went on so that a system of punishment had to be introduced.[165]

Mencius avowed the goodness of human nature, that is, from the feelings proper to it, it is constituted for what is good, and that, if men do evil, it is not the fault of their natural endowment. He further held that men are led into evil because they allow themselves to succumb to passion or environment. Hence in years of plenty the common people are mostly well behaved, but in time of dearth they become lawless. Mencius also denied in man the existence of a positive principle of evil, so that if a man sins, he is not regarded as moved by a positive principle. Thus Mencius' attitude towards evil is akin to that of many Western philosophers and theologians. Christians hold that by the grace of God man's nature can indeed be raised up into conformity with the mind and will of God, but they insist on the inherent weakness and imperfections resulting from "original sin", which balks growth towards perfection. Augustine believed the story of the Fall to be literally true and thought that the original sin inherited from Adam and Eve corrupted human nature.[166] To Augustine reason raised men above animals.[167] Thomas Aquinas described man in metaphysically dualistic terms, that is, as composed of a body with its passions and a soul with its reason. It was the passions that distorted reason and allured man to sin.[168] Confucius would come into line with Aquinas on this point. Muller pointed out that Augustine sought to reduce the notion of evil to that of negation. Leibnitz stated that the tendency of the will is essentially towards the good. Jung dismissed evil, "a privatio boni" as a non-sensical doctrine,[169] a "euphemistic petitio principii"[170] and a "regular tour de force in sophistry."[171] We should bear in mind that the flow of Mencius' doctrine of human nature consists not so much in holding that all this is true of human nature as in taking a partial truth for the whole. His teachings account for the evil, while neglecting to explain that evil and goodness co-exist in the world and are poles apart and in conflict with each other.

Tzu Tze, the grandson of Confucius is the well-known author of the book Chung Yung, the Doctrine of the Golden Mean or Central Harmony. It contains mostly quotations from the sayings of Confucius, but there are some parts which Tzu Tze claimed to be his own. The doctrine of the Mean says: "Perfect is the virtue which is in accord with the Mean."[172] Elsewhere it is said: "The superior man embodies the course of the Mean; the mean man acts contrary to the course of the Mean." [173] Tzu Tze thus described virtue as laying at the mean point or medium between two extremes. In other words, if the passions extend beyond the proper bounds, there will be a sin of excess. If they are not developed to reach the mean or medium, there will be a sin of defect." In the opinion of Tzu Tze nature is that which Heaven has dictated in man. Evil that is conceived by excess and shortcoming or defect is exemplified in the schools of Yang Chu and Mo Ti. Yang Chu was the apostle of egoism and Mo Ti of altruism. Whereas Yang Chu in his egoism did not come up to the Mean, Mo Ti in his doctrine of universal love went beyond the Mean. In other words, while Yang's principle "each for himself" fails to acknowledge the claims of sovereignty, Mo Ti's principle "to love all equally" gives no due consideration and peculiar affection for the father. Akin to Mo Ti's love, Christian love, falling short of the Confucian requirements for different ranks, would offend his sense of good taste and would run, in Mencius' belief, against the ethics of the Golden Mean.

Confucius disapproved Yang because even though he might have benefited the whole empire by plucking out a single hair, he would refuse it. On the other hand, he opposed Mo Ti because if by rubbing smooth his whole body from crown to heel, he could do good to the whole empire, he would not avoid it. It is perhaps for the same reason that Paul said that the cross was foolishness to the Greeks. Jean Jacques Rousseau held that man was "instinctively and naturally good."[174]

The Golden Mean of Confucius clearly bears resemblance to Aristotle. Although Aristotle may have maintained a more liberal attitude than Confucius, he would insist on the Golden Mean of temperance between the extremes of self-indulgence and insensibleness. "A man's moral worth", he said, would be destroyed by excess and defect and preserved by the mean.[175] In Confucian doctrine, if man fails to discharge filial duty, he will commit a sin of defect. The principle of filial piety lies not in one's parents, but in one's own mind which is the same as Reason. If I seek the Reason of filial piety in my parents, it is crystal clear that after my parents are defunct my mind will not in consequence lack the Reason of filial piety. This principle is expounded in the Analects of Confucius: "The dutiful son adheres to the principle of propriety in serving his parents when they are alive and in burying them and sacrificing to them when they are dead." [176] Here again, Tzu Tze's doctrine is in conformity with what the Stoics hold, namely, that virtue or moral rectitude consists in living in accordance with nature.[177] In line with Tzu Tze's doctrine, Aristotle stated that a man's moral worth would be destroyed by excess and defect and preserved by the mean.[178] In contrast, in the Old Testament sin, as I mentioned previously, means to miss the mark or fall short of the target or goal God sets for mankind. In the New Testament sin is conceived as a deviation from the goal; it is the missing of a target and refers to wrongdoing of man, but above all sin is committed against God-the source of 'Good'.

Kao Tze held that 'human nature is neither good or bad or evil, but indifferent to both'.[179] Man's nature may be compared to a willow, and benevolence and justice to the cup of a bowl; as the tree may be made into a utensil so may human nature be fashioned benevolent and just.[180] It follows that benevolence and justice arise not from human nature but are shaped or formed through education. That is to say, human nature must be hacked and bent to achieve those virtues. Again, he said: 'The nature is

like a rushing stream; make an aperture on the east side, and it
will flow eastward; make an aperture on the west side, and it will
flow westward; as water is indifferent to the east or west, so
human nature has no preference between virtue and vice, but is
indifferent to both'.[181]

Kao Tze contended that, considering the indifference of
human nature to good or evil, it is the education of the good that
makes a good man, whereas the education of the bad makes a
wicked man. We should bear in mind that in the light of Kao
Tze's comparing human nature with a rushing stream, the good
or the evil into which the nature is carved depends on external
agencies, such as education and training. Apart from education,
an agency in the formation of human character, the nature of
some is good, while the nature of others is bad. Here Kao Tze
attached importance to environment which mold human nature.
Kao's theory fails to account for phenomena in which men
brought up in the most favorable environment turn out to be the
vilest. Every individual admits that he himself is accountable for
his conduct, and not the environment in which he happens to be
brought up.

Hsun Tze's theory is in conflict with Mencius. Hsun Tze
(320-235 B.C.) chose to give us a depraved portrait of human
nature, but contended that it was not totally depraved, as in the
teachings of Calvin. It was Calvin's belief that man was totally
depraved and naked of all virtues.[182] Luther spoke of a "relic" of
"Imago Dei" to elucidate the difference between man and other
animals.[183] All Christian teachings in respect to the Fall which
resulted in original sin, concurred in holding the uninterrupted
existence of the "Imago Dei" in man. Iranaeus held that the
Imago Dei' had not been destroyed or there would be no "relic"
of ethics among thieves themselves. Paul said: "All have sinned,
and fall short of the glory of God", so that no one has his
personality intact.[184] Carrying further his arguments, Hsun Tze
said that because human nature was prone to evil, each man must
strive to develop his own nature towards the right. He added that
as man seeks virtue it is a proof that he is devoid of it by nature.
What man lacks in himself he seeks outside, and whatever man
has within himself he does not go out to seek; the deformed
desire to be beautiful and the poor, rich. The holy emperors Yao
and Shun were identical in nature with the nefarious emperors
Kieh and Chow. That Hsun Tze and Ming Tze, two of
Confucius's disciples excelled others in filial piety is not owing

to any particular blessing of Heaven; they were reputed for this virtue as a result of their indomitable efforts. Hsun Tze's teachings are in accord with what has been taught in Christianity that man has the ability to do good because he has been made in the image of God, although this has been defaced. Niebuhr has viewed man as a paradox, as both good and evil, because he innately possesses freedom to make decision. But where there is freedom, there is sin. [185] The writer is of the conviction that human nature is both good and evil because human beings are endowed with the freedom of reason and will, and the freedom of choice and decision. Man has the ability to do both good and evil. But whether man leads a laudable life or a wicked one depends on the individual's own making. Evil or sin is the creation of man. Man's original nature has been degenerated by unbridled passion and desires, so that stringent discipline must be imposed to restore its original goodness. But I think what comfort man can derive on the point at issue is that as man brings about evil, he can also destroy it. Confucianism, however, teaches the possibility of man's transmitting evil himself and in this light it denies the idea of original sin and of forgiveness.

As for the improvability of human nature by the dint of education, while the Confucians attached much importance of education and training, Hsun Tze said that if human nature is good, there seems little purpose to education. Rousseau's method of letting the child develop without training is the logical method to use. In the West, it is admitted that human nature is bad. Hebrew and Christian theologians have gone much farther than Hsun Tze. We have found that combination in both Catholic and Reformation Protestant theology and in Hobbes as well as in Hsun Tze. Hobbes asserted that morality only arose after the social contract had been made and hence he could not pass a moral judgment upon men in the state of nature, but he described human nature as evil, though he could only call it brutish. The Catholic theologians were confronted with the same difficulties and, while the authority of the Bible fell short of adequacy they added that of the Church Fathers, then that of the councils to define what the Bible and the Fathers taught; and finally it was in the Pope that they found an ultimate authority.

Hsun Tze and Mencius were poles apart. They adhered to opposite aspects of human nature, each choosing a particular aspect for the whole. Like the doctrine of Mencius, the Bible declares that nature corrupted by sin is an enmity to God and that the Gentiles who lack the law do the things in accordance with nature, that is, those who lack the law are a law unto themselves. Paul's Epistle to the Romans says that one has raised the question: "Will the Torah, the law of Sinai not protect Israel from the wrath of God? On the day of God's judgment sin will be punished as sin against God's will (law) as read in the Torah or voiced in man's conscience. [186] In contrast to Christian teachings as regards human nature after the Fall, Hsun Tze was right when he said that human nature is prone to evil, but was mistaken in denying a "moral nature" to man and an innate principle of greatness. As a utilitarian Hsun Tze may be ranked with Bentham, whereas Mencius was the moralist of conscience.

Yang Tze seems to have been influenced by the writings of both Mencius and Hsun Tze. Mencius professed that man possesses a moral nature - something that voices its reproof on behalf of truth and justice on the one hand and brings its verdict to bear on wrongdoing on the other. Hsun Tze argued convincingly that there is such a strong propensity to sin that nothing short of laws and punishments can restrain men from plunging into the depth of vice and sin. Yang Tze appears to have adopted the positive and rejects the negative aspect of each of the two extreme theories. He subscribed to the opinion that human nature is both good and bad, and that both elements are mixed in it. He who makes an effort to cultivate the good side of his nature will become a good man; he who fails to eschew the vicious side of his nature will be a vicious man. Yang Tze admitted the existence of contradiction in human nature, but he was unable to explain it. However, his ideas afford a deeper insight into the moral nature of man than those of his predecessors.

The Concept of Human Nature and Sin among the Philosophers of the Sung Dynasty

. Since I have presented the ideas of Confucian philosophers about human nature and sin I need to put forward the theories of Chu Hsi and other philosophers of the Sung dynasty (960-1279 A.D. the Northern and Southern Sung). They have explored human nature in relation to the concept of sin. Here our attention must be called to the meaning of the word "hsing" (nature), the material principle and its counterpart "k'I", the immaterial principle. The immaterial principle is the order of the universe;

the law which pervades all things. Hsing is the all-pervading immaterial principle existing in man as well as in all animated beings. Chu Hsi said that benevolence, justice, propriety and wisdom are contained in nature, and that though these are considered the principal elements of nature, they do not exhaust it. What is decreed by Heaven is united to the material principle, and both are essential -to the production of things. According to Chu Hsi, man is a being composed of two principles: the one an entity and the other a law. Evidently he ignored the existence of a spiritual entity in which the immaterial entity inheres. The immaterial principle, nature or man is perfectly good, though the actions of the emperors Kieh and Chow in the Yin and Shang dynasties (1523 B.C.) were wicked. Supposing the immaterial principle is good, whence does evil come? Chu Hsi replied that evil is rooted in the material principle. The immaterial or essential nature (goodness) is like pure water, and the- physical or material nature like a pond. Whether water is pure or turbid, the water is one, but it is the pond of the channel which makes the difference. Even when the water is muddy or turbid, the water is itself clear. Likewise the nature, despite being conditioned by the physical or material nature, remains in itself pure. Chu Hsi argued by analogy that filial. piety is inherent in human nature as it is coterminous with human affection or benevolence. Whenever filial piety is put aside on account of selfishness or wickedness, it will disown the principle of affection and lose the child-like heart. [187] This resembles the water stream which becomes turbid after it has proceeded some distance in its course. Matter or material pursuit_ is the source of all vice, not as an active force opposed to goodness and wisdom, but simply as a negative obstruction to their perfect manifestation and realization.

According to Christian thought the eternal law is not divorced from the nature of things, which amounts to nature or the immaterial principle (universal, eternal, always good) or Heaven-conferred nature conceived by Chu Hsi and Sung philosophers. The sinner who infringes the eternal law does violence to his individual natural order of which he is a part. In this sense, sin is seen not as a violation of God's law, but as an act of self-destruction. When man places himself within God's love which is shown by the natural and the positive divine law he makes his way towards perfection. However, when he rejects God's plan and loves and substitutes in its stead his own selfishness and wickedness, he commits sin. In every sin two elements can be distinguished, one positive and the other negative or privative. The positive element consists in the sinner's pursuit of some created or material good in the sense that he has the predilection for it to the rejection of the divine good. Paul said that one sins because he loves money that is the root of all evils.[188] In other words, attachment to the worldly and anything that can detract one's interest from the divine good is evil or sin. The aversion from the divine good constitutes the privative element in sin; it would not bring about a sinful act if it did not entail aversion from the divine good. In fact, when man seeks an illicit material good which is incompatible with the divine good, he means to all intents and purposes the privation.

Furthermore Chu Hsi conceived the "Heaven-conferred nature" as referring to the essential or immaterial nature with which man is originally endowed. This is congruent with Mencius' notion that "nature is good". Both Mencius and Tillich were speaking only of the "Heavenly-conferred nature". Tillich says that "human nature" is essentially good.[189] On the other hand, when Confucius said "men in their nature are nearly alike, but by practice they grow wide apart",[190] he was speaking of the physical nature. John Dewey was in agreement with Confucius that environment and habit play an important part in human conduct. He said: "We perceive the better and we follow the worse."[191] Again Mencius regarded the physical nature as the appetite of the senses.[192] We should keep in mind that in the view of Chu Hsi the physical nature is not a different or second nature, but the same original or essential nature.[193] When the good is mingled with evil which is found actually in man, it is not a different good but the same good that exists before any evil has emerged.[194] Mencius asserted that if we look at the feelings flowing from the nature, there is no mistaking that they are destined to do what is good. The knowledge of a wicked man that his actions are evil is the proof of the existence in him of a nature that would lead him astray.

The physical nature is inferior to the essential or immaterial one, and thus it must be subordinated to the latter. The work of subordinating the physical nature is cumbersome, since the earnest seeker will have to make unremitting effort to achieve success. The method by which this subordination or transformation can be achieved is self-culture, education or sublimation. By a grim determination and indomitable perseverance the noble will gain ascendancy over the physical nature, rectify it and at long last reach the Golden Mean. Again as the source of evil is the disturbance of the equilibrium of the Golden Mean, the self-culture of the noble man strives to restore the equilibrium. When there are no stirrings of pleasure, anger, sorrow, and joy the mind remains in the state of equilibrium; but when those feelings have been disturbed, but restored in due course to calmness, there ensues the so-called state of harmony. Equilibrium and harmony should in all cases be maintained and pursued. Then the immaterial nature will be in dominance over the physical nature.[195] In this sense, sin is thought of by Chinese scholars and philosophers as an infraction of, and deviation from, the Golden Mean. In other words, evil is not evil originally, but it comes to be such by excess or by defect.[196] Confucius reproved his disciple, Tseng Tze, for filial impiety because he allowed himself to be beaten by his father to the extent that his life was endangered, and his inordinate conduct was derogatory to his father's kindness; Tseng Tze thus committed the sin of excess. In the Autumn and Spring Era (722481 B.C.) Duke Hsien of Chin showed undue partiality for the son, Hsi Ch'i of his concubine. Li Chi and banished his son Shen Shing to Chu Wo. As the concubine Li Chi fabricated an accusation that Shen Shing had plotted patricide, Duke Hsien became infuriated and harboured thoughts of killing his older son Shen Shing. Shen Shing's younger brother I Wu attempted to convince him of the imminent danger and advised him to escape. But Shen Shing refused it and in the end he committed suicide under duress.[197] Shen Shing committed the sin of excess. On the other hand, those who die without male issue to continue the family line and perform ancestor worship commit the sin of filial impiety, that is, a sin of defect. Such are the sin of monks, nuns and of unmarried people in traditional Chinese society.

We should bear in mind that sin in the Biblical sense has not been accepted by Chinese philosophers. The contrast of good and evil or virtue and vice, resolves itself into a difference in degree. If the immaterial principle is not obstructed by the physical nature or material principle, it will be a virtue; otherwise it will he a vice. This shows a striking similarity between the doctrine of the physical nature and Paul's doctrine of the flesh chiefly in the struggle between the higher and lower natures which both set forth. Paul spoke of an inner inclination to evil expressed by the term "flesh" which sets man against what good reason and the law prescribe. The flesh is the internal factor for sin, while the law is an external factor and makes man awake to his sinfulness. Here the innate depravity is recognized and shifted from what may be regarded as the real "ego", or the essential or immaterial nature of man to that which is external to it or the physical nature. Christian dogma teaches that sin lies in the heart, the inmost center of life,[198] that is, the seat of inclinations and self-determination, and hence it contaminates man. The Chinese philosophers confess with the Christian teachings that our failure in abiding by the law of God is accounted for partly the flesh in which we are entrammeled and partly our own self-indulgence in allurements or a giddy _life of pleasure. Sung philosophers have already laid down the principle that sin originates from a sphere of life, i.e., from the union of the essential nature with the physical nature; as a result, sin is thought of as an earthly impurity arising from "without" by which the true form of the interior life may be thwarted and its manifestations balked. Such is the doctrine of human nature and sin laid down by Sung philosophers. In brief, Sung philosophers believe with Mencius that human nature is good on the grounds that it is not conditioned and contaminated by the physical nature, external environment or tainted by fleshly entanglement. They also go along with what Christian philosophers teach that as an aftermath of the Fall of Adam and Eve, human nature which was originally pure, became corrupted. The immaterial principle is essentially good, while the physical nature or material principle is bad and gives rise to vice.

Chapter 7

The Chinese Natural Religion: Confucianism and Taoism

This paper investigates those Chinese ideas which were strikingly conveyed by Confucianism and Taoism in the early Han dynasty and Neo-Confucianism in the Sui 隋 (A.D. 581-619), T'ang 唐 (A.D. 618-907) and Sung 宋 (A. D. 960-1278) dynasties. It is evident that a number of the elements of Confucianism were viewed as an elaboration of the ancient Chinese tradition and owned their authority to the exemplary character of the sage kings Yao 堯 and Shun 舜. Confucius himself showed due respect to the Duke Chou 周公, son of King Wen 文王 as his inspiration: the Duke Chou was also considered by Chinese the founder of Confucianism, which developed in Wu Ching (Five Classics). The theory 'never too much' in 'I Ching' 易经 (Book of Changes) furnished the principal argument for the Doctrine of the Golden Mean which was cherished by Confucians and Taoists. On the other hand, Confucius drew his moral value from the Shih Ching 诗经 (Book of Poetry or Odes), which, he said, 'contains three hundred poems, 'the essence of which can -be summed up succinctly in one sentence: 'have no depraved thoughts'. The Ch'un Ch'iu 春秋 (Spring and Autumn Annals) was a year by year record of events in the State of Lu 鲁 Confucius took a leaf out of the Li Chi 礼记 (Book of Rites) in that harmony or moral order is the universal law of the world. As for Shu Ching 书经 (Book of History), one of the inserted chapters of the Shu Ching says:'.... And goodness itself has no constant resting place, but accords with perfect sincerity'. This notion is similar to what Confucius treated at length on the concept of Jen 仁 (sincerity or love) in Lun Yü 论语 (the Analects of Confucius).

Taoism existed at the beginning of the fifth century B.C.; but it was not espoused until the first century B.C. Among Taoists, Lieh Tzu 列子 laid an emphasis on pessimism, fatalism and self-interest while Yang Chu 杨朱 (c. 440-366 B.C.) held that Taoist spirit was simplicity and harmony. We can readily point out in Lu Shih Ch'un Ch'iu 吕氏春秋 (A Compendium of Various

Schools of Philosophy written by Lu Pu-wei 吕不伟 in the third century B.C.) the root and source of the two main trends of Chinese thought, Taoism and Confucianism. Both in the realm of nature (Taoism) and in that of man (Confucianism), when anything moved to its extreme, a reversal to the other extreme inevitably came about. In speaking of Neo-Confucianism, there are three lines of thought in its main sources. The first is Confucianism; the second is Taoism along with Buddhism through the medium of Ch'anism; the third is the Taoist religion, of which the cosmological views of Yin and Yang school are of paramount significance and interest.

To understand the Chinese natural religion, there should be a study of what the Chinese consider to be 'Nature' and man's relationship with it. The word 'Nature' can hardly be understood unless we probe most especially Confucianism, Taoism and Neo-Confucianism. I, for one am quite aware that the Chinese philosophy of life and Western philosophy are poles apart; it is certain that the former is unlike the Christian religion to say the least; to bring this into better relief, it is necessary to expound the concept of 'Nature' in the context of the Chinese philosophy.

Indian thought is characterized by profound metaphysical speculation and asceticism; Hebrew-Christian thought by a theocentric approach; early Greek thought by semi-materialistic speculation in regard to the essence and origin of the universe. Chinese thought is described by an ethical realism that conveys deep-rooted beliefs: (1) both the universe and man's life are real, and running through the universe and life is a pervading ethical principle, i.e., man's duty is to follow the natural order of the universe; (2) the world must be transformed into an ideal pattern and axiomatic unity of supreme perfection, which consists of developing one's nature and in the end culminating in a well-ordered state; (3) the human propensities, such as selfishness, attachment and worldliness are out of accord with the perfect philosophy of life; (4) the universe is a macro-micro cosmos while man a micro-macro cosmos-a world in miniature so that 'Sheng-Jen (圣人), the sage or living saint, who is of help in transforming and nourishing the power of heaven and earth, forms with them a triad; (5) in Taoism all forms of change arise from the interaction of two opposite forces-Yin and Yang (阴阳). The vicissitudes of Yin and Yang account for the regular succession of day and night and the alternate waxing and waning of the four seasons, so that man has his days and nights, and the prime of life and its decline.

Confucian Monism and Human or Social Harmony

The metaphysical aspect of Confucianism and its ethical implication can be thought of as monism; to Confucians, a thing's activity is to be guided by its essential nature, and its activity as a whole lies in the form of a harmonious and co-operative relationship. 'All things live together without injuring one another', says Chung Yung, the Doctrine of the Mean, and 'all courses are passed without collision with one another'. A natural order or social order are two faces of a single order: well-being for the individual and for society at large depends on the continuance of this harmonious order. The theologians who have treated religious concept often refer to what cannot be experienced by the senses. This is inadmissible in Chinese religious thought and practices which are a projection of their social life.

The perfect state of life in Confucianism is understood in terms of universal principle, namely, natural relationship between man and cosmos, not a supernatural being of any kind; as the Confucians do not believe in God, immortality conceived in the Confucian tradition and the eternal life Christianity has preached are two separate things. Most Chinese people crave for something which is immortality in this natural world, but not beyond this present life, for in no Chinese philosophy be it Confucianism or Taoism or Neo-Confucianism, is there the Western conception of personal immortality. True, there is the realm of immortals in the Taoist cult, but his belief which I suppose we should call 'secular' or 'mundane' is a conception of man's place in the universe, that is, salvation or long life and lasting vision in this world. Likewise, in Confucian doctrine, the sage or saint and the moral order which are bound up with the cosmic order do not transcend this world. Lao Tzu, the founder of Taoism was one of the prophets of life according to nature; he sought to bring the human Tao into harmony with the Tao of the cosmos. For the Chinese the philosophy of life is in this world simply because daily human relationship and activities give life meaning and can be experienced.

Confucian Summum Bonum and the Way of Life

Realization of Tao is the summum bonum or self-realization above the material world. This being so, a man can become a superior man or sage, who is the combination of the good man who has no sorrow, the wise man who has no perplexities, and the courageous man who has no fear. (Lun Yü, 14 'Hsien Wen', 14a). The Chinese recognize that it is not the possession of worldly things. Whatever their economic value might have been, nor their utility, however great it may be, that constitutes the 'summum bonum'. Although the pursuit of worldly pleasure has not been altogether dismissed in Confucian ethics, it must always be held in check by higher moral standards. The most weighty point is that we should have higher regard for morality than life itself, and its appurtenances. The spiritual and moral inspiration of Confucians is that man can make truth and not that truth can make man great. (Lun Yü, 15 'Wei Ling-Kung', 5b).

Chuang Tzu and, later most of Taoists maintained that the ideal of life must be secured by leading a spontaneous life that is, letting nature take its course; for nature is its own design which man can on no account circumvent. Like Taoists, the Neo-Confucians directed their attention to incessant transformation, a sober reality, which was looked up as a matter of duty for man so dovetail with the scheme of events; on the contrary, he should abide by his destiny whatever it may be, engaging in the universal law so as to live in conformity with the general pastern of the universe and foster social life accordingly. Benevolence, righteousness, sincerity and wisdom paved the way for reaching what the Chinese scholars have thought of as the paragon of human life.

Taoism on Universe and Harmony

The universe or Yü Chou 宇宙(the world) is conceived of as embracing within itself a physical world as well as a spiritual one; the physical world stands for matter, while the spiritual world for Tao or Reason. The universe is also conceived of as a comprehensive realm wherein matter and spirit have become entirely unified so as to form a coalescence of life, which continues with creation unlimited by space and time. The word 'Yü' is a constellation of a three dimensional series of changes in succession: the past continuing itself into the present and the present into the future.

The universe is a spiritual whole in which there is only one world, the objective, or actual world that we ourselves actually experience. Romantic Taoism conceives the universe as a harmonious whole: there exists a harmonious relation between the universe and man, an identity of attributes under the form of reciprocity, and the principle of creativity, that is, the universe and man are equipotent in creation. (Fang, 1957, 135) This point can well be illustrated by the following Figure 1.

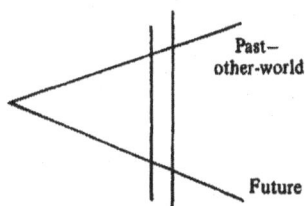

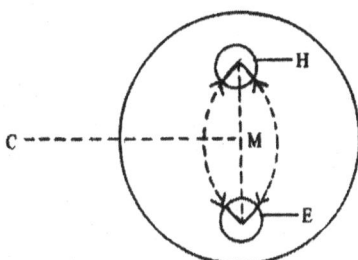

Figure 1   Figure 2

This Figure 2 symbolizes the comprehensive harmony of the cosmos, the ordered universe in which man (M) forms a center of creation and participates as a generating power of creation along the line (CM). The upper hemisphere Heaven (H) is endowed with the eternally dynamic Tao and embraces all the 'celestia' making them coalesce spirit and matter.

(E) stands for the terrestrial or earth kingdom which, being a receptacle of the heavenly creative life, has the power of creation. The central track included within (HE) constitutes the sphere of human action entwined with the procreative forces of Heaven and Earth.

Man and universe stand in a relation of harmony, though they are not identical. And the theory of harmony between man and the universe can be better understood if we compare it further with Western thought. The ancient Greeks also established a theory of harmony; man formed an insignificant part of the universe which was bifurcated into ideal and actual realms, the latter being weighed down by the evil effects of matter. Men living in the actual universe can barely overcome natural forces and social allurements so as to ward off evil. Thus when the Greeks contemplated supreme good they had to disentangle themselves from the shackles of the material world.

Here again, modern Europeans have set man against the universe and have done their level best to gain ascendancy over nature, and. in subduing nature, to harness all natural forces to human purpose and needs. Such a state of hostility between man and nature looms large quite clear in the whole of modern European thought. As a result, many moral ideas have caused torment and war; good Europeans have often seemed to mistake assertiveness for justice and the exercise of power for beneficence, (Tagore, 1928, 96; Russel, 1928, 105). This point of view is at best arbitrary, and at worst fallacious and self-defeating.

To understand better the above ideas we can compare Western philosophy, Confucianism and Taoism as follows:

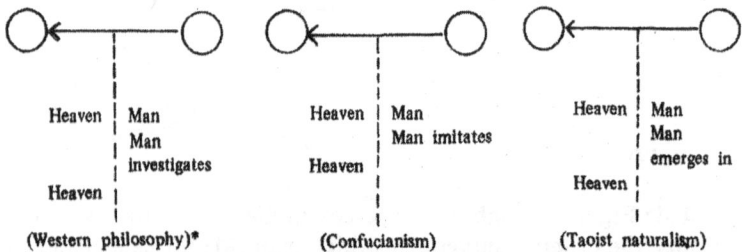

O ◄——┬——— O	O ◄——┬——— O	O ◄——┬——— O
Heaven ¦ Man	Heaven ¦ Man	Heaven ¦ Man
¦ Man	¦ Man imitates	¦ Man
¦ investigates	Heaven ¦	¦ emerges in
Heaven ¦	¦	Heaven ¦
(Western philosophy)*	(Confucianism)	(Taoist naturalism)

*Man's knowledge of nature and power over it. (Plato's Republic, 1966, Book II,51-57). Man, relinquishing the kingdom of Heaven, established a kingdom of man on earth. (F. Bacon, The Advancement of Learning and New Atlantis, 1960, 271-72).

Now what is this kind of morality? Nietzsche gave a clear answer: 'The condition of existence of the good is falsehood: morality is the idiosyncrasy of decadents, motivated by a desire to avenge themselves successfully upon life. Morality is just immoral.... morality is in itself a form of immorality'. (Nietzsche. 1966, 215, 308).

Chinese philosophers by contrast have conceived the universe as a plane of the confluence of universal life, in conjunction with heaven, makes up the cosmos within which all men come to be in harmony with heaven and earth, in sympathetic unity with one another and in perfect equilibrium with all things. In the Han dynasty (206 BC – 221 AD.), it was the people's belief that there was a unity between heaven and earth and man. And disturbances in the heavens or earth were inseparable from human actions and acted as a warning of impending catastrophes. The 'hui-hsing' or comet which was seen for 70 days from the second month of 5 B.C. was linked, perhaps retrospectively with an important and potentially treasonable suggestion put forward in the sixth month (Han Shu, IV, 144). The Chinese people ascribed the disturbances of the natural order to the social disarray. Hence to make every form of life congruent with the comprehensive harmony is the prospect of the universe. The Chinese by following 'nature' strive to the best of their ability for the attainment of the supreme good in imitation of cosmic order, radiance and splendour. All that need be said here is that they, while being men, have their philosophy to abide by the fundamental principle 'Tao', to identify themselves with the sentiments of compassion, righteousness, benevolence and love, and to eradicate what is regarded as ignominy in selfishness and prejudice and violence. The sages are respected as ideal personalities with attributes from heaven and earth, leading to the eminence of universal love.

Tao and the Ideal, Moral Conduct of Man

In the book Tao Teh Ching, Medhurst subscribed to the opinion that benevolence righteousness, filial piety, paternalism, loyalty and devotion degraded when the 'Tao' receded from view (Medhurst. 1972, 30). Tao is in fact Jen, love and righteousness and is not something enigmatic, or a vague incomprehensible. Arguing against a false mysticism about Tao, Chu Hsi said that Tao, a mystical love paradox is still more conspicuous. 'The Tao which can be expressed in words', said Lao Tzu, 'is not the eternal nameless Tao: but with a name, it is the mother of all things' (Giles, 1972, 19). Medhurst wrote glosses on this passage like: 'That aspect of God which is hidden in eternity, without bounds. without limits, without beginning, must be distinguished from that which is expressed in nature and man, the one apparently subjective, certainly unknowable, the other, self-manifestation, or the commencement of our knowledge as of our being'. Here Chu Hsi insisted that Tao should have a real existence and not be so transcendental as to lack any connection with men, that is, the transcendental Tao should be the principle of right conduct in everyday life for all men, and be akin to a road which is tramped upon by innumerable masses of people within the nine continents.

Tao is in fact the moral law written upon the heart of man. What differentiated Confucianism from Taoism was that in the former the fulfillment of life goes with the development of man, while the latter holds that simple and harmonious life comes from following 'Nature'. What is of concern to the Taoist is not so much succession of events as moral exigence and brilliance; it tends to be timeless, placed in thought beyond or above historical time. This is what is meant by the aphorism: Wen Shou Wu Chiang (万寿无疆), Life world without end. Ching Hsin (calmness of mind) and serenity undisturbed by any worldly allurements, including death, were reiterated in philosophical Taoism.

Kuo Hsiang argued that everything has its own nature in that things exist and transform according to 'nature'. The gigantic roc can soar high and the quail can fly low not because they take any action, but because 'nature' fashions them that way. The word 'nature' means that things come into existence spontaneously. If, then, all things come into being by themselves and their transformation is their doing, atheism inevitably ensues.

In short, when Taoism lay emphasis upon a simple and harmonious life, we are able to see why this naturalistic and atheistic philosophy should have a relationship with a superstitious religion, and it is this religion that lends support to the practice of alchemy and countenances immortality in this world, that is, in search of the elixir of life. This Taoist religion leads men to a negative philosophy at the loss of self-confidence. The Confucian attitude towards the metaphysical and transcendental question tends to widen the gap between Shang-ti (God) and men, especially when the terms 'Heaven' and 'Earth' come to the fore. Chu Tzu relegated God to a position of infinite remoteness, though he admitted the existence of a supreme power.

Taoism and Monism

Chinese monism corresponds to, and supplements that of the West: monism in Chinese philosophy and Western philosophy brings out the same points: the rejection of the view that attaches ultimate value to the individual, and the introduction of a higher principle. 'Tao', the only reality, is one and it produces many, although they are but appearances. In the view of Plato, the 'many' which are only appearances gain what is called reality by virtue of their participation in the 'one'. The subject of the 'one' and 'many' was broached in a Buddhist essay 'the Golden Lion' by Fa Tsung (A.D. 643-712). In the Golden Lion the gold and lion are of one substance, the lion being inlaid with gold; every part of the lion penetrates the gold and vice versa. Since 'Tao' is the moral law and the principle of life, it is the universal principle (one) of ail things (many) and is similar to Plato's idea of God that the world would be most real if all things conformed to the idea of God.

A question arises whether promoting longevity is contrary to nature; the answer is negative in that nature's time-scales are variable. As the slow growth of minerals could be achieved by the alchemists, so man's short life could be slowed down and often be unending. A man might defer death without going outside nature if only he could find out certain natural processes (Needham, 1974, 82). We cannot control nature but must obey her. Hence Tao abhors competition or any effort to expand oneself beyond the natural bounds of one's nature. To the Western thinkers, naturalism implies competition and control, but the Taoist mode of thought views nature as a harmony.

The 'Tao' or law corresponds to ethical perfection and is termed by Chu Tzu 'Good' in heaven and earth, man and all things. There is only one 'Tao' which is received by every individual in its entirety and undivided, like the moon shining in the heavens. When it is reflected on rivers and lakes, and is thus visible everywhere, we would not say that it is divided (Chu Tzu Yü Lei, I, 10b). Here the Tao bears resemblance to what Plato called the idea of 'good' or what Aristotle called 'God.' Chang dwelt on the comparison between Chu Hsi and Aristotle. 'While Chu Hsi', Chang said, 'is an Aristotelian in the field of nature, he is a Platonist in the field of moral values, recognizing that there exists an eternal unchanging truth'. (Chang, 1957, 255-56)

Two Modes-Yin and Yang and Moral Order

The principles 'Yin' and 'Yang' coexist and function together. When activity 'Yang' reaches its limit, it becomes tranquil, producing the passive principle 'Yin'. The two principles Yin and Yang are in fact two aspects of the one reality; as a result, the 'many' is ultimately 'One', and 'One' is differentiated in the 'Many'. The principle of the 'One' and of the 'Many' is akin to what Hua Yen said that the ocean consists of many waves, and the many waves are from the ocean, each involving the other. This metaphysical principle may be illustrated in the ancestral individual-group rites in which all male descendants (the many) of an ancestor took part, each having the proper position in accordance with seniority and performing them under the direction of the head of the family (the one). In ancestral cults where there is a lineage system, the cult group consists of lineal descendants from the same ancestor; the clan acted as unity and each member collectively; the male had his unique place and function, and his sentiment and sincerity towards his ancestor were personal and direct,

Furthermore, the Neo-Confucian philosophy of One-in-All and All-in-One was based on 'Li' (reason or law). Reason, as Swift put it, enables men to see truth impartially, unclouded by passion; only through his own reason man grasped what he needed to know. Like the ancient Stoics, deists found man's reason confirmed and supported by the rational structure of the universe (Swift,1961, XI). Reason cannot operate without the substantiating principle 'Ch'i' (vital force), which works in the form of Yin and Yang principles. It is due to the coordinating function of reason and the vital force that the universe is made a cosmos. Much the same could be said of the universe which in all its manifestations is a harmonious system; the order of the universe is central, and harmony is its immutable law, and so reason stands for cosmos, a moral order.

The Change in the Universe and the Self-transformation in Human Life

The philosophy of change in the universe lays the foundation of Neo-Confucianism. In terms of change in the universe Buddhists compare the universe with a sea wave, and made considerable efforts to cross the sea of waves to arrive at the other shore where the perpetual becoming will cease (Chang, 1967,135). Taoists who compared the universe with a galloping horse consider this drama with detachment. Confucians think of the universe as a great current which plays a leading role in the drama with pleasure. One of Confucius' disciples, Tseng Hsi enjoyed going swimming, adult and children together enjoying the breezes and returning home singing, Confucius was delighted and said: 'You are one after my heart, (Lun Yü, VI, I I .'Hsin chin', 7a).

Needham holds that Neo-Confucians arrive at essentially an organic view of the universe which, though neither created nor governed by any personal deity, was completely real (Needham, 1956, 412). Needham saw a striking similarity between Chinese organism and that of Whitehead; nevertheless, there is an absence of Whitehead's God in Neo-Confucianism. As for the change in the universe Taoists maintain that time travels in a circle, and since a thing comes from non-being, it will return to 'non-being'. Ancestors exist in the changeless dream time of the past, and wherever our ancestors are now, it is there that we are going too. The eternal changeless past and future time tend to coalesce (Leach, 1964, 5). In the process of production and reproduction, Confucians contend that time never comes to an end or repeats itself. Yet Neo-Confucians relish a metaphysical flavour and undoubtedly agree that the universe is good because it involves the greater acts of love. The universe embraces all things, and what moral act can be better than identification with everything? In the Doctrine of the Mean the principle 'Ch'eng' (sincerity) means the beginning and the-end of things, leading to activity, change and transformation (Chung Yung, XXII, 17a). Lao Tzu spoke of Ti (Lord), yet, if the idea of God is insinuated in Taoism, it is overshadowed by the cardinal doctrine of self-transformation. In Confucianism, heaven is of anthropomorphic character and is identified with Shang-Ti, who, not being the personal God as held by Christians, implies the greatest mystery in the process of production and reproduction. Christians preach that all beings but God are imperfect, whereas Taoists say that men can become perfect through self-transformation.

Hence man can strive to be perfect whether he is called 'sage' or a perfect man; it means that perfection is accessible to man without being what is thought to be transcendental or other worldly. Here we speak of the pragmatism of self-cultivation or edification which is in an anthropomorphic way a substitute for the worship of, and dependent upon God. Humanism, in the sense of attaching importance to human interests and affairs and classical scholarship, is founded upon the dignity of the individual; it is compatible with, and a partner of Christianity, but Christianity is not a philosophy or metaphysical system. In Confucianism, man depends upon other men for self-cultivation and perfection; the relation of fatherhood is not external to the son, but enters into his very self and becomes part of his very nature.

The Mind and Jen (Love) of the Universe

The character Jen (仁) consists of two parts, of which one

'人' refers to man, and the other '二' means two; two persons can establish human relationship. Jen (love) or moral perfection, as Ch'eng Tzu put it, is the principle of affection and the virtue of the mind. Jen is also the vital impulse which is translated 'Shing-Yi'. The two words 'shing' (life) and 'yi' (purpose) combined together convey the principle of life, such as exists in the grain of wheat, in peach and apricot kernels, although they seem to be dead (Chu Tzu Chüan Shu, 47, 3a). For to live without Jen, man is dead. We can in no way move or melt the hardhearted man, just as we can neither sow seed in a block or stone or reap fruit from it. The vital impulse carries more weight' than the principle of life as it is latent in the seed or kernel which will under favourable conditions burst full-blown; this is certainly the case we see in the budding life of spring when all nature is shooting. In the four seasons, spring is the birth of the vital impulse, summer is its development, autumn is consummation, and winter is the storing-up of the vital impulse. This impulse, whether in man or in the universe, is 'Jen', which imports the delight of creator in creating things; it is to the same 'Jen' that whatever is in the world owns its origin. The 'Jen' is the gentle mind which loves mankind and other creatures alike; it also extends human feeling and experience to animals because when a man hears the cry of an animal that it is to be slaughtered, he cannot help having instinctive compassion. Chu Tzu was even reluctant to allow anyone to cut the grass in front of his window (Chu Tzu Chüan Shu, 48, 8b). These feeling and experience bespeak the innateness of the heavenly nature within man.

On universal love both Spinoza and Wang Yang-ming are, I suppose, of the sane opinion. Wang approved what was preached by Mo Tzu about universal love. The love between father and son is the starting-point of the love spirit; hence it extends to love people and all things. Spinoza spoke of universal love as the intellectual love of God: this love is eternal. He said: 'He who lives under the guidance of reason makes every possible effort to render back love or kindness for another's hatred, anger and contempt towards him' (Spinoza. Corollary 'love and Tao', 168). When man sees his parents, he naturally knows what filial piety is and acts upon it. If man is remiss in filial piety, it is due to his selfish motives which besmirch the original nature of the mind and put him outside the pale of society. In short, to be a true man is to love all men and to possess the attributes: propriety'. 'modesty', and 'honesty'. Propriety is the basis of man's conduct: modesty, his starting point, and honesty, his goal (Lun Yü, VIII, 15 'Wei Ling-Kung', 14a).

Now we may ask what becomes of existence beyond this world or what would be the future of man after death? It is clear that Western idea of personal immortality hereafter does not exist in Confucianism. Taoism and Neo-Confucianism; none of them has anything to say on this matter. It was only Mo Tzu who believed in spiritual beings and founded a religion in ancient China (Hu Shih, 1963, 57). In the belief of Chinese philosophers, at death man's soul returns to the heavenly paradise from which it comes, and his spirit returns to the earthly or passive universal principle from which it takes birth. Man's soul and spirit dwell apart. It is taken for granted that people have some sort of existence after death, social immortality, though the Chinese do not pretend to know where and what kind of life it is that they have.

Now what is social immortality? Influenced by Buddhism in a land which promised eternal life in paradise the Chinese masses had no doubt that the individual continues to live. after death. Yet the Chinese intellectuals speak, as I understand it, of their belief in a personality that survives after death, namely, social immortality or immortality of inspiration. Both Lao Tzu and Confucius have been thought to live still not so as physical persons as spiritual beings, because at death certain attributes continue, such as influence, work, doctrine and example. For the idea of life among the Chinese is not just restricted to one's body, we live not simply as ourselves alone, but we depend on those of the past and have the duties to those living in the present and to those of the future who will depend on us. In other words, our blood, fresh in our children will persist. Dubs does not believe in earthly immortals as put forward by Lao Tzu, but he insists that Lao Tzu understood the word 'immortality' to mean an 'immortality of influence' (Dubs, 1954. 149-161).

The continuation of a life for individual families and for the society at large depends on a male heir. For a male heirdom has symbolic meaning as well as is ceaseless family link; it is projection of one self, the self being identified with the large self. Although Chinese people are devoid of a formal religion, they do entertain the idea of religion in a rather anthropomorphic way; their ancestors are spoken of as spirits and stand for the collective strength to which the person belongs. The ancestral rites are performed unbroken in Chinese society because they are part of the mechanisms by which an orderly and harmonious society is sustained, serving as they do to produce certain fundamental social values. To render service to the living is embellishing their beginning, to send off the dead is beautifying their end. When the beginning and the end meet, the service of the dutiful son is well recompensed and the way of the Sage is achieved.

Confucius, however, neither denied the existence of spiritual beings nor ignored ancestors; he urged his pupils to serve parents, when alive, according to propriety; bury them, when dead, according to propriety: and sacrifice to them after death, according to propriety (Lun Yü, I, No. 2 'Wei Cheng', 8a). As a result of Confucius' emphasis on rules of propriety, spiritual beings had been relegated to obscurity. Hence to all intents and purposes Confucius apparently weakened, if he did not destroy, the belief in personal and spiritual survival after death.

One may raise another question: if human nature is good as both Confucius and Mencius insisted upon, whence comes the evil in the world? Taoism imputed the appearances of evil to man's ignorance which engenders inevitably false knowledge and pernicious desires. Confucianism and Monism as well account for evil in terms of selfishness, delusion and deviation from the Golden Mean. No one would dispute, I think, that when men are liable to be tossed hither and thither by pursuit of selfish and sordid interests, evil will certainly ensue. Chinese philosophers have on the whole agreed that since evil is produced by man, it is within his power to eliminate it; this being so, it may be clearly seen that the idea of original sin and its atonement are out of place in Chinese philosophy. Man perpetuates wicked actions which entail his own downfall but he can also ascend to perfection in life.

Conclusion

The Confucian concept of 'Jen' (humanity or love) has been central in Chinese philosophy. The man of 'Jen' is the perfect man, a man of the golden rule, for, wishing to mould his own character; he 'also fashions the character of others, and wishing to be eminent himself, he also helps others to excel. The harmony of self and society in 'Jen' is expressed by 'Chung' (conscientiousness) and 'Shu' (altruism), which is essentially the Golden Mean or the Golden Rule. The extended idea of Jen inspired the Neo-Confucian doctrine of man forming one body with Heaven, the universe or the unity of man and nature; this idea entails balance and tranquility of mind. The Chinese have held that the world embodied in ultimate goal of the present life should be transformed into an- ideal pattern pranked with the axiomatic unity of supreme perfection. They have aspired to the transfigured world of edifying morality and of contemplative truth; any other world will be a sphere of anxiety and dismal disquietude for us. On this basis the Confucians have aspired to the continually creative power of the heavenly 'Tao'-the way of reality on a par with Plato's idea of God-to mould the whole cosmic order; this, however, can by no means be achieved unless man lives in accord with the general pattern of the universe and fosters moral life, namely, benevolence, righteousness, wisdom and propriety. Obviously these four virtues are the manifestation and moral fulfillment of the ideology of human life. This is simply what Mencius said: 'To dwell in the spacious habitation of the universe (to practice benevolence), to stand in the right place of the universe (conform to propriety or moral rules of correct conduct), and to walk on the grand path of the universe (to observe righteousness), these are the marks of a great or perfect man' (Mencius, 4 'Li Lou', Pt. i, 7a-7b).

Chapter 8

Fire Ancestor Worship in China

In ancient China (ca. 2000 B. C.) not only did the emperors provide temples for the expression of their people's fond respect for their ancestors through sacrifices and ceremonies, but peoples improvised their own domestic shrines as well. The first ceremonies involved the kindling of a fire. Incense was burned in the ancient Chinese temples; and even in more modern Chinese households the 'joss-stick' censers were lit to do honour to all divine beings, from the ancestral manes[199] to the great gods of heaven and earth.

Fire and Ancestor Worship

In such worship, the Chinese called their ancestors 'chu' (主) ; its form is ' 坐 ' coming of ' ｜ ' which is symbolized by a frame or by the wick of an oil lamp above it. [Hsü Shen, (许慎), Analytical. Dictionary of Characters (说文解字) Vol. 5, 19b.] Although the ancestor worship in the form of a wooden tablet shaped thus ' 上 ' is a metamorphosis of that early fire worship, there are very few accounts of this worship in writings on fire.   The character 'tsu' (祖) for ancestor is composed of two parts: one pictophonetic and one adding meaning or knowing. The part ' 示 ' of the character 'tsu' stands for spirit or god, and another part '且'portrays both a phallus ' 且 ' and ' 且 ' the female organ. The paleography of the character ' 示 ' , includes three parts: ' ノ ', ' し ', and ' ｜ ', whose vertical strokes symbolize the sending down of light and blessings on earth. The light represents the ancestral spirit bestowment of blessings upon the descendants.

This paper seeks to investigate the development of ancestor worship from its early symbolizing in the form of fire to its later symbolizing a wooden tablet. I must emphasize that this is a study of religion. The influence of ancestor worship, however general as a religion of humanity, has been so strong that without understanding it, we should be hard put to comprehend the traditional Chinese social structure, particularly in relation to the family, its most fundamental institution. No serious attempts have yet been made, so far as I am aware, to prove the existence of the link between fire and ancestor worship, but their linkage will become clearer as this paper proceeds. I do not feel obliged to describe how Homo Sinanthropus or Peking Man discovered fire half a million years ago; for on no definition of religion can that be regarded as relevant to this study.

The sources to which I resort principally are palaeography, bone or tortoise shell inscriptions and historical documents. We should note that inscriptions on ancient bones, and oracle inscriptions of the Shang dynasty (ca. 16th-11th century B.C.) are regarded as the best sources for this study; but palaeography is also undoubtedly of great ethnographic value, and particularly so the remarkable Chinese script. Such classical sources are of inestimable value for this sort of research; in fact, the quarrying of them for their bearing on the origin of fire is fundamentally relevant to this study, and will throw light on the development of ancestor worship in the form of a wooden tablet.

1. *The relationship between fire and wood.* There is no denial that fire and wood are bound up with each other; this has been illustrated by an old Chinese legend. Once upon a time a great man went to walk beyond the bounds of the moon and the sun. He saw a woodpecker at a tree and making fire issue from it. Wonder-struck with what he saw, the sage himself took a branch of the tree and produced fire from it. (Lo Pi, Lu Shih (路史) , Peripatetic, Vol. 5, pp. 4b-5a.) The sage was then called Sui-Jen Shih (燧人氏) . The character 'sui' (燧) means an instrument to bring about fire, and 'mu-sui' (木燧), signifies eliciting fire from wood by rotary friction or by boring into it. It was the sage - Sui Jen Shih who drilled with sticks and produced fire with which to transform rancid or rank and putrid foods. The people thrilled with joy and made him the ruler of the world, calling him 'the Drill Man'. [Han Fei-tzu (韩非子), Vol. 19 ' Wu Tu' (五蠹), p. la.]

Now which trees were prescribed from whose wood to kindle fire? There is a distinction between those trees that could be used impeccably for this purpose, and those it was impious to make use of. (Virgil, Vol. 71; Plutarch, Numa). The sanctity ascribed by the Chinese to fire springs from the custom of kindling it with the wood of their ancestral trees, and hence the cult of fire resolved itself into a form of ancestor worship. Chou Shu recorded: 'The elm and willow were used for spring; the date, almond and mulberry for summer; the green shrubs for autumn; and locust and sandalwood for winter.'[200] This seasonal changing in woods parallels a custom of the Greeks and Romans: amongst whom every first of March every family was under an obligation to extinguish its sacred fire and to light a new fire immediately.[201] In India the god 'Agni' was a typical example also of a deified personification of fire, which was to be produced by friction between two pieces of the sacred fig tree called 'Arian'.[202]

2. There is a further relationship between fire or flame and the origin of life. The question is what is this relationship? It is concerned with how fire should be kindled and how the method used bears symbolically on male and female congress. In ancient times fire was obtained by means of the fire drill consisting of two dried sticks of the elm and willow trees; the former was sharpened vertically as a drill, whereas the latter was shaped into a horizontal tray. The sharpened end of the elm stick was placed into the top notch of the willow tray and spin rapidly around in the tray by twirling it with a cord until it burst into flame. Chuang Tzu described how friction between woods can thus be made to kindle fire,[203] and that the drill and the hollow for it were an expression of male and female function.[204]

The vertical elm stick was symbolized man and the horizontal willow slot woman. The two sticks which were used to kindle the fire by friction represented a definitive ancestor of the paternal clan. As wood produces fire - which is, as previously described, the origin of life - the ancestor is the progenitor of his later descendants. In the light of what has been said above, it is quite sensible for there is to be such a tangible link between fire making and the worship of the dead. We find the same custom among the Hopi Indians, who kindle fire ceremoniously by the friction of the two sticks standing for male and female respectively. The female stick with its notch is laid flat on the floor, in the notch of the female stick the point of the male stick is inserted, and by twirling the stick between the hands, fire is made to come forth.[205]

3. How fire-making comes to symbolize an ancestor in relation to the form of the reproductive organs is worth further investigation. (1) The origin of fire. Marin-Anim explains that it is based on the analogy which is traced between the process of kindling fire by the means of a fire-drill on the one hand and the intercourse of the sexes on the other. The drill consists in rubbing together a split bamboo as a male and a flat stick which is bored by it as a female.[206] (2) That fire is a pictograph of a phallus is illustrated by the legend of the birth of King Servius Tullius. Once upon a time, a virgin of Ocrisia, a slave woman of Queen Tanaquil, the wife of

King Tarquin the elder, was offering the customary cakes and libations of wine on the royal hearth when a flame in the shape of the male organ shot out from the fire. Taking this for an augury that her handmaiden was to be the mother of a king, the wise queen Tanaquil bade the girl array herself as a bride and lie down beside the hearth. Thereupon Ocrisia conceived by the god or spirit of the fire, and in due time brought forth Servius Tullius who was the reputed son of a slave mother and a divine father, the fire god. His birth from the fire was attested in his childhood by a lambent flame about his head during his sleep at noon in the king's palace.[207] (3) It remains to say a few further words about the myths which are relevant to those of the birth of Servius Tullius and of other Latin kings; often virgin mothers had come to them conceived through a contact with a spark or tongue of fire. It is still believed that the fire which originates life may impregnate human beings. Mr. Brown of the Canadian Baptist Mission to the Telugus said that in Hindoo temples in South India sometime a scaffolding is erected over a fire; man and woman are got to copulate on it and allow the human seed to fall into the fire.[208] This ceremony is another way of conveying the fertilizing virtue of the fire to the woman.

4. The paleography of the character for 'fire' (火). The pictogram of the character for fire is described as follows: (🔥🔥🔥🔥[209]).

According to the inscriptions on bones or tortoise shells of the Shang dynasty (c. 16th century B. C.) the ellipsis or abbreviation of the character fire is '⊥' and 'L' which stand for the ancestor and ancestress respectively, viz. ' 且 ', ancestor, and ' 𝔖𝔖𝔖 ', ancestress. [210] These symbols as the Analytical Dictionary of Characters suggests, represent man and woman in the form of reproductive organs.[211]

(1) The character 'fire' (火) was an ellipsis of 'mu' (母 mother) ; the symbol 'jen' (人 man) comes originally from man (人) and the two dots ':' in the character '母' is taken after what are 'mana' of the reproductive organs in various European regions.[212] In relation to the word 'fire' the word '夹炗奐' is composed of three parts: (a) man (人), (b) the great (ta 大), and (c) fire with two dots '••' '山 山' '业业'; this is so although the oracles inscriptions of the Shang dynasty (16th-11th century B.C.) and some ancient bronze objects, differ from this paleography. Nevertheless Kuo Mo jo, an expert on the inscriptions on bones and tortoise shells was of the opinion that

these figures '∧ ∧ 山山 ㅛㅛ', are the metamorphosis of mu (母), which symbolize the worship of the reproductive organs. The character 'mu' in connection with 'fire' (火) gives us a further understanding of the origin of life.

(2) We are faced with another problem: the relationship of the 'fu' (父 ❧ father) to fire. This very problem is derived from the function of the father, the head of the family in terms of the sacrifice of fire. The word 'fu' (父 ❧ ❧)[213] stands for the father who holds a stick; the symbol '❘' a stick, which is the paleography of 'fu' (父) occurs with much the same range of meaning as 'father's holding a stick'[214] as well as the form of flame. The relationship between the father and fire brings me to an extremely important concept, understanding of which is necessary to a correct appreciation of Chinese religious thought and family structure. In the Chinese patrilineal structure it is the father (fu 父) who makes sacrifice to his ancestors; for the founding ancestor of a lineage is visualized as its father.

(3) In the Analytical Dictionary of Characters the word 'wang' (王) standing for grandfather or priest or king, is written in the form of '壬';[215] the form '壬' was the Chinese script before the Ch'in dynasty (221-207 B. C.) and consists of '壬' and '△' which is taken as the character 'fire' (火). The character '壬' is derived from '⊥' and '△';[216] it bears resemblance to the subterranean fire signifying a strong flame rising up, and is also identified with fire. The '△' like '⊥' is in fact the character '且', a form of phallus.[217]

Furthermore the character 'chu' (主) for spirit was originally written as '生'; the symbol '生' is considered as a picture of a lamp with a flame or wick '❘' rising up as a symbol of a prince. The character 'wang' (王) emperor represents a lampstand without which there will be no stand for a wick.[218] It follows that the character 'wang' is derived from fire simply because in ancient times the emperor was also the priest of sacrificing sacred fire.

In the light of the above discussion it will be seen that as fire is the origin of life the domestic fire is only the symbol of an ancestor; the fire is lit in the house to honour him, and this fire is to all intents and purposes kindled to preserve life in him, or stands for his soul being always vigilant.

Seeing that ancestors are regarded as gods, one may ask: is fire endowed also with a sacred nature? It is believed that a sacred nature was also attributed to that fire which preceded ancestor worship centered on a wooden tablet. It was to the fire endowed with divine nature, not to the fire as a physical or material creature that the Chinese offered real worship, since they saw in sacred fire a beneficent god-ancestor who maintained their life and protected their house and family, and brought them good fortune. The Chinese poured out wine to the fire in front of the ancestral image simply because the ancestors were conceived as a sort of apotheosis. Under an obligation to make offerings to their ancestors the Chinese do act at their own sweet will. Cicero said: 'Our ancestors desired that the men who had quitted this life should be counted in the number of the gods'.[219]

Among the Hindus this divinity of the fire importing the creator of the world, is called 'Agni'. In one of the hymns addressed to the divinity of the fire it is said: 'O Agni, thou are the life, thou are the protector of man'.[220] Agni contains three bodies: his terrestrial essence (the domestic fire), his atmospheric essence (the lightning), and his heavenly essence (the sun). The Agni god was a typical example of a divinized personification of fire.[221] In the Bible on several occasions the divine fire spurts forth and consumes the flesh lying upon the altar.[222]

5. *Fire and kitchen god (the Shen 神,竈神)* On the morning of the twenty-third day of the twelfth month, the most devoted, filial and kind-hearted son, Yin Tzu-fang, made a sacrifice to the kitchen god with a yellow sheep; radiant with satisfaction at the offering and invocation, the kitchen god conferred upon him a special blessing: to make him henceforth a prosperous man with, as an apanage, seven hundred acres of land.[223] The story undoubtedly suggests the kitchen god being pleased by his offering under an obligation and in some way constrained by the sacrifice to grant the favour asked for. Speaking of the sacrifice it is implied that god or a spirit is placed by the sacrifice under the obligation to give suppliants blessings. The god of fire[224] or the kitchen god or the Prince of the Oven is of exceptional importance in China. Few of the gods are older than he, and none are more universally worshipped, for it being he who was identified with the inventor of fire - heaven's greatest material gift to mankind - he has grown to personify the hearth, pivot of the home.

The shrine, a little niche behind the cooking stove, was the altar of the kitchen god, god of the hearth, upon which a little lamp was forever kept alight and was akin to Vesta who was none other than the hearth fire or the divine flame.[225] As the protector of the hearth, the kitchen god stood in tutelary relationship to the family of the owner of the homestead, and also with the ancestral ghosts or manes. In the light of what has just been said, it stands to reason that the kitchen god is the source of fire, the metamorphosis of the ancestry.

In the similarity to the Chinese kitchen god, Hestia - the Indo-European goddess of the hearth, protectress of the home and domestic life was symbolized by a fire kept eternally burning in each house. Just as fire which has been domesticated, as it were, has the eternal place in the sacred hearth, so Hestia was venerated as a symbol of the continuity of life in the home and state.[226] There was the cult of Vesta, the Roman goddess of the hearth fire, which corresponds in name and fact to the Greek Hestia. In Rome the first adoration was addressed to Vesta who was none other than the hearth fire. In Christianity the Holy Spirit is symbolized by fire at the Pentecost, when there fell upon the apostles cloven tongue-like flames; this tongue stands for the Holy Spirit who gave them the power of xenoglossy - the ability to speak and be understood in foreign languages. [227] The Lithuanians also appear to have worshipped the fire on the domestic hearth; and in some places they cherished a domestic god called Dinastipan, i.e., the Director of the smoke or chimney.[228]

We have so far discussed Hestia, Vesta, the Holy Spirit in Christianity and the fire god on the domestic hearth among the Lithuanians. Now one may ask what would there be to corresponding with Hestia, Vesta and the Holy Spirit, the family figured as the guardian of the family and lineage.[229] Although belief in him began in the remote past, the kitchen god has not fallen into desuetude; instead he still retains his popularity among the peasants as hearth guardian, spirit, helper and censor, who metes out to every member of the family alike the length of his days and his share of worldly wealth.

The kitchen god is represented by a paper inscription placed in a little niche on the stove. It is to this little niche, where the kitchen god is believed to dwell, that the sacrifice is made, and religious reverence is observed by laying dishes on the platform before this little palace. In this place also a lamp or a pair of candles are kept alight and a bundle of incense kept burning as an invocation.[230]

On the twenty-fourth day of the twelfth month a farewell sacrifice will be made; then, this being done, the paper inscription will be burnt with pine sticks. Through the fire, as indicated by the flame, the god returns back to heaven. The criterion for pleasing and displeasing the god consists in the observance and non-observance of certain taboos. These taboos, as far as I am aware, fall into three categories: the first is based on reverence to rice; rice should not be tramped under foot or wasted. The second category of taboo is related to a concept of sexual functions as being unclean, nothing to do with which may thus impinge upon the kitchen. It is rigorously taboo for women during menstruation to touch anything in the platform of the kitchen god. The third category deals with respect to learning; any paper with written characters of any kind should be burned, but never in the kitchen, only on the open ground or in a special furnace in the temple.[231]

We begin now to discuss how the concept of ancestor worship came to be symbolized in the form of a wooden tablet; and this will be more clearly seen when an account of the meanings of wooden tablets, the character of ' tsu' (祖) and 'shih' (示) is given in the next paragraph.

Ancestor Worship[232] in a Wooden Tablet[233]

In China there is not an established church with well-formulated dogmas, but there is a body of religious-philosophical beliefs in ancestors. These beliefs lay the foundation of the official religion, which consists in ancestor worship. On the basis of historical evidence, ancestor worship has been thought of as falling into the category of a low type of religion and has marked a first stage of development from earlier nature worship and animism.[234] Spencer held that ancestor worship was at the root of every religion, and the earliest manifestation of man's aspirations, from which idol and fetish worship and belief arose.[235] In the Roman Empire man-worship in the deification of emperors was a great falling off from a simpler faith of earlier times. Augustus, who was the son of the deified Julius, was believed to be theanthropic and thus was worshipped as god. He was the savior of the whole race of man.

1. The wooden tablet. I t is related to 'chu' (主), ancestor and was made of the ancestral trees; the men of the Hsia (2100 - 1600 B.C.) dynasty planted pine wood trees so as to signify exhilaration; the men of the Yin (c. 16th-11th century B.C.) dynasty planted cypresses to express mourning; the Chou (1122-249 B.C.) dynasty used a tablet made of chestnut so as to inspire people with awe.[236] The oldest descriptions of the ancient 'chu' (主) ancestral tablet, as

Karlgren states, occurs in Ho Hsiu's (何休) (2nd century A.D.) commentary to Kung Yang Chuan (公羊传) late 3rd and early 2nd centuries, Wen Kung-duke 2nd year. 'the shape of the 'chu' is quite square, a hole is made through the centre'.[237]

The ancestral tablet is simply a piece of wood, chestnut being the most orthodox of varied dimensions: its twelve inches chih (尺 foot) in length represents the twelve months, its four inches in width denotes the four seasons and its one inch and two ts'un (寸) in thickness stands for the twelve hours.[238] Now one may raise the question: what exactly was the origin of the wooden tablet? Ancestor worship in the form of a wooden tablet occurred as early as the Eastern Han dynasty (A.D. 25-220). Ting Lan (丁兰), who lived during the Han dynasty has been taken to be the originator of the ancestral tablet. While he was working in the fields his mother brought him some refreshments, but she stumbled over the root of a fir tree, she fell to the ground and died forthwith; whereupon Ting took that root from the fir tree and carved on it the image of his parents.[239] Again it was to Ting Lan that the worship of deceased parents under some visible form has commonly been attributed.

Chavannes stated that the tablet 'chu' (主) was originally a living image which was sometimes engraved on the back of the wooden tablet.[240] Likewise Erkes attempted to prove from ancient texts that the ancestral tablet was an image.[241] In the Orient an image is an accepted symbol for worship. At the request of the Jewish people, Aaron manufactured an image of golden bull which symbolizing Yahweh, was an accepted symbol of divinity.[242] To elaborate upon the worship of deceased parents, Wang Chung (王充) holds that according to the rites the tablets in the ancestral temple are made of wood, one foot and two inches long, to betoken deceased ancestors. A dutiful son on entering the hall worships them with all his soul. Although he knows that these wooden tablets are not his parents he must show them the greatest respect, and they call for his veneration.[243]

Ancestor worshippers have attached importance to the tablet in two ways: The first has been in that at a man's death, his bodily form can no longer be seen, but his descendants have a longing for him. For the satisfaction of this longing some visible objects must be used, which, being ever before their eyes, will keep the departed one in constant and vivid remembrance. The second has been in that for fear of their departed ancestors being deprived of any settled place, their descendants set up tablets in which their spirit may rest.

Being aware that a mere piece of wood, as such, may not serve as the abode of the spirit, when the tablet is set up some important personage is invited to dot in, with red ink on a brush, the character 'wang' (王) which then becomes 'chu' (主) , meaning the dwelling place of the spirits. Thus by means of a living person or a personification, the departed soul is called back. Before the dotting, the writer breathes upon the brush using the following form:[244]

The spirit rests in this wooden tablet
And the wooden tablet is spiritualized by its resting
The spirit and the wood together dwell In ages of unending spring!

2. The character 'shih' (示)

(a) The character 'shih' has its derivative form: '丁 禿 于 票' in the bone inscriptions.[245] In this character 'shih' the stroke 'J', as I said earlier, stands for the sun, the 'ᒪ' for the moon and the 'I' for the stars. The three vertical strokes of the character 'shih' symbolizes sending down their light on earth.[246] This is a spiritual being who observes human affairs and terrestrial changes, and manifests auspices and calamities to man. This is conceived as a hypostatization of his methods and attributes; there is a strong belief why in ancient Chinese divinities, spirits and ghosts are all called 'shih'.[247] Kuo Mo-jo said that whatever is reckoned as divine can easily be accounted for by the character 'shih'.

(b) The radical 'shih' which originally represented a wooden tablet has two forms: the cone-shaped '且', a phallus (menhir) and the triangle shaped '△' for the female vulva (dolmen).[248] The Chinese character 'tsu' (祖) is equally applied to both male and female: a dolmen called 'frog stone' which was discovered in Shantung at Chih-Chuan five miles to the west symbolized male and female megaliths.[249]

(c) Furthermore the character 'shih' (示) is an image of a reproductive goddess: given this, the pictograph of the character 'si' (祀) symbolizes man's kneeling before a divine image and of the character 'chu' (主) 祝 , kneel before a divine image with invocation.[250] The character 'shih' may also be taken, in form, as symbolizing a Chinese flag-pole, which resembles an ancient writing of the character 'shih'; on top of a flag-staff or pole appears a bottlegourd or calabash, written in the middle, a buttress below which there is a square base. This staff or pole is the relic of ancient worship of generative organs;[251] it has the sense of male symbol, and is really a phallus. In the light of what has been said above, it is quite sensible that shih as the spirit or the soul of ancestor, was worshipped.

   3. The character '且' (chieh) of the right part of the character 'tsu' （祖） represented by the symbols such as ' 且 △ 且 且 且 ' phallus[252] symbolizes the origin of life. In the temple the character ' 且' is identified with 'tsu', an ancestor; as the Li Chi said: When his (ancestor) place is given to him in the ancestral temple and his spirit-tablet is set up he is styled on it the 'god'.[253] Kuo Mo-jo holds that the 'mu' (牡 male) and 'bi' (妣 female) were the etymology of the character 'mu' （牡） and 'pin' （牝） In the Shang oracle inscription '牡' 牡 is a picture of the head and horns of an ox. The left part of the character 'mu' is the character 'niu' （牛） cattle, which is used as radical, while the right half (土) symbolizes the genital of a bull.[254] The character 'pin' (牝) is a picture of the head of a cow; the character 'pin' consists of the same radical 'niu' （牛） cattle, but either the left or right of this radical is a symbol of the genital of a cow.[255] The standing for 'tsu' （祖） and 'bi' （妣） have the following figures: 且 且 △ (male) whereas (5 ' 7 ' 5) for 'bi' (female). We may see the character '且' is the symbol of male and female.

   We find the character 'tsu' , earlier written as a simple drawing '且', which means the ancestor, the procreator of the race; and here there is a priori a great probability that we have a phallic picture. The word 'tsu' (ancestor) written with this character '且' occurs in thousands of inscriptions ever since the Yin (殷) dynasty (1300-1028 B.C.). This character ' 且 ' has a triangular top and a rectangular low part: by making the whole pictograph triangular the side strokes are more easily drawn. The triangular or tooth-like pictogram ' ▲△ ', must, according to Dr. Rydh, be necessarily a phallic design. (Dr. Rydh cites B. Karlgren's paper. Some Fecundity Symbols in Ancient China. Bulletin of the Museum of Far Eastern Antiquities. No. 2, p.1 Stockholm, 1930)

   Now one may ask: is the phallus idea limited to the script or are phallus elements to be found in real life, in the ancestral cults? As departed ancestors have been worshipped since the immemorial by sacrifices to the ancestral tablets, these tablets, even in such modern forms as ' 且 △ 介 ', bear a considerable resemblance to some of the most ancient variants of the character 'tsu', the phallic pictogram; it seems quite likely that the ancestral tablets originally were none other than phalluses symbolizing the procreative force of the family, for the ancestral cult was above all a fecundity cult.

The characters for 'tsu' (祖) and 'she' (社) are all the same meaning. The character 'she' is written with the radical 'shih' appearing in many religious characters and 'tu' (t'u 土 the soil).[256] Shou Wen Chich Tae mentions an old variant ' 示坐 ' in which a tree is added, alluding to the sacred tree, always attaching to the 'she' altar; the altar; beside a sacred tree, had a pole which represented the god of soil himself. The technical term both for the ancestral tablet 'tsu' and for the pole of the 'she' was 'chu'; the characters 'tsu' and 'chu' (主) are polyonymous. Chou Li records that the portable tablets carried in war were called 'tsu'.[257] We can now come to the conclusion that the symbols ' 且 ' and ' 介 ' are essentially the same. While a pole forms a fecundity and fertility symbol, ' 且 ' stands for the ancestral tablet 'tsu'.[258] The symbol ' 介 ' for the god of soil, both cases being a striking male phallic symbol,[259] for the god of soil is a tellurian spirit providing food.

The significance of the phallic symbol as an artifact is unearthed at Ch'uan Hu Ts'un (泉护村), Hua Hsien, Shensi as well as the Ching-Ts'un Lung Shanoid findings, has corroborated the etymology of the character '且' of the 'tsu'.[260] Ancestor worship is thus essentially male-ancestor, a requisite for which, as has been said earlier, might have been patrilineal descent.

Again the worship of male and female organs serves to expound the 'yin-yang' philosophy of ancient China, which can be summed up by the phrase 'yih-yin yih-yang wei chih tao' (一阴一阳谓之道), that is, one yin, the female, and one yang, the masculine, make the word ' tao' - the ordered whole.[261].This yin-yang philosophy laid down the foundation of the religious beliefs and social life of the Chinese. We can see here, as Professor Fortes holds, that the primary responsibility in ancestor worship devolves up on these who stand in filial relationship to the ancestor worship from generation to generation.[262]

Further light can be shed on the religious thought in ancestor worship. It has sometimes been said that ancestor worship, in its similarities to Christianity in concepts of sacrifice and rites, seems to be a religion in the true sense. In fact, on no level of thought is the ancestor thought of as something altogether the same as the God conceived in Christianity. The dread of death fits in with ancestor worship's total lack of eschatology; for it is exclusively a domestic religion. A stranger or outsider cannot participate in the religious rites of another family or hearth; every one has his own personal gods and knows them at his own hearth. In this world-wide religion, man never supplicates any other man's god.[263] A Greek proverb points to a time when all religions, being around the hearth or domestic shrine, had not passed beyond the narrow circle of the family.[264] There is nothing the Chinese can say of the nature of god than that he is their ancestor in their own hearth. By contrast to Christians, God is the God of the universe and has no chosen people, and who makes no distinction in race, families or states; God is to be worshipped by all men whoever they are and wherever they are.

What is more, the Chinese find their principal divinity within the house, where a domestic shrine is erected.[265] A shrine to ancestors - as god of the hearth in whatever further modifications he may figure in successive generations of the family. A man loves his house in the way a Christian loves his Church; in other words, the ancestor is thought of as god in a tutelary relationship to particular clan of family group.

Ancestor Worship and Chinese Social Structure

We have so far expatiated upon the relationship between fire and ancestor. Now the question arises of ancestor worship and its function in Chinese society.

1. It is in ancestor worship that we are most easily able to discover the social function of a religious cult. In the rites of ancestor worship it is sufficient that the participants should express their reverential gratitude to those from whom they have received life,. and their sense of duty to those not yet born, to whom they in due course will stand in the position of reverend ancestors. The ancestral rites are performed unbroken in Chinese society because they are part of the mechanism by which an orderly and harmonious society is sustained, serving as they do to produce certain fundamental values.[266] The memory of a dead man is thus kept alive by its being constantly on the people's lips through favored patronymic usage during the life-time of his children and afterward in the recitation of living descendants.

In fact, every family has at least one son and through this son the ancestor's name is forever a link in a line of descent. This is the only form of immortality that the Chinese are interested in; they think of the dead as continuing in this way in the living.[267] This refers to what was said by Hsun Tzu (筍子): "To render service to the living is embellishing their beginning; to send off the dead is beautifying their end. When the beginning and the end meet, the service of the dutiful son is well recompensed and the way of the sage is achieved."[268]

2. Ancestor worship and its complement, filial piety, form the core of Chinese religion. Among Chinese of all places and of all kinds there is a close connection between the tending of ancestors and filial piety. The Chinese owe their ancestors a debt for the gift of life and sustenance; they pay them respect during life, and their duty in this regard does .not come to an end when death removes their elders from among the living. There was an emphasis upon the necessity for continuing after death the reverence and respect toward their ancestors. Now by consulting the classical sources, a rational anthropologist was able to find his views on the role of religion confirmed in the Chinese attitude to the cult of ancestors.[269] Again, the continuation of the family and ancestor worship are intertwined; it is said that the family had to be perpetuated so that the ancestors could be worshipped by sacrifices. This given, an unmarried man or a married man without a son was considered unfilial. Mencius said that "there are three unfilial acts; the most serious is to be without descendants."[270]

3. Ancestor worship is the religion of humanity. The term "The religion of humanity" was coined by Thomas Paine. He held that the only way we can serve God is to make a contribution to the happiness of the living creature that God has made. He affirmed a religion of humanity based on the authentic divinity of that which is supreme in human nature and distinctive of it.[271] Religion, as he believed, directs itself from the universal family of mankind to the divine object of all adorations. What he said meant that ancestor worship contributes to the happiness of the living being on earth. Paine's thought and expression as regards the religion of humanity are inevitably constructed out of, and inextricably bound up with, his experience of the world around him.

Comte was a founder of the religion of humanity. The religion of our age must be a positive inspiration and answer the needs of humanity; that is, the religion of humanity is in search of unity and love.[272] The humanity Comte asks us to love is not all men, but those who survive in their descendants. This humanity we must love is worthy of what Comte called "subjective immortality". As he said: "The worship of truly superior men forms the essential part of the worship of humanity."[273] Such an idea is doubtless to some extent analogous to Confucius' humanism of ancestor worship.

4. The most important part of religion in China was the worship of ancestors. It is ancestor worship that has formed the bond of every family. Confucius was humanistic in that he showed a reasonable interest in religion; he himself sacrificed to his ancestors and felt as if his ancestors were actually present,[274] saying: "If I am not present at the sacrifice, it is as I did not sacrifice at all.[275] Nevertheless, Confucius frankly preferred the welfare of men to religion. The subjects which the master jibbed at discussing were: "strange phenomena, feats of strength, disorders and spirits."[276] When his pupil asked about serving the spirits, he replied: "We do not know how to serve men, how can we know how to serve the spirits?"[277] Confucius urged his pupils to serve parents when alive according to propriety; to bury them when dead according to propriety and to sacrifice to them after death according to propriety.[278] Given the rules of propriety toward ancestors, spiritual beings in Confucius' doctrine, were relegated to obscurity. Man, and man alone, engaged Confucius' primary attention.[279]

It needs not surprise us that on the basis of Chinese classics, such as the Analects of Confucius and the works of Mencius, ancestor worship is the religion of humanity because salvation takes place only in this world. In Chinese philosophies, the symbols of perfection, namely, the sage and moral order do not transcend this world. The Chinese, in general, are interested in the problems of life; they are chiefly occupied with the problems of this world.[280] As I said earlier, Confucius was loath to answer inquiries about the hereafter; the answer to the question of existence beyond this world has an entirely different complexion and in no Chinese religious doctrine can the Christian conception of personal immortality be found.[281]

Here again, in a classification of Chinese philosophies the dominant one is, as we have already seen, of an essentially religious kind dominated by the prevalence of a cult of ancestors. Therefore, the Chinese neither pretend to know nor do they care, I think, what happens to them in an after-life. Chinese ancestor worship which strives, by and large, to add to our understanding of the nature of Chinese natural religion which we espouse, does not have to appeal for justification to immediate utility.[282]

Chapter 9

Ancient Egyptian Religion and Christianity

Abstract: There is no denial that Christianity sprang out of the Jewish tradition, but was undoubtedly conceived as a higher dispensation than Judaism. A painstaking examination of Christianity debunks the root that its existence was paved not simply in the course of centuries but of millennia. In this vein, Gerald Massey traces the Christ back 10,000 years B. C, to the lands drained by the Nile River on the continent of Africa, particularly in Egypt. It is quite clear that as Charles Finch holds, there is at least a 4500 year connection that leads Christianity out of Africa and through Remit (Egyptian) - the cultural products of Egypt. Historical Christianity was an elaboration of Kamitic religious and symbolic ideas. It is in this vein that I propose to explore the relationship between Kamitic religious beliefs and Christianity, which occurs passim.

The article is intended as a contribution which it is hoped may be helpful to better understand the influence ancient Egyptian religion has exerted on Christianity. The western worlds and Christian civilization has typified the cultural melting pot of the near East; particularly, there exists a potent factor in the cultural borrowing from the religion of Egypt. [283] The influence of the Egyptian religion on posterity is keenly felt through Christianity and its antecedents.[284] The cult of Isis, her temple and her associates, had an inestimable influence on various faiths, particularly Christianity. Morenz holds that the concatenation has been traced between both the Old and New Testaments and Egyptian religion. Essentially, Christianity and Judaism differ fundamentally from Egyptian religion: while the former are concerned with scriptural religion revealed to mankind, the latter is centered around ritual and cultic practices. Nevertheless, there is no denial that a number of Christian elements were more than likely developed from the Egyptian tradition.

There have been many studies of Egypt's links with both the old and New Testaments. The Judaistic and Christian doctrines of creation through the word was likewise influenced by the Egyptian creation myths. [285] Some of the Egyptian ideas and images were transmitted via the Old and New Testaments and thus became part of early Christianity. Some Christian practices can be traced back to Egypt and Hellenistic forms and, in the end to the religious beliefs of Pharaonic Egypt. Embarking on the relationship between Egyptian beliefs and Christianity, we shall not leave out kinship, without which we would be hard put to understand it.

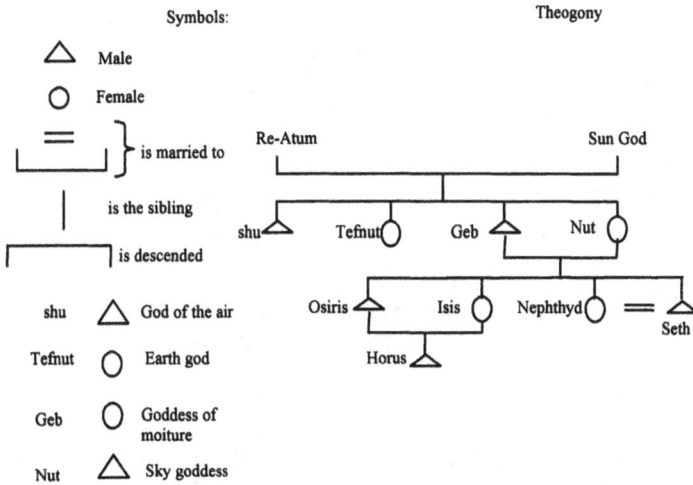

Biblical texts are conceived as mythology, not as history, as James Frazer has demonstrated. The Bible stories also have close parallels in folklore: none of these stories though recorded either in the Old Testament or in the New Testament are likely to be true as history,[286] but many millions consider the Bible to be a sacred tale; it is certainly a myth. The original authors of the Bible have drawn on a variety of actual human institutions. For example, in the Pentateuch the model used is that of the Egyptian Pharaoh. In Egyptian mythology the Pharaoh was treated as a divine king. The pattern of kinship for which Egypt offered the prototype prevailed throughout the Middle East. That in the Bible certain of the Patriarchs are identified with Pharaoh does not suggest that the Jews simply borrowed their religious belief from the Egyptians. But at the level of structural pattern the Jewish and Christian versions are the transformations of the Egyptian version.

Now we take a close look at the relationship between the stories about the Patriarchs appearing in Genesis and Exodus and the Stereotyped form of the saga of Osiris, Isis and Horus. In myth the god Osiris is married to his sister Isis, the goddess, and is killed by his brother Seth: the god Horus is the son of Osiris and Isis but posthumously conceived. The living Pharaoh of Egypt was regarded as an incarnation of Horus, In mytho-logic, the queen mother and the queen sister-wife were both representations of Isis.[287]

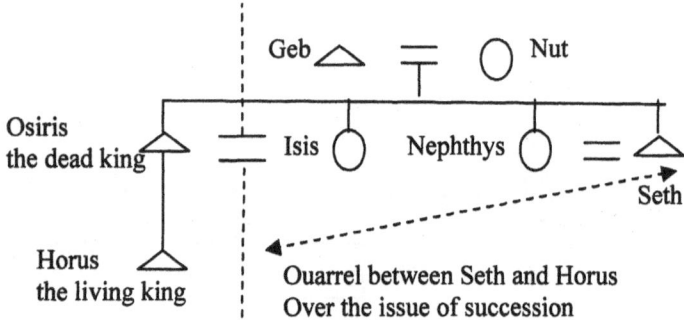

This is the ramifying elaboration of the Osiris-Isis-Horus mythology. The siblings spouse pair Osiris and Isis is matched by another siblings-spouse pair Seth-Nephthya and all four characters are immediate siblings to one another.

Moses and the Pharaoh's daughter - Thermutis

As Moses is the adopted son of Pharaoh's daughter, Thermutis this would imply that Moses' father should be the equivalent of the husband, the Pharaoh's daughter. This can be illustrated by the following figure:

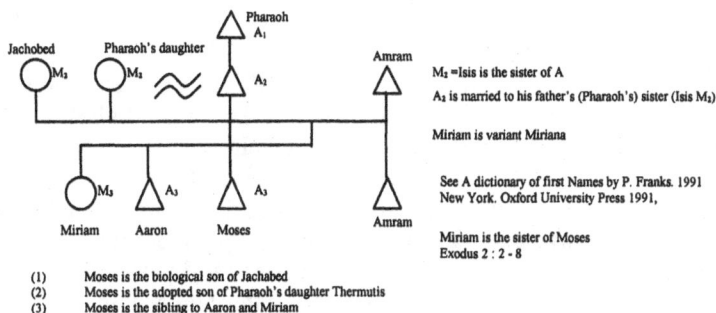

M₂ =Isis is the sister of A

A₂ is married to his father's (Pharaoh's) sister (Isis M₂)

Miriam is variant Miriana

See A dictionary of first Names by P. Franks. 1991 New York. Oxford University Press 1991,

Miriam is the sister of Moses
Exodus 2 : 2 - 8

(1)   Moses is the biological son of Jachabed
(2)   Moses is the adopted son of Pharaoh's daughter Thermutis
(3)   Moses is the sibling to Aaron and Miriam

Moses is Jachobed's first born son (Exodus 2, 1-2), yet the mother and sister play slightly different roles: Jochabed, the mother of Moses, hides the child in the bulrushes (Exodus 2. 2-3) while the sister (Pharaoh's daughter or princess) discovers the child Moses. This is the story about death[288] and rebirth with a change of witnesses in between.

Moses is the water-born: the name, according to Josephus, signifies one who has been taken out of the water. Pharaoh's daughter called the name of the child "Moses" and said: "because I drew him out of water. (Exodus, 11, 10)[289] According to the legend, the young child Moses was saved from the river in the ark and adopted and named by Thermutis, the princess.[290] Likewise, from the pregnancy of a virgin mother Isis, is born Horus: the infant is also hidden in the reeds of the Nile Delta so as to evade the vengeance of Seth.[291] Dealing with the resemblance between the "infant Moses in the bulrushes", and "the infant Horus is the reeds" we see clearly that the Pharaoh who orders the midwives to kill the male children of the Hebrews is Seth, the usurper King, brother, murderer and perpetual enemy of Osiris - Horus.[292] The gospel of St. Mattews of which I now turn says that King Herod orders the massacre of the innocents of whom Jesus is the sole target: this episode is a close copy of what the Pharaoh orders in the slaying of the male children of the Hebrews.[293]

As both Moses and Jesus are Horus figure so we are therefore led to speculate regarding possible connections between Mary (Miriam), the virgin mother of Jesus. Miriam, the virgin sister of Moses, and the archetypical figure of Isis who manages to be simultaneously mother, sister, wife and daughter.[294]

Now the question arises: what was the origin of Christianity in olden days? What was the series of things or events which linked together between Egyptian religious belief and Christianity? Through these moot questions can long-buried truths be brought to light? There are a myriad of Christian truths, but they are buried under gnostic and esoteric opinions. Catholic Christendom invokes many saints in its polyhagiodulia, but our interest is to think of such religious beliefs and practices as we find in the zoolatry of Egypt and the anthropomorphic cults of Greece and Rome as outworn crude falsehood or numbo-jumbo.[295] There is no denial that, however bogus their belief, they have a good deal of modern Christian belief.

The Christian creed convives of the existence of one God and of the Lord Jesus Christ, whereas Egyptians are polytheistic as well as pantheistic. The test of orthodoxy is a monotheism: in consequence, Christian theocracy stamped out of the Sarapeum of Alexandria[296] and obliterated officially the polytheistic ideas so long and strongly held in the Craeco-Roman world.

Now we denote our chief attention to investigate how the Egyptian beliefs in many gods and goddesses are bound up with Christianity: we should also consider Egyptian pantheism, myths and cosmology and their bearing on Kamitic[297] religious drama which concatenates Christianity.

The drama of Osiris

1. The religious concept of the Christhood was starkly influenced by the drama of Osiris. The Egyptian name of Osiris is "Asar" and its components "As-ar" can be translated "of Isis" (Ast). As-ar is the great ancestor of the dynastic Egyptians. He was drowned in the Nile by Seth but he rose from the dead and became the king of the dead and gave immortality to all who believed in him.[298] The myth of the death of Osiris and the search for his body by his widow or sister Isis establishes the whole range of Egyptian religion. Osiris is the aspect of the all-seeing sun regularly rising and setting. But he is at the same time the power that resuscitated and regenerated by his wife or sister Isis. As the god of resurrection, Osiris is the judge of the dead, the Lord of eternity and the hope of every person for rebirth after death.[299] The dead god Osiris is sufficiently vivified to have sexual intercourse with his sister Isis leading to the conception of his avenging son Horus.

2. The second important deity is Isis, the sister and wife of

Osiris (Fig. 1): her Egyptian name "Ast" means "throne" or "abode".[300] Isis is the greatest goddess of the Egyptian pantheon: she is the virgin-mother of Horus and mourns Osiris in his death. She seeks his dismembered body cut into 14 pieces by his brother Seth and in the end she re-instills the body with life.[301] Isis is the goddess of the moon and the most influential queen of Heaven.[302] She is also the mother of stars, the parent of seasons and the ministries of all the world.

3. The third drama involves Horus. Before Osiris had risen from death, the child Horus had been miraculously conceived by Isis in a necrophilious union. Horus is represented as an infant son of Isis sitting in her lap suckling her breast. Another aspect of - Horus is that he is the personification of light while his uncle Seth is the personification of darkness; Horus and Seth become mystically the warring twins and, as the avenger of his father's murder, Horus is Seth's implacable enemy.[303] Osiris was murdered by his brother Seth. When Horus was fully grown he avenges his father's death and fought Seth. Seth was condemned as the personification of evil and became a reviled outcast. Seth was regarded as a symbol for illegitimate confusion and became the storm on the horizon. If Osiris is to Seth as order is to confusion, then the death of a reigning king is appropriately represented as "the murder of Osiris by Seth". The new regime is established by the triumph of Horus over Seth and the binding of Seth in chains.[304]

Given the mythological arid symbolical and symbolic bearings of the principal actors in the dramas of Osiris, Isis and Horus. I have attempted to show how certain parallels, if any, to the Christian arrest our attention. As I have said earlier, there is no avoiding the fact that Egyptian religious have mutatis mutandis influence on the Christian theology. To delve for the parallels at the issue is not an unworthy undertaking. More than ever, it can be seen that Christian belief and practices in both the Old and New Testaments are inevitably constructed out of Egyptian religious belief. It cannot be denied that there is a moral identification imposed on individual Christians by the Egyptian culture and inextricably bound up with its religious values.

The composite entity of Osiris, Isis and Horus is the prototype of the Old Testament and the Gospel of Jesus Christ. Comparing the Kamitic archetypical figure to Christ, we have him who born of a virgin mother, and contends against Satan as analogous to Seth.[305] Isis is compared to the Virgin Mary who gives birth to the divine child Jesus.[306] Dealing with Isis and the Virgin Mary, Sir Budge tells us that the early Christians bestowed some of Isis's attributes, as the mother of Horus, upon the virgin.[307] Further Macquitty assures us of the influence of Isis throughout the world and says that it was from Alexandria that Horus and Isis entered the legend surrounding Buddha in Gandhara in northern India and then travelled to China where the Goddess Isis bears a resemblance to the Chinese Kwan-Yin.[308]

As for foil to the kinship of Osiris, Isis and Horus it behaves me to chart patently the pedigree or the family tree of the Holly family: Mother Mary. Joseph and Jesus and interpret it intelligibly as the system of kinship goes passim. This being so, the difficulty in the point at issue will undoubtedly be hurdled.

The Pedigree of the Holy Family: Mary, Joseph and Jesus

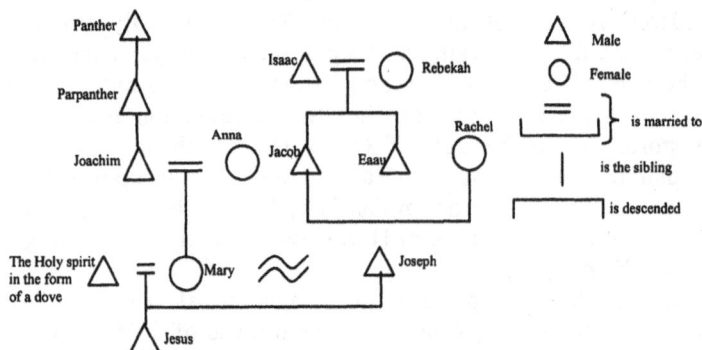

Panther

Parpanther

Joachim   Anna

Isaac   Rebekah

Jacob   Eaau   Rachel

The Holy spirit in the form of a dove   Mary   Joseph

Jesus

Male
Female
is married to
is the sibling
is descended

1) Joseph is descended as the eleventh son of Jacob and Rachel
2) Joseph's grand father and grandmother are Isaac and Rebekah
3) Joseph is legal or foster not biological father of Jesus

Here we can say that there are more than just parallels and analogies to be plumbed and link up with the Kamite mythos - the Osirian drama and Gospel Christianity. Horus is more than once represented as lame and deformed because, as Neumann holds, he is born of the mother only, without fatherhood.[309] Similarly, Jesus in Christianity is a paragon because he is of the "Father" through the foster or legal Joseph as well as of the mother Mary. In this regard it seems that the nativity of the infant Jesus comes right out of an Egyptian original. In this sense Thoth,[310] the messenger of the gods, announced to the royal mother (Isis) the impending birth of Horus who is descended from the God Amen and will reign as the divine king, Likewise, in the gospel of Luke (1,26-28) the messenger Angel Gabriel announced to Mary the impending birth of a divine king, the son of God. In the gospel of Matthew, Mary is made pregnant by the power of the Holy Spirit. The Holy Spirit is represented by a dove [311] which denotes the mystery of all mysteries about the origin of the Egypto-gnostic Christ.

Another scene is one of salient contrast: In Egyptian beliefs the gods gather around the infant Horus to adore him and in the New Testament the heavenly hosts gather above the infant Jesus to praise and adore him, In addition to the Angles adoring the infant Jesus, there were three Magi who came far afield to offer three gifts: of gold, frankincense a myrrh. [312]

Jesus and Lamb

In the Book of Revalations Jesus is the lamb that has been slain as the foundation of the world. [313] The slain lamb for ages annually was a type of the foundation laid in blood sacrifice. Here Sebeck or Jesus in Egypt had been the lamb that was slain as the foundation of the world. The lamb was one of the sacrificial types: Orisis in the human form of his son Horus is another; from Osiris mysteries we may undoubtedly learn that the foundation of the world has been imparted into the Christian belief. In the New Heaven the mother and child are re-enthroned in glory as the lamb of Gold, the Mighty. [314]

Jesus and the son of God

There is a need to labor the process of revealing to Kamite astronomical symbolism in the Gospels. This leads us to state patently that Jesus assumed the attributes of the sun gods of antiquity, the protype of which was Horus. It is all the more a fact that the solar character is exemplified by the Palm Sunday procession of Jesus into Jerusalem on the back of an ass and with his way strewn by palm branches. [315] Horus fought his battle against Seth with a branch of palm, the symbol of victorious renewal of life. The righteous also have the branch of palm given as typical of their conquest over death and Hadas; the branch of palm has occurred in the imagery of heaven and the typology of the eternal. [316]

The ass was one of the zootypes of the god Aiu who led the Israelite people out of Egypt. The ass-headed god is a form of Ra. the sun and is represented as the golden ass who carries the disk of the sun on his head between his ears. [317] Jesus riding the ass moves to his ultimate crucifixion: this is a figure of the sun moving toward the equinox symbolized by the palms at the Easter or Passover when he will be crucified on the cross.

The Cross and Christianity

The cross is the symbol of Christianity. The cross, the fundamental symbolism is itself as incomparably old as the Kamite symbol. The form of the ankh ⚲)[318] known as the "crux ansata" is the symbol of life, uniting masculine and feminine images.[319] The ankh-the ansata cross-is the sign of life; this sign was Christianized as a form of the cross. The presence of the ankh sign on some medieval tomb-stones in the Balkans may have an Isaiac connotation. Since in antiquity the ankh sign was also associated with the Mother Goddess, probably of Egyptian origin. In Christian iconography is found the peculiarly looped form of cross which is undoubtedly derived from the hieroglyphic writing of the Egyptian word "ankh". The earliest Christians, as we will see, adopted the "ankh" as their symbol of the cross. It is quite interesting to note, as an aside, that in a number of West African religions the cross-road is, to many who have knowledge of them, a place charged with numinous power; that is, a place of union between human and divine material and spiritual, living and dead.

The Tat-cross, as Marsey holds, is a type of the eternal and denotes the dead, i.e. those who have crossed over. [320] In Christian dogma, Jesus was dead on the cross, viz., he was crucified on Mount Calvary.[321] In Christian iconography Christ and cross are identical as were Horus and Tat. The cross takes the place of the Tat as a symbol of supporting power and the god as a sustaining force within the Tat may account for the legend of the gospel: Jesus being the hearer of the cross on which he was to suffer death. Thus the Genesis of the legend of the cross resembling that of the Christ is traced in Egypt to the cult of Plah at Memphis where the religion of the cross originated.[322] Jesus is the king of Israel, but is persecuted by his own people by being put to death by hanging: he first descends into the lower world and then ascends into heaven by an act of self resurrection.

Jesus and the word

Speaking about the relationship between Jesus and the word there is a fact to be taken into consideration, the Christian cult is invariably founded on the mysteries of incarnation; the doctrine of the incarnation is Egyptian, and to that wisdom we ought to appeal to fully understand it.

1. The incarnation as such has no adequate explanation without resorting to Egyptian origin. The doctrine of incarnation had evolved and had been established in the Osirian religion at 4.000 and possibly 10.000 years before it was portrayed in Christianity. In the Gospel of the Evangelist St. John, the word and the Christ are thought to be identified by a mystical bond. It is read in the Gospel: In the beginning was the word, the word was with the God, and the word was God."[323] John informs us that the "word was made flesh" in the person of Jesus Christ. Likewise, Osiris was the "great word i.e., the word of what cometh into being and what is not.

Osiris, the word, as Budge holds, spoke the words through which all things in heaven came into being from non-existence. Because he was the first man who was raised from the dead, he became the type and symbol and hope of every dead man.[324] In the Kamite universe conception, the power of life and re-birth rested in the word which was commanded by Osiris. As foil to Christ before the incarnation the Son of God was simply the word (Logos)[325] and the wisdom (Sophia) of God; that is, the creative power by which the world was to be made. Here the Nicene Creed is well quoted: the world proceeded out of the invisible, by the power of the "world" or Logos, true God of true God... by whom (word) all things were made." Osiris the word, as Budge holds, spoke the word through all things in the world.

Christianity and the Messiah

The Messiahs lays down the foundation of the Christianity. I feel that I am bound to discuss the "Messiah" which is found lucidly in the Kamite religion in the person of Horus. Now the question is posed concerning what light is shed by taking account of the Messiah and Christianity under the aegis of Horus. Mess[326] was the root of the Messiah by nature and by name. In the mythical representation, Horus was reborn each year as the Messu and the re-birth was celebrated by the festival called "Messiu". Messu is an Egyptian word meaning the anointed and to be anointed. The anointed is typical by Christ. As Jewish religion failed to establish the earthly kingdom under the Messia, Christians would fain have changed the earth kingdom to one of a heavenly kingdom under the messiaship of Christ.

The doctrine of messiaship was founded on the ever-coming Messu or child of the inundation in the pre-anthropomorphic phase of symbolism. In Egypt the first Horus came by water in the inundation; the second Horus came in the Blond of Isis: the third was the Horus of the resurrection who came in the spirit.

2, The Mes-ia is the Great Prince or Great Man while retaining the connotation of re-birth and the sonship. This is on a par with the sense inherent in the term "Messiah" as used by Christians and Jews. Further, "Mes" or "Mas" denotes "anointing" in the hieroglyphics: the mess becomes Messiah in Hebrew.[327] Tertullian claims that the name of "Christian" came from the unction received by Jesus Christ: this is in perfect accord with Christ anointed with oil, its embalment. It is read in the gospel of the woman who poured the ointment upon Jesus's body in Bethany to prepare him for his burial.[328]

3. As the Messiah Jesus was the "Kristos" or Christ, so in Egypt the "Krst" or "Karast" was the anointed mummy standing for the reborn re-arisen Osiris. In contrast Jesus is the arisen anointed one. This reflects the story of Lazarus in the Gospel of St. John.[329] Lazarus[330] is the dead brother of his two sisters Martha and Mary who bewail him. Jesus was then far from Bethany so that it took two more days to get where Lazarus lay dead. Jesus arrived in Bethany four days after Lazarus had been buried. By contrast, Annu is the sepulchre of Osiris whereas the cave for Lazarus is in Bethany.

Horus, the deliverer of his father Osiris, reaches him in the train of Hathor who is Meri. Thus Horus follows Meri to the place where Asar lies buried in the sepulchre[331] as Jesus follows Mary who had come forth to meet Jesus on the way to Bethany.[332] Jesus reached the tomb of Lazarus in the train of Mary and Martha. A loud voice was heard upon the horizon as Horns lifted the truth to Ba and the way for Osiris to come forth at the rising from the cave.[333] In like manner Jesus cried with a loud voice: "Lazarus come forth"!; the dead man came forth at once bound and foot with grave bands. Mary, the sister of Martha is witness to the resurrection of her brother Lazarus.

Egyptian religion and the Christian eucharist

The core of the Christian religion is the re-enactment of the sacrifice of Jesus in the Eucharist, i.e., the giving of his body and blood,[334] in the form of bread and wine so that sin may he forgiven. Now Osiris is god of viticulture, and wine is the spirit of the grape on the one hand and on the other it is the blood of the grape; thus to drink wine is to participate in the blood and spirit of Osiris.[335] Jesus, as it is read in the gospel, changes the water into wine in consequence of which the sacrifice today at the altar is the essential feature in the ancient idea of eating and drinking together: again the sacrifice, as such, is formalized in the Mass which is translated to an Egyptian "Mess". The "Mess" of sacrifice, the prototype of the Roman "Mass"[336] is called the sacrifice of the Christ: the dead body is typified by the raw flesh, bread without leaven and blood wafer. [337] The living mess signifies the generative spirit, still typified by the wine of the Eucharist, the blood of grapes and the wine, the branch of the new life.

There is an association of the Christian Last Supper with the dead Pharaoh Unas. The dead Pharaoh Unas ate the bodies of the gods and drank their blood. [338] The ancestors of the dynastic Egyptians partook ritualistically of human flesh and blood. Unas is said to have eaten gods so as to become gods himself, in this sense we would doubtless be right to say that the Eucharist of Christianity is nothing but a refinement of the Egyptian idea.

What is more, prior to his death Jesus instituted the Eucharist: in this ceremony what was noteworthy was that according to the Gospels. Judas, the brother of Jesus in one character, is the betrayer on the night of the last supper. By contrast, Judas the son of perdition, answers to Seth the twin brother of Osiris, who is his betrayer at the last supper called the "messiu" meal that was eaten on the night of the old year or the reign of Osiris.'' [339] One of the most striking of the various episodes in the gospel was the scene at the last supper in which Jesus washed the feet of the disciples. Washing the feet was one of the mysteries pertaining to the funeral of Osiris when the feet of the disciples of Horus were washed. The washer Jesus was one who was confronted with Judas who was waiting for his destruction and beseeched a speedy burial.[340]

Isis and the virgin Mary

A brief glance at Isis's attributes makes known her common characteristics with the Blessed Virgin whom Catholic Christianity has always revered as the Mother of God. Yet there are many parallels that an unprejudiced mind must he struck by. The pictures and sculptures wherein Isis is represented in the act of suckling her child Horus (Fig. 2). lays the foundation for the Christian figures and paintings of the Madonna and child. The image of the Virgin Mary, as we have seen, originates from Kamite typological antecedents. The Egyptian word 'men" imports "beloved" or "one who loves-" or "is beloved."[341] The bulk of the people in Egypt and Nubia who professed

Christianity transferred to Mary the Virgin, mother of the babe Jesus, the attributes of Isis, the everlasting mother of Horus.

We have already identified the Virgin Mary and the Virgin Isis; the Kamite Goddess Hathor and the name "Her" is the form of the mother of Horus; she carries the epithet "meri" as Hathor the "beloved". Hathor is personified as a dove and likewise the Holy Spirit comes down on the head of Jesus in the form of a dove.[342] In the "Legenda Aurea" Christ addresses his mother as his dove and says: "Arise my mother, my dove."[343] The cult of Isis exerts a strong influence on the religious development of the West where as a harbinger of the virgin the goddess Isis was to make her salient mark on Christianity.

To Isis, a patroness of mariners, the Virgin Mary owes her beautiful epithet of the "Stella Marls" or star of the Sea under which she is adored by tempest tossed sailors.[344] In this episode two major stories of Christian religion have been told, i.e., the resurrection savior and the immaculate conception of virgin birth:

And what is more, were I not to point out that lamentation of Isis and Mary for the beloved soul (Fig. 3). I would leave out one important episode. The Isis's dirge song is sung at mortuary ceremonies and before the dead Osiris: "Look thou upon me, I am the sister who loveth thee, go not far from me. I do not see thee, my heart weepeth for thee. Come to thy beloved one. Come to thy sister, come to thy wife.[345] Bearing a striking resemblance to Isis, the blessed Mary also bewails the death of her son Jesus. Mary laments for him crying: "those scalding tears our Lord shed..Tears that Jesus's sorrow fed. Jesus who for us did die. My eyes have failed with weeping and my heart is troubled. I weep bitterly in the night. Tears on my cheeks. My face is swollen with weeping." (Fig. 4).

Ancient Egyptian belief and the Christian Trinity

1. It can hardly be doubted that some of Egyptian ideas and images were transmitted from the Old Testament to the New Testament and as a result, became part of early Christianity; but it is to be noted that Egyptian influence had exerted an effect upon Christianity through the influence of Egypt to Egypto-Hellenistic world. Some Christian concepts were then traced back to Egypto-Hellenistic forms, and ultimately to the religious beliefs of Pharaonic Egypt.[346]

2. The concept of the trinity was of cardinal importance for early Christianity, and it has been claimed that this was

undoubtedly Biblical in tradition we are talking here about. The understanding of the "three-in-one in which God is conceived in three forms, but is regarded as a single Deity. This conception has been transmitted from principle of the Egyptian "triads" which can be dated from the New Kingdom.[347]

3. Now what is the idea of the one God as a Christian concept? The one God of Christianity is a father manifesting through one historic son by means of a virgin Jewess (Jewish woman). The son of one God in Egypt was not historic or limited to an individual personality: it was instead the divine nature manifesting as a soul of both sexes. The one God of Christianity is a trinity consisting of the Father, Son and the Holy Spirit. These "three" constitute the one God in the religion which is at least as old as the Osiris living eternally, king of the double earths nearly six thousands year ago.[348]

In the trinity of Osiris, Horus and Ra in which three are one, the first person is imagined in the likeness of both sexes. The oneness of the Godhead is unified from all the goddesses and gods in whom all others are absorbed: the father, the son and the holy spirit.[349] In Christianity the three persons are the one God and all three exist from all eternity. No one comes into being before or after the other. For always and always the son is begotten by the Father and for always and always the Holy Spirit proceeds from the Father and the Son.

4. The Egyptian doctrine of the "triad" affords an important area of controversy during the early centuries of Christianity. The same proposition is implicit in a well known mythology: Osiris, Horus and Isis in ancient Egypt. If the total deity is conceived of as bisexual triad-God the Father, God the Son, and the God the Mother of God, then theology claims that God the Father and God the Son have been consubstantial and coeternal from the beginning. The system by which God the Father begets God the Son through the body of the Mother of God replicates itself indefinitely. In fact, the Mother of God is also the spouse of God, the sister of God and even the daughter of God.[350] The mythology of Osiris, Horus and Isis mapped the relationship between religious ideology. The reigning king was Horus, the deceased king was Osiris and the Queen Mother was Isis.

The theological triad in Egyptian mythology is illustrated by the following schematic form.[351]

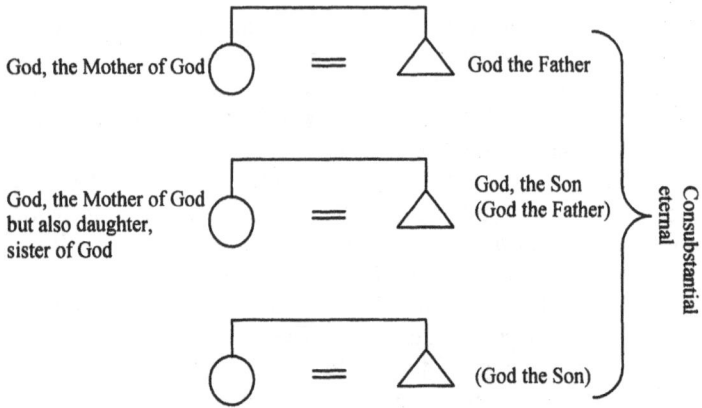

5. From time immemorial there was the Holy, blessed and glorious Trinity, three persons and one God. Patristic writers speak more often than not of the divine economy whereby the Three Persons of the Trinity have different function the Father is God "above us", the Son is God "with us", and the Spirit is God "in us".[352]

I now advance the important part of this survey. One striking resemblance as I have said earlier between the Egyptian religion and what followed, i.e., Christianity, is the holy mother on her throne with her babe. Theologically, there exists the likeness, viz., there is an excellent example of Egyptian type of Isis suckling Horus which affords a prototype of the Christian Madonna.[353] (Figs. 5 & 6).

a) The Gospel, regardless of the exact date of its existence, was written for the Church of Alexandria: here Egypt has been uncanonically claimed the land where the founder of Christianity lived his yearly year. There is another tale that St. Mary of Egypt, our Lady, holy and pure virgin, Mother of God, on the Archangel Gabriel's bidding took her son to dwell in the fayum far to the south in Kom Ombo.[354]

b) The nineteenth century Egyptology of England has claimed W. R. Copper as one who took as his theme the Horus myth in its bearing on Christianity. He says: "the works of art, the ideas, the expression and the heresies of the first four centuries of, Christian era can hardly be well studied without resorting to the nature and influence of the Horus myth.[355]

c) I believe that as far as the myth goes, the child Horns would not exist without his mother Isis. It is in the light of

Egyptian mythology that we must not ignore emergent Christianity's struggle at Alexandria against what was its most contumacious and insidious foe, Isis. It is certainly no exaggeration to say that the Egyptian goddess Isis was the forerunner of the Christian Virgin Mary, Mother of God. This being so. I venture to say how, we may ask, could it be otherwise'? Both in the ancient world and these latter days, as Witt has put forward the argument, humanity was being prepared for a dispensation never previously known.[356]

Egyptian religious Ceremony - the root of Christianity
Now more consideration arises from what is acknowledged in regard to the roots of Christian churches. Isis's stately ritual with its tinkling music, its baptism and aspersion of holy waters presented many points of similarity with the pomps and ceremonies of Catholicism.[357] Again, the priest sprinkles blest water in the temple of Isis. He resembles the minister of Mithras.[358] In the fabric of religious ceremony the distinction between the 'ankh' - the ansata cross-sign of life and the cross was blurred: later, the ankh in Coptic art was Christianized as a form of cross and its uniquitous use in modern theosophy and occultism is well known.[359]

b) In Christianity, the "Sanctus" (holy, Holy) bell still tinkled like the Isaic sistrum.[360] A sistrum is a metal rattle or noise-mar which the Egyptian priests of Isis used to shake at the festival of that goddess.[361] The use of the crotalum or rattle certainly was heard by Bruno at Church on a Maundy Thursday.[362] As I have said earlier, there certainly exists a resemblance between Isis and Jesus. The stock of explanation of this relationship is that for a myriad of men and women in the Graeco-Roman world. Isis the Egyptian goddess, has remained doubtless that she had been in the Black Land of the Pharaoh: that is, many centuries prior to the Christian era Isis had been revered in the Nile Valley as the unique and unparalleled.

Given the influence and the relationship that Egyptian religious belief has had on Christianity, we may surely pose the question: what is the Egyptian intrinsic belief? Does Egyptian religious belief have the basic doctrine of Christianity? Is the Egyptian religious belief nothing but a magical cult? There is no religious concept, as Morenz has shown among others, which would convey adequately the meaning of the Latin tern "religio", this term developed out of the syncretism of Roman paganism and Christianity.[363]

c) Whatever it may be, we should bear in mind that the structure of Egyptian religion differs clearly from what we understand as regard Christianity. This leads us to classify it among the cult religions which stand in stark contrast to Judaism. Christianity and Islam: these religious denomination, strongly sported by many, take shape in scriptual creeds in which God speaks and reveals.[364] So much as that the Egyptians have a belief we are right to supplement "cult" as to make up what is called their religion.[365]

d) To the Christians, a man's everlasting life should by all accounts be based upon God: nevertheless other religions such as those of Isralites and of ancient Greeks teach that God's power does not extend beyond the bounds of this earthly existence: it cannot penetrate the dark realm of Sheof.[366] If the Egyptian of the late period became sceptical towards their belief in the beyond, it does not imply that they became stark unbelievers. In fact, far be it for the Egyptians to deny their faith that God acts in the world of the living that he caters for justice within it and also that he is the lord of fate and is supreme over life and death. In spite of all these scepticisms about the immortality of the dead, they were anything but lacking in reverence. Moreover, the Egyptian, whatever was his anticipation of the hereafter based on equation with Osiris, seems by no means to have possessed a yearning for death in joyous hope in the way early Christians experienced it during the age of martyrs. The hope as such was expressed by St. Paul from prison: "for to me to live is Christ, and to die is gain."[367]

Egypt succumbed to Christianity and finally to Islam: here we are in agreement with the basic outlook of the ancient Egyptians in that they also promised eternal life Again. Egyptian links with the religion of the Old Testament have been known and studied for a long time, yet there has hardly been any serious consideration given to the fact that the religious forms of Egypt had an effect upon the New Testament and thus upon early Christianity. For whatever reason, scholars have been remiss in sufficiently appreciating the Egyptian influence which was destined to be embodied in Christianity. Apart from what we have analyzed, we should make it clear that the contributions Egypt has made to Christianity should not be seen in any way as morphologically akin to Christianity. The evident case: "Jesus's parable of Dives and Lazarus" which is read in the New Testament was originally Egyptian and occurred by way of

Jewish material.[368] In sum, we can speak again as a platitude of an Egyptian religion which despite all its structural differences from the scriptural texts quite similar to us, has one fundamental point in common with Christianity: "the reality of a God who is in man and above man."[369]

Given the enormous influence ancient Egyptian religion has exerted on Christianity, what topic has been left undone in this paper? We have to consider two basic questions: 1) What are the steps by which the transition of the Egyptian religion to Christianity takes shape? 2) What are the social and cultural sequels thought to be chiefly resulting from this transition?

The doctrine of polytheism, pantheism and festishism was never heard of in Christian Europe: it had been purged of the errors of Egyptian religious belief. Although Christianity involves many saints in its polyhagiodulia (the inferior kind of saints and angels paid attention by Roman Catholics), such beliefs and practices found in the zoolatry or fetishim of Egypt and the anthropomorphic cults of the Graeco-Roman era are nothing but superstitious falsehood. The ancient Egyptian religion is reckoned as pre-eminently polytheistic as Egyptians worshipped a plurality of gods, such as Re. the sun god. Geb, the earth god and Nut, the sky goddess. The national character of the Egyptian religion had begun to lose its vigour in the Hellenistic age. The Graeco-Roman period (352 B.C.) reflected the final stage in the development of ancient religion before Egypt was converted first to Christianity and in the end to Islam.

1) Here what we can do is to point out a direct transition from ancient Egyptian religion to Christianity. and the range of influence of the Greek translation of the Old Testament made at Alexandria known as the Septuagint; this became, in the end, almost a kind of Holy Writ for Christians.

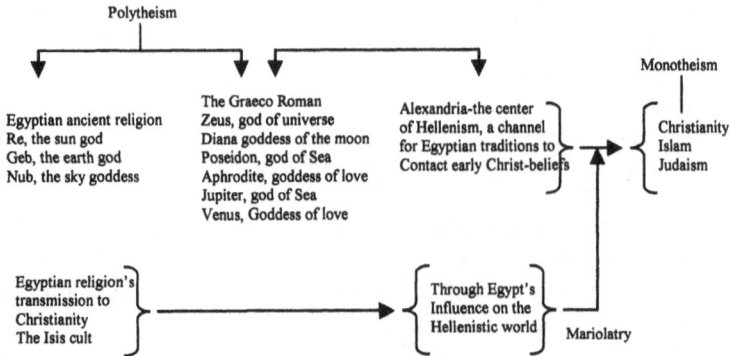

2) As the Egyptian influence was felt as an undercurrent throughout Hellenism, we may consider Alexandrian theology as an intermediary between the Egyptian religious heritage and Christianity. The only direct evidence for Christianity in Egypt during the first century is the tradition that the Church of Alexandria was founded by St. Mark; there is no doubt that the Gospel reached Alexandria well before the end of the first century. Inhabitants in Egypt were those who at Pentecost hear the apostles speaking in tongues.[370]

3) Cyril, the Archbishop of Alexandria, adopted the dogma 'the Holy Virgin. Mother of God' at the council of Ephesus in A.D. 431.[371] He also perceived the evil spirit of Isis arid brought the typical transformation of Iseum into a Christian shrine.

4) The catechetical school of Alexandria at the end of the second century involved some of the ablest of the Christian apologists.[372] Clement (c. A.D. 160-215) was born in Athens and converted to Christianity at Alexandria; his work in the Christian way of life was achieved by deepening understanding of the Christian faith, Alexandria, the great center of Hellenism would have served as a channel for Egyptian traditions to pave the way for early Christian beliefs.

(B) Now the question is: what are the social and cultural consequences of such a transition from the Egyptian religion to Christianity?

1) From the beginning of the sixth century A. D. as Harris holds, Neoplatonism had not ceased to exert a striking influence through its impression on Christianity. The myths of Egypt, then, did not sink into oblivion; instead, they survived the transplantation from paganism to Christianity by adopting

themselves to the new spiritual climate by subtle change and modification.

2) The resemblance between the teachings of the Hermetic corpus and those of Christianity were pointed out by medieval scholars.[373] Many of the most popular motifs, such as fables and legends, were of hieroglyphic origin, such as the eye symbolizing divine justice, the pelican plucking its breast for Christian charity. They were used side by side with the new Christian symbols and had themselves become root and branch Christianized.

3) There can be hardly a denial that the myriad figures of the enthroned Isis nursing her son Horus paved the way, on account of Christianity, for the Byzantine and later images of the Virgin Mary.[374]

4) In the third century A. D., a Christian writer stated that. "What were once Egyptian are now Roman deities." The widespread Christianity in Egypt and its eventual victory toward the end of the fourth century marked the final stage in which the age long tradition of Egyptian religion became retrograde and succumbed to the influence of Greek philosophy and thought.[375]

5) The Christian victory disrupted the connections with past Egyptian religion, creating a wide hiatus between the old Egyptian tradition and the new. What the ancient prophet predicted now came true: "Egypt was dead, her children were recognized as Egyptians by their tongue alone, but their actions seemed to be men of another race. Likewise her religion had become nothing but empty, so much so that only the stones told of her ancient piety."[376] This notion doubtless supervenes an account of the existence of Christianity.

6) Language and religion set out in Egypt upon new career under the Christian aegis, and even though they now speak Arabic, the Copts, being Christian, have preserved to the present day their inveterate consciousness which has prevented them from being submerged in Islam and which made them to be, in the nineteenth century, the intermediaries between the West and Islamic Egypt.

7) Cyril, the shepherd of Christ who saw the guile of the evil Isis and observed the harm done to the faithful entreated the savior to put an end to the scandal. Christianity had impinged on the ancient Egyptian culture, specifically religious, in that polythesim, fetishism, idolatry and pantheism had been largely rooted out. Furthermore, the absorption of Egypt into the Roman

Empire in 30 A.D. marked the decline in the political and social status of the native Egyptians. It is interesting to note that there was a change of beliefs and practices between the Egyptians and their conquerors embracing, so to speak, Christianity, viz. the Isis cult and Mariolatry.[377] In Egypt, Christianity and finally Islam, however different their religious practices have agreed with the basic outlook of the ancient Egyptians in that they also promise eternal life.[378]

A Coptic stele from the Fayum, showing the mother and child- the basic iconography of Isis and Horus / Mary and Jesus

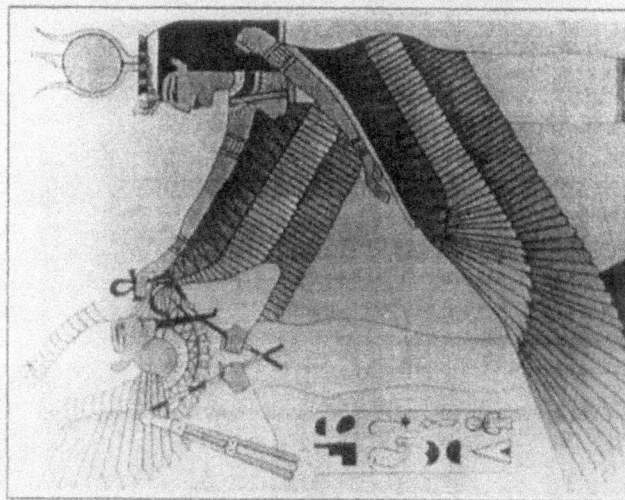

Fig 1 Osiris and Isis

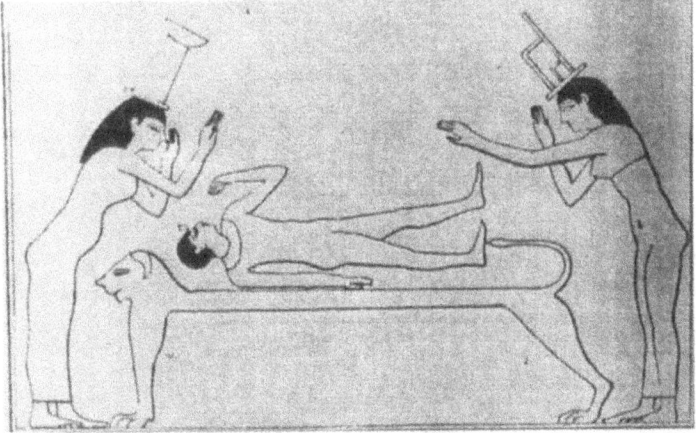

Fig. 3. Isis and Nephthys bewailing the death of Osiris

Fig 4. The Entomhent of Jesus Christ: Saint Sebastian (left), Saint Anthony (right)

Fig 5. Old kingdom statue of Isis suckling Horus

Fig 6. Madonna and Child, ca.1660.Kunsthitorisches Museum Vienna.

References

Addison, J.T. 1925. Chinese ancestor worship. Shangai.

Badley, J.H. 1951. Form and Spirit. London

Bocckh, A. 1886. Encyklopadie und Methodologie der Philologischen Wissenschaften. Leipzig.

Botsford, G.W. 1901-1902. History of Rome. New lurk.

Cham, W. 1953 Religious Trends in Modern China.

Chang, C., 1957. The Development of Neo-Confucian Thought. New York: Book Man Associates.

Chang Wing-tsit, 1963. "Synthesis in Chinese Metaphysics," The Chinese Mind. Edited by C.A. Moore. Honolulu: The University Press of Hawaii.

Cheng Chung-ying, 1973. "Ewligious Reality and Religious Understanding in Conficianism and Neo-Confucianism" International Philosophical Quarterly 13: 51ff.

Ch'eng Shih I-shu, The Posthumous Writings of the Ch'eng Brothers. Co. 13, 3.

ChouLien-his, I T'ung shu – Explanation of the Book of Changes. Col. 6 2a.

Chou Tun-l, Tai chi T'u shou-Explanation of the Diahram of the Great Ultimate: Chou Lien His Work.

Fei Hsuao-tung, 1939. Peasant Life in East China. London.

Forde, A. and Wang Ch'ung, 1911. Lung Heng. London.

Freeman, M. 1965. Lindeage Organization in Southeast China, The Athlone Press London.

Freeman, M. 1965 Lineage Organization in Southeast China. The Athlone Press London.

Fung Yi 1938. New Ratuonal Philosophy. Shanghai. The Commercial Press.

Good, J. 1962. Death, Property and Ancestors. California: Stanford University Press.

Heimisch, P. History of the Holoy Testament. St. Paul, Minn: The Liturgical Press.

Hubert, H. and Mauss, M. 1964. Sacrifice, Its Nature and Function. London: Cohen and West.

Huges, E.R. and K. 1950. Religion in China, London: Hutchinson's I Ching; the Book of Changes. Vol. 7, 7a in Ssu eu pei yao edition.

Hu Shih, 1933. The Chinese Renaissance, Haskell Lectures. Chicago

Hu Shih, 1928. The Development of the logical Method in Ancient

China. Shanghai, Oriental Book Company.

Jackson, J. 1907.   Ancestral Worship.   Centennial Missionary

Conference: Shanghai.

Kuo Mo jo.   1954   Chin Wen Ts'ung-kao.   Peking People's

Publishing House.

Leach, E. 1964. Time Concepts of Primitive People. A Lecture

delivered at Cambridge University.

Legge, J. 1880. The Religions of China-Confucianism and Taoism

described compared with Christianity. London.

Loewe M. "Han Dynasty Happenings" London Times. December

21 p.13 Lu Shih Ch'un ch'iu-Master of Lu's Spring and

Aruman Annals, Compendium of Natural Philosophy,

Chou 239 B.C. by Lu Pu-wei.

Lum Yu the An-lect's of Conficius or Conversations and discourses

of Confucius (Chou, Lu state) c. 465-450 B.C. compiled by

disciples of Confucius.

Mencius (the Book of Mensius) Chou. C. 290 B.C. by Mencius in

Ssu pu pei yao edition.

Munchen C. Hauser. 1964. Plato's Republic ed. And trans. By I.A.

Richards Cambridge University Press.

Needham, J. 1956. Science and Civilization in China. Cambridge
University Press.

_____ 1974. Science and Civilization in China.
Cambridge University Press.

Russell, B. 1956. Skeptical Essays. London: Allen and Unwin.

Shih Ching (Book of Odes or Ancient Folksongs) Chou, 9th to 15th
centuries B.C.

Shu Ching (Historical Classic or Book of Documents) writers
unknown.

Spinoza, B. 1910. "Definitions" Ethics. New York: E.P. Dutton
Compnay.

Swift. J. 1974. Gulliver's Travels. The World's Classics. Oxford
University Press.

Tagore, R. 1928. Creative Unity. New York. W.E. Norton and
Company.

Yang N. 1948. A Chinese Village. Taitou, Shantung Provonce.
London.

Note

[1] F. Engels, *The Origin of the Family, of Private Property, and the State* (New York: International Publishers, 1942), pp. 49-50.

[2] *The Marriage Law of the People's Republic of China*, Art. 1, pp. 1-2.

[3] Feng Ting, "Love and Support of Parents is Also Necessary Virtue in the Socialist Society", *Chinese Youth*, No. 24, December, 1956.

[4] "Care for Parents Should Not Conflict with the Interests of the State", *Chinese Youth*, 1957, 4, February 16, 1957.

[5] In criticizing the disrespect for the old on the part of youth the Communist Party has emphasized the important role of the old in terms of socialist construction. The old technician Wu Fu-min worked on textile machines for 20 years and taught 30 young workers the methods of manipulating and repairing the machines. *Workers' Daily*, April 20, 1963.

[6] Peking, *Chinese Youth*, May 12, 1962.

[7] On the Chinese New Year's Day (1964) a dinner party was arranged by the government to entertain and pay respect to all officers and their wives aged over 70 years. There were 248 present this year, in contrast to 218 of 1963. Mr. Chou En-lai wished them New Year greeting and toasted their health. *People's Daily* (Jen-min Jih-pao), January 2, 1964.

[8] "Social Problems in Communist China Juvenile Delinquency", *Union Research Service*, Vol. 28, No. 5, July 17, 1962.

[9] Engels, *The Origin of the Family, of Private Property, and the State* (New York: International Publishers, 1942), p. 148.

[10] Lenin, *Works*, "Programme and Statute of the Communist International", IV, p. 3.

[11] Chai Shang-tung, "How Should We Regard Communist Family Life", *China Youth*, No. 22, November 16, 1958.

[12] Engels, Op. cit., p. 72. One case can be cited as evidence to challenge the Communist pure love theory. One official of a certain factory was promoted to a higher post. The promotion made him feel that his spouse could not match his new social status, and so he divorced her. "Some Young People in Tientsin Involved in Hasty Marriages. Divorces", Peking, *People's Daily*, March 9, 1957.

[13] To the extent that Western capitalist societies have become increasingly a women's world, the Communist doctrine and the Western democratic idea of 'equality' of the sexes exhibit a rapprochement. A man and a woman may be equal as persons in

society, but as husband and wife, playing their masculine feminine roles in marriage, they are different. David and Vera Mace, *Marriage East and West* (New York: Doubleday and Co., 1960), p. 328.

[14] Ch'en Chien-wei, "The Breaking Down of the System of Feudal Patriarchy", *Hopei Jih-pao*, April 8, 1959.

[15] "Industry and the Urban Communes", *The Times*, July 11, 1960. The title 'collective living' may mean that, on the basis of division of labour, men and women work under the same roof of factories. This factory system was created in Western industrial countries.

[16] In the light of M. Jones' report, "in two communes, Hsin Chiao near Canton and another near Hangchow, there is no sign of men and women living in separate dormitories, or even of communal kitchens, and eating halls." M. Jones, "China Now", *The Observer*, May 19, 1963.

[17] Peking, *People's Daily*, July 29, 1962.

[18] *The Times*, January 13, 1964.

[19] Engels, *Op. cit.*, p. 72.

[20] Lenin condemned 'free love' as a reflection of the decay of bourgeois society, of 'lower class radicalism'. *Documents* 1 and 5.

[21] "Some Young People in Tientsin Involved in Hasty Marriages, Divorces", Peking, *People's Daily*, March 9, 1957.

[22] Simone do Beauvoir, *The Long March* (New York: The World Publishing Company, 1958), pp. 153-54.

[23] *China Youth*, No. 6, March 6, 1962.

[24] Canton, *Yang-ch'eng Wan pao*, February 25, 1962, p. 1; Wang Kung and Wang Chih, "Breaking Up With Romantic Love", *Women of China*, No. 1, 1963, p. 23.

[25] Yang liu, "Reform of Marriage and Family Systems in China", *Peking Review*, March 13, 1964, p. 19.

[26] *Chung-kuo Fu-nu* of China (Women of China), No. 12, December 1, 1962.

[27] Mao Tze-tung asserted that Communist theory should be welded to the particular national background. That means the sort of blending of Communist ideas with national culture. Mao Tzc-tung, *China Is Yew Democracy* (Bombay: People's Publishing House, 1950), pp. 40-41.

[28] It should be clear that the tendency to revive traditional marriage does not indicate the restoration of the old family system. The process of family system has gained too much momentum to be arrested.

[29] Canton, *Nan-fan Jih-pao*, May 12, 1962.

[30] *Women of China*, No. 5, May 1, 1964, p. 29.

[31] Yang liu, "Reform of Marriage and Family Systems in China", *Op.*, cit. p.19.

[32] K. Marx, *The Communist Manifesto* (Chicago: Charles Kerr and Company, 1947), p. 44.

[33] Anti-Dhrung, p. 171.

[34] "The Civil War in France", *Selected Works*, I, p. 51.

[35] The theory of uninterrupted revolution is adopted in the Soviet Union, but is now greatly emphasized in Mao's declaration in the post-revolutionary period.

[36] K. Marx, *Selected Works*, II, p. 20.

[37] The production teams were essentially the same as the small co-operatives created back in 1956, and their formation constituted a noticeable ideological revisionism for communism.

[38] *The Observer*, October 14, 1962.

[39] "Communist China's Economy Falters On", *Current Scene-Developments in Mainland China*, Hong Kong, April 1, 1963, p. 5.

[40] "Peking to Tighten Political, Economic Hold on People", *New York Herald Tribune* (International edition), March 26, 1964.

[41] Marx. *Selected Works*, I, pp. 50-51.

[42] M. Jones, "China Now", *The Observer*, May 19, 1963, p. 21.

[43] "Friesian Bull in a Chinese Commune", *The Times*, May 12, 1964.

[44] "Friesian Bull in a Chinese Commune", *The Times*, May 12, 1964.

[45] Ibid.

[46] "Life Inside a Showpiece Commune in China", *The Times*, May 10, 1965, p.12.

[47] "Flattening China's Social Pyramid", The Times, April 27, 1965.

[48] Marxists contended that the labouring population produces, with the accumulation of capital, the means by which population is not a problem. This is the law of population peculiar to the capitalist mode of production. R. L. Meek, *Marx and Engels on Malthus*, trans. by Dorothea L. Meek and R. L. Meek (New York: International Publishers, 1954).

[49] T. C. Wickbom, "Learning the Value of Incentives", *The Times*, January, 14, 1964, p. 9.

[50] The United Nations Demographic Year Book, 1963. Cited by The Times, September 1, 1964. The world's population is 3,135 million half way through 1962, increasing at an average rate of 2.1 per cent a year, or 63 million. Next to China, the biggest populations in million are:

India	(449)	Indonesia	(98)	Brazil	(75)
The Soviet Union	(221)	Pakistan	(97)	West Germany	(55)
The United States	(187)	Japan	(95)	The United Kingdom	(53)

[51] Robert Trumbull, "China's Birth Rate", *The New York Times* (International edition), June 20, 1963.

[52] M. Jones, "China Now", *The Observer*, May 19, 1963.

[53] *Women of China*, No. 5, May 1, 1964, pp. 30-31.

[54] The emperor K'ang Hsi commanded people to perform ancestor cult as a part of piety and duty, while popes condemned it as superstition and idolatry.

[55] Objections to my treating the Chinese society as "static" may be raised. I am emphasizing this debatable point. In clarification of the term "static" I make a distinction between two terms "kinetic~" fold "dynamics". the former amounting to "operation of" a social system and to economic movement as used by economists, while the latter to "change n" a social system and to economic development. The terra "static" Corresponds to kinetics. fn speaking of Chinese social structure, the Western scholar Wilkinson said : "It may be that such a lapse of time (two thousand years) without much change in social structure of village and Family life is inconceivable to the Western mind accustomed as it is to change, arid prone to confound movement with progress. A. 1'. Wilkinson, The Family in Classical Chance (Shanghai : Kelly and Walsh, 1920), p. 471. The basic assumption of Chinese scholar Dr. Chü T'ungtsu is that during the last two thousand years Chinese society was static. In spite of all growth and change, the fundamental conditions which determined the structure of Chinese society remained unchanged........ During these centuries authors, notwithstanding their great historical sense, consciously or unconsciously assumed that Chinese society was static. The influence of the ancient structure of Chinese society and of ancient Chinese law.... remains to this day pre-1949, i.e., the Communist regime. This is clearly shown by a recent development in family law and in criminal law. A.F.P. Hulsewe, "Forword", in Law and Society in Traditional China (Paris : Moulton and Co.. La Have, 1981), p.12. On the basis of no perceptible alterations in the essential features of the Chin se social structure during two thousand ,years I have no scruple in treating side by side the teachings of Confucius and the idea of contemporary Chinese scholars, and making them. speaking of the same culture.

[56] A lineage is a group of agnates, dead or alive, between whom kinship can be traced genealogically.

[57] Leviticus, IV: 9 ; VII: 14

[58] Li Chih - the Book of Rites includes the Chou King, the official book of the Chou dynasty, the I Li - the Book of Decorum, and the Records

of Rites completed under the, Han dynasty in the reign of Wu Ti (1.40.87 B.C.).

[59] Lun yü Chu su – The Analects of Confucius, "Wei Ling Kung", Book XV, Ch. 38 in Ssu pu pei yao (ed).

[60] Motzu, Vol. II, Ch. 2 "Shang Hsien", in Ssu pu pei yao (ed.) pp. 2a and 2b.

[61] Plato. Statesman, translated by Benjamin Jowett (London: Oxford University Press. 1892), 297.

[62] Plato, The Republic, translated by Benjamin Jowett (London: Oxford University Press, 1892), 398 E, 412.

[63] Plato, The Republic, 412.

[64] Kuo-yü, Ch. I, p. 16a in Ssu pu pei yao (ed.).

[65] Tso chuan Chu-su, Ch. 30. p. 16a in Ssu pu pei yao (ed.).

[66] Mencius, "T'ang Wan Kung", Vol. V, Part I, p. 11a in Ssu pu Tc'ng kan (ed.). (Shanghai, 1942).

[67] Plato, *The Republic*, translated by Benjamin Jowett, third edition (London: Oxford University Press, 1892), 369 B.

[68] Li Ki (Book of Rites), "The Li Yun", Ch. IX, in Ssu pu pei yao (ed.), Vol. XXI, p. 2a.

[69] Lun Yü Chu su, "Ke She", Book XVI, Ch I, p.1b in Ssu pupei yao (ed).

[70] Mencius, "Yang Wan Kung", Part I, Vol. V, in Ssu pu Ts'ung kan, Vol. XIV, pp. 7a-8a.

[71] Chou li (Book of Chou), t'se 6, Ch. 12 in Ssu pa Ts'ung kan (ed.), p. 18b.

[72] Joseph. R. Levenson, "I11 Wind in the, well-field: The Erosion of the Confucian Ground of Controversy" in The Confucian Persuasion, ed. by Arthur F. Wright (Standford University Press, 1960), p. 270.

[73] Shih-ching (Book of Poem), Ch. 21 "Fu t'ien chih shih" in Mo shilr Clru-su, Vol. XIV in Ssu pre pei vao ed., p. l0a.

[74] Ku Yen-wu, Jin Chih lu - Record of Knowledge Day by Day (Shanghai, 1933). I, Ch. 3, p. 12.

[75] L. C. Thompson, trans. Tai T'ung shu-The One World Philosophy of K'ang Yu-wai (London, 1958), pp. 137, 211.

[76] T'anc Ssu-t'ung, "Jen Hsieh"-Study of Benevolence in Tang Ssu-t'rrng Chuan Chi-Collected Works of T'ang Ssu-t'ung (Peking, 1954), p. 69.

[77] Mencius, "Hwuy of Leang". Part I. Ch. 3, Book 1 in Ssu pu pei yao ed., p. 4b-5a.

[78] Lun yü Chu-su, "Wei Ling King", Book XV, Ch. 38 in Ssu pu pei yao (ed.).

[79] R.H.S. Crossman, "Plato and the Perfect State", in Plato: Totalitarian or Democrat. Essay selected and Introduced by Thomas L. Thorson (N.J.: Prentice-Hall, Inc., 1963), p. 33.

[80] Mencius, "T'ang Wan Kung", Part I, Vol. V, in Ssu pu Ts'ung kan (ed.,) p. 18b.

[81] R.H.S, Crossman, "Plato and the Perfect State", op. cit., p. 34.

[82] Mencius, "T'ang Wan Kung" Part 1, Vol. V, in Ssu pu Ts'ung kan (ed.), p. 11a.

[83] The Republic by Plato, translated by Benjamin Jowett, third edition (London: Oxford University Press, 1892), 370 B.

[84] Plato, Statesman, translated by B. Jowett (London: Oxford University Press, 1892), 303.

[85] "The Forum on Confucius", in Jen Min Jib Pao - The People's Daily, January 10, 1967, p. 4. The report "The Forum on Confucius" is published in The People's Daily in Chinese and here translated into English.

[86] The Book of Odes (Shih Ching), The Book of History (Shih shu), The Book of Change (I Ching), and The Book of Rites (I Li).

[87] The Analects of Confucius (Lun Yu), The Book of Mencius (Meng Tze), The Book of Filial Piety (Hsiao Ching), the Doctrine of the Mean (Chung yung), The Great Learning (Ta hsiao).

[88] J. A. Cuoq, Lexique de la langue algongquine (Montreal, 1886), pp. 312-13.

[89] John Long, Voyages and Travels in the Years 1768-1788 (Chicago . The Lakeside Drive, 1922), p. 110.

[90] M. Naeterlinck, Pelleas et Melisande, Act I, scene 2. Paris Durant et Cie p. 38.

[91] Andrew Lang, The Secret of the Totem (New York: AMS Press, 1970), p. 29.

[92] John F. McLennan said that totemism is fetishism plus exogamy and matrilineal descent. Fortnight Review, vols. 6 and 7, 1863-70

[93] Li Chi chu shu, Vol. 26 'Kiao Te shing', p. 9b in Shih san ching edition.

[94] 'Translations from the General Code of Laws of the Chinese Empire', The China Review, Vol. IX, July 1881 to 1882, p. 95.

[95] A. Henry, 'The Lolos and other Tribes of Western China', Journal of the, Royal Anthropological Institute of Great Britain and Ireland, 33, 1933, pp. 96-107.

[96] Julius H. Klaproth, Memoires relatifs a l'Asie, Paris : Dondey and Dupree, 1824, 2 Vols., Vol. I, p. 203,

[97] I Li chu shu, Vol. 10, 'Chin li', p. 11a in Shih san third edition with the commentary of Chong Kan-ch'eng of the Han dynasty and the exposition of Kia Kung-yen of the T'ang dynasty.

[98] Mao Shih chu shu, Vol. 10 Ta Yan, 'Cheng min', p. 81a in Shih san ching edition.

[99] Chou Li chu shu, Vol. 21 'Ch'un kuan', p. 7a in Shih san ching edition

[100] J. J. M. de Groot, The Religious Systems of China, Leyden, 1901, Vol, IV, p. 271.

[101] Tso Chuan, Vol. 2 'Duke Ying' eighth year, p. 6b. Commentary by Tu Yüand Lin Yao-shou.

[102] Shih Ching chu shu. Vol. 1 Chou nan 'Lin chi', p. 56b in Shin San ching.

[103] Timothy Dwight, Travels in New England and New York, London, 1823, Vol. IV, p. 184.

[104] Henry R. Schoocraft, The American Indians, Philadelphia, 1856. p. 95.

[105] Mao Shih chu shu, Vol. 30 Shang Sun, 'Lieh Tso', p. 13b in Shih San ching edition.

[106] F. Poole, Queen Charlotte. Islands, London, 1872, p. 136.

[107] Mo Shih chu shu, Vol. Ta ya 'Yun Han', p. 50a in Shih San ching edition.

[108] Tso Chuan, 'Duke Chao' seventeenth year, Vol, 39, p. 13a, Commentary by Tu Yü and Lin Yao-shou.

[109] Shu Ching chu shu, Vol. I, 'The Book of Yü', p. 426, Ts'ai Shen's commentary.

[110] Baldwin Spencer and F. J. Gillen, The Native Tribes of Central Australia, London, 1895, pp. 143-45, 151.

[111] A. Morel and George Davy, Des Clans aux Empires, Paris, 1922, p. 71.

[112] Mao Shih chu shu, Vol. 30, 'Shang sting', p. 13b and 14a in Shih San ching edition.

[113] Mao Shih chu shu, Vol. 4 'Shang sung', p. 14a in Shih san ching edition.

[114] Li Chi chu shu, Vol. 15 'Yueh ling', p. 4a in Shih san ching edition.

[115] Bruno Schindler, 'On the Travel, Wayside and Wind Offerings in Ancient China', Asia Minor, Fasc. 2-4, Vol I, Leipzig 1924, p. 625.

[116] Bruno Schindler, Op. cit., pp. 626-27.

[117] H. Doré, Recherches sur les superstitions en Chine (Shanghai, 1911-1919), Tome XI, pp. 99sq.

[118] A. R. Radcliffe-Blown, 'The Comparative Method in Social Anthropology', Journal of the Royal Anthropological Institute, vol. 81, 1951, p. 20-21.

[119] Claude Levi-Strauss, The Savage Mind University of Chicago Press, 1966, pp. 131 sq.

[120] A. R. Radcliffe-Brown, Loc. Cit., p. 21.

[121] Victor Segalen, Gilbert de Voisins, 'Lartigue, Pl. XVIII' in Mission archeolo gigue en. Chine Paris, P. Geuthner, 1923.

[122] Victor Segalen, Gilbert de Voisins, 'Lartigue, Pl. XVIII' in Mission archeolo gigue en. Chine Paris, P. Geuthner, 1923.

[123] Tso Chuan, vol. 6 'Duke Chuang', twenty-second year, p. 14b.

[124] Shan Hai ching, Vol. 14, p. 7a. The crow and the Fu Sang Tree are carved on a porcelain vase discovered from a brick tomb, which dates back to the Late Han period. The vase was excavated near Sze Kien Tao village, Tzi Yuan district, Honan Province in November 1969. Wen Wu Quarterly, No. 3, 1972, p. 8.

[125] E. James, Annual Third Report of Bureau of Ethnology (Washington, 1884), p. 238 sq.

[126] R. H. Codrington, The Melanesians (Oxford The Clarendon Press, 1901), pp. 57-58.

[127] Codrington, Op. cit., p. 49.

[128] Tso Chuan, Vol. 18 'Duke Hsuen', third year, p. 10b.

[129] Tso Chuan, Vol. 23 'Duke His', twenty eighth year, pp. 12a and 12b

[130] Tso Chuan, Vol. 12 'Duke His', twenty-fifth year, p. 11a,

[131] Ch. Keysser, 'Aus dem Loben der Kailouto', in R. Nouhauss's Deutsch New Guinea, iii, 111-112.

[132] Li chi chu shu, Vol. 46, 'Ch'i fa', pp. 9a and 9b.

[133] George Turner, Samoa, a Hundred Years Ago and Long Before, with a preface by E. B. Tylor (London, 1884), p. 70.

[134] Antonia de Herrera, General History of the Continent and Islands of America trans. into English by Captain John Stevens. IV (London, 1726), pp. 138 sq.

[135] Otto Stoll. Die Ethnologie der Indianerstame iron Guatemala (Loyden, 1889), p. 58.

[136] Tso Chuan, Vol. 18 'Duke Hsüan', third year, p. 11a.

[137] G. Dolourp, 'Huit jours chez les M'Bengas', Revue d'Ethnographie, ii, 1883, p. 223; P. Barnet, L'Afrique Occideniale (Paris, 1888), ii, p. 173.

[138] Tso Chuan, Vol. 34 'Duke Ting', tenth year, p. 15a.

[139] Mao Shih chu shu, Vol. 25 Ta Ya 'Sun kao', p. 62a, Shih san ching edition

[140] I Li chu shu, Vol. 5 'Hsiang she', p. 61a.

[141] Ibid., Vol. 12 'She Sang li', pp. 9b-10a.

[142] Tso Chuan, Vol. 53 'Dukc Chao', twenty-ninth year, p. 5b.

[143] A. C. Haddon, Headhunters, Black, White and Brown (London, 1901), pp. 95-116.

[144] Goerge Turner, Samoa, London, 1884, pp. 21, 24, 60.

[145] R. Firth, 'Totemism Polynesia', Oceania, Vol. I, January-March, 1931, No. 4, p. 391.

[146] A.R. Radcliffe-Brown, Structure and Function in Primitive Society (Illinois, Glencoe: The Free Press, 1952), p. 207. Radcliffe-Brown said: 'While in modern western civilization a sin is usually regarded as necessarily a voluntary action, in many simple societies an involuntary action may fall within the given definition of sin.'

[147] Frederick Starr, Confucianism (New York: Covici-Friede, 1930), p.8.

[148] John B. Noss, Man's Religions (New York: Macmillan Co., 1956), p.340.

[149] Hsiao-ching chu-shu, 6. 2a

[150] Oliver Goldsmith, Vicar of Wakefield, Ch. XIV

[151] Mencius, Vol. IV, "Li Lou", pp. 26b-27a. This passage encourages men to repentance and self-reformation.

[152] E.E. Evans-Pritchard, Nuer Religion (Oxford University Press, 1962), p. 191.

[153] The Analects of Confucius (Lung Yü), Vol. VIII, 'Wei Ling Kung', p.7a.

[154] Mencius, Vol. III, 'Kung Sun Ch'ou', p. 13a.

[155] Han Fei Tze, Vol. II, (in 2 vols), p. 6b.

[156] Proverbs, 20: 20.

[157] St. Matthew, 25: 4.

[158] F. Hsu, 'The Problem of Incest Tabu in a North China Village', American Anthropologist Vol. 42, No. 1, January-March, 1940.

[159] Meyer Fortes, The Web of Kinship among the Tallensi (Oxford University Press, 1957), pp. 28, 101, 110.

[160] Mencius, Book V 'Wan Chang', Ch. 2, 3.

[161] By Hsu's account on West Town, Yunnan province, a bucketful of human excreta was thrown over the young man and his bride walking hand-in-hand in the street. F. Hsu, Under Ancestors' Shadow (London: Routledge and Kegan Paul, 1949), p. 225.

[162] Samuel 6:607.

[163] Joseph Buttler, Bishop of Durham, Fifteen Sermons, "Preface" p.7 Preached at the Rolls Chapel and published in London, 1856.

[164] Ibid., "Sermon I", pp. 41-42.

[165] Wolfram Eberhard, Guilt and Sin in Traditional China (University of California Press, 1967), p.21.

[166] Augustine, The City of God (New York: E.P. Dutton and Co., Inc., 1947), p.93.

[167] Ibid., p.367

[168] Thomas Aquinas, The Political Ideas of St. Thomas Aquinas, ed. Dino Bigougiari (New York: Hafner Publishers Co., 1957), p.50.

[169] C.C. Jung, Symbols of Transformation in Collected Works, XI, p.383.

[170] Jung, Carl G., Oion, (Zürich, 1951), p.85.

[171] R.J.Z. Werblowsky,. Lucifer and Prometheus in Collected Works, VII, p.513.

[172] Chung Yung - The Book of the Mean, p.4a.

[173] Ibid., pp. 3b-4a.

[174] Jean Jacques Rousseau, The Social Contract and Discourses, trans. G.D.H. Cole (New York: E.P. Dutton and Company, Inc., 1950), p.273.

[175] Aristotle, Nicomachean Ethics, Introduction to Aristotle, ed. Richard McKeon (New York: The Modern Library, 1947), p.333.

[176] Lung Yü - The Analects of Confucius, Vol. II, p.5.

[177] In speaking of the innate rectitude of human nature, Tzu Tze used the word 'chung' (middle) instead of the word 'ching' (goodness).

[178] Aristotle, Nicomachean Ethics, p.333.

[179] Mencius, 'Kao Tze', p.4b.

[180] Ibid; p:1b.

[181] Ibid; p:1b.

[182] John Calvin, John Calvin on God and Political Duty, ed. John T. McNeil (New York: The Liberal Press, 1950), p.5.

[183] Emil Brunner, Man in Revolt (Philadelphia: The Westminster press, 1939), p.95.

[184] Paul, Romans, 3:23.

[185] R. Niebuhr, Nature and Destiny of Man (New York: Charles Scribner's Sons, 1955), Vol. II. p.80.

[186] Paul. Romans, 2:14.

[187] Mencius. 'T'eng Wen', Part I, p.15b. Cited by Chu Hsi in Philosophy of Human Nature trans. by J. Percy Bruce (London: Probsthan and Co., 1922), pp. 128-29.

[188] Paul, I Timothy, 6:10.

[189] Paul Tillich, Theology of Culture, ed. Robert C. Kimball (New York: Oxford University Press, 1959), pp. 117, 119.

[190] Lun Yü, The Analects of Confucius, 'Yang Huo', p.1b.

[191] John Dewey and James E. Tuft, Ethics (New York: Henry Holt and Co., 1908), p.219.

[192] Mencius, 'Chin Hsian', p.25a.

[193] Chu Hsi, The Complete Works (Imperial edition, compiled under the direction of the Man-chu Emperor K'ang Hsi and published in the year 1713 A.D.), Vol. 42, p. 10b.

[194] Ibid.

[195] The physical nature refers here to what Paul propounded as an excessive indulgence in material or worldly pursuit, especially money. When the pursuit of riches takes a full possession of man, he will deserve sordid reproach and fall into sin. He said., 'We should not be condemned with the world'. I Cor. 14:32.

[196] Chu Hsi, The Complete Works, pp. 13b-14a.

[197] Pictorial Tung Chou Lieh Kuo Chih - Annals of East Chou States, Vol VI, Ch. 25, pp. 4b-5a.

[198] Matthew, 14:18-19; Mark, 7:21: "The heart as the seat of moral life is the source when proceed the evil thoughts and affections which bring about depravity or defilement."

[199] Manes are human souls deified by death and what the Matins called 'lares' ancient Roman household deity. Manes are lares when ancestors were benevolent and propitious. Lares, as de Coulanges put it, were no other than the souls of the dead to which man attributed a superhuman or divine power. The sacred death of ancestors was always attached to the hearth fire; the descendants, when they spoke of the hearth fire, recollected the name of the ancestor. We may assume therefore that the domestic fire was in the beginning only the symbol of the worship of the dead. Coulanges, de Fustel, The Ancient City. Doubleday Anchor Books, 1956, pp.21, 24.

[200] Chou Shu (周书) (the Book of Chou) Vol. vi 'Yueh Ling' (月令); The elm and willow are blue standing for spring, the date and almond are red representing summer, the green shrubs are white symbolizing autumn, and locust and sandalwood are black figuring winter. The seasonal proper trees serve to avert the periodical epidemics and bring blessing. The ancestors are concerned with what we call 'nature' or on the regular succession of the seasons. Lun Yü reads: 'Within a year the old grain is exchanged, and the

new grain has sprung up, and in producing fire by friction, we go through all the changes of wood for that purpose'.

[201] J. Frazer, The Golden Bough, Vol. II, Part I 'The Magic Art and the Evolution of Kings', g. 267.

[202] Sir William Monier, Brahmanism and Hinduism. London, 1891, p.9.

[203] Chuang Tzu (莊子) , Vol.9, p. 1 in Ssu pu pei yao edition.

[204] W. Weisskopf, The Psychology of Economics. London, 1955, p. 144.

[205] J. Frazer, The Golden Bough, Vol. II, The Magic Art and the Evolution of Kings, Ch. XV, 'The Fire Drill', pp. 208-09. Hopi Indians kindle fire ceremoniously by the friction of the two sticks'. J. W. Fewkes, The Lesser New Fire Ceremony at Walpi. American Anthropologist, Vol.3, N. S. 1901, p.445. B. Spencer and F. J. Gillen, Northern Tribes of Central Australia. London 1969 p.621.

[206] J. Frazer, Myths of the Origin of Fire. London 1930, p.46.

[207] Plutarch, De Fortuna Romanorum. 10; Ovid, Facti, vi. pp. 627-636; Pliny, Natural Historica, 11, 141-xxxvi, 204.

[208] J. Frazer, The Golden Bough, Vol.2, 'The Magic Art', Ch. XVI 'Father Jove and Mother Vesta', p.231, note 6.

[209] Yin Hsu wen tzu kia section (殷虚文字甲编) , p. 2130; and yi section 4100.

[210] Kuo Mo-jo (郭沫若) Kia ku wen tzu yen chiu (甲骨文字研究), People's Press, Beijing, 1952, p.10.

[211] Ibid., p. 21: The male phallus is clearly enhanced, as the paper proceeds, by the etymology of the character for ancestor 'tsu' (祖); ancestor worship was essentially male-ancestor which is, as it has always been associated with patrilineal descent system.

[212] Mana was a virgin who conceived by putting a ripe almond in her bosom and gave birth to Attic - the god of vegetation. Mana was itself a form of the world-wide for mother. Arnobius, Adversus Nationes. ed. Aug. Reifferscheid, Vienna, 1875, Vol. 6 and 13. Frazer, Op. cit. , Vol, v. p. 163.

[213] Li Ke Fu Ting Yi (立戈父丁彝) and Shih Kui Fu Ting (师奎父鼎)Yin Hsu Yi Ts'un (殷虚佚存) , p. 844.

[214] Yin Hsu Wen Tzu Lei Pien (殷虚文字类编), and the Analytical Dictionary (说文解字).

[215] The Chinese script before the Ch'in dynasty (221-207 B. C.) and Inscriptions on ancient bronze objects. Kia Ku Wen (甲骨文), Vol. 1, p.7.

[216] Kuo Mo-Jo, Kia Ku Wen Yen Chiu (甲骨文研究) > Beijing: People's Press. 1952. p. 10.

[217] Kia Ku Wen (甲古文), Vol. 1, p.8.

[218] Yin Hsu Wen Tzu Lei Pien. Vol.5, p. 11 in Wen Tzu Ki Yao (文字基要), Hong Kong: Cheng ('hung Press, 1975, p.58.

[219] Cicero, De Legibus, 22; St. Augustine, City of God, 9x, 11, vii, 26.

[220] Taittiriya, Bramana, 1, 1 3 and 5.

[221] Sir William Monier, Brahmanism and Hinduism. London, 1891, p.9.

[222] I Samuel, ii, 13.

[223] Hou Han Shu (後汉书), History of the Later Han Dynasty. (A. D. 25-220). By Fan Yeh (范晔), Vol. 22 'Yin Tzu Fang' (阴子方), p. 1133. Taiwan; Chung Hun Press; Po Hu Tung (白虎通), Book of the Preservation of Solidarity-Vol. 6, p.3b; Ching Chu Sui Shih Chi (荆楚岁时记), Annual Folk Customs of the States of Ching and Chu) by Tsung Lin (宗懔), pp. Ila-I Ib in Ssu pu pei yao ed.

[224] Po Hu Tung, Later Han Dynasty, by Pan Ku, Vol.2, p.14 In Ssu pu pei yao ed.

[225] Ovid, Fasti, vi, 291.

[226] Reinhold, Past and Present - the continuity of classical myths. Toronto, 1972, p.85.

[227] Exodus 3:2; Acts, 7:30.

[228] Gomme, Sir G. L. , Folklore Relics of Early Village Life. London 1883, p.9.

[229] Johnston, R. F. Lion and Dragon in Northern China, London 1910, p. 192.

[230] Fei Hsiao-tung, Peasant Life in China. London 1976, p. 101.

[231] Ibid. pp. 100-101.

[232] The term 'ancestor worship' in its widest and loosest sense refers to any sort of rites relating to dead persons. The cult group consists solely of persons related to one another by descent in one line from the same ancestor or ancestors- Radcliffe-Brown, Structure and Function in Primitive Society. 111. The Free Press, 1952, p. 163.

[233] The tablet is a visible sign of spirit which is conceived as separate from the materical substance tablet on which the spirit has its abode. It is to the tablet that people attach their feelings of affection for the

deceased. Again, the wooden tablet is taken as the altar of ancestral spirit within the house spirit of the hearth. Every member of the family will in invocation speak in reference to the name of the ancestor of the family, just as the Old Testament speaks of the God of our Fathers the God of Abraham, Isaac and Jacob.

[234] Tylor, E. B., 'Animism' , Primitive Culture, Vol. I, 23 and II , 9, 11, 84.

[235] Spencer, H., Principles of Sociology. Vol. II, Part VI 'Ecclesiastic Institutions' New York, 1885, pp, 20, 23, 26.

[236] Lun Yü(The Analects of Confucius). Vol. 2, 'Pa Yih' , p. 6a in Ssu pu pet yao.

[237] Kung Yang Chuan (公羊传) Master's Kungyang's commentary on the Spring and AutumnAnnals) 'Wen Kung' (文公) 2nd year, Vol. 18, p. 4b in Ssu pu pei yao ed.

[238] Chu Tzu Kia Li 朱子家礼 'Yi Ch'uan Shen Chu' (伊川神主) - ancestor spirit. See Ling Shun Shing (凌纯声), 'Ancestral Tablet and Genital Symbolism in Ancient China' Bulletin of the Institute of Ethnology, Academia Sinica, Vol. 8, Autumn 1959, p.16.

[239] Sun Shing (孙盛), I Jen Chuan (逸人传) in Tai Ping Yu Lan - Imperial Encyclopedia, Lit. , Emperor's Daily Readings, Sung dynasty A. D. 983, VoL 414. p. 2038. When Ting Lan's neighbor caught sight of uncanny image carved on the tree root, he broke the tablet at one fell swoop.

[240] Chavannes, E., Le Tai Shan (泰山), essai de monographie d'un culte Chinois.

[241] Erkes, E., Idols in Pre-Buddhism China, Artibus Asiae, 1828, no.1.

[242] Heimisch, P., History of the Holy Testament. Minnesota: St. Paul, 1952, pp. 93-94.

[243] Addison, J. T., Chinese Ancestor, Shanghai, China, 1925, pp.50sq.

[244] Kuo Mo-jo, 'Shih Tsu Pi' (释祖妣), in Kia Ku Wen Yen Chiu, 1919, 1, 11.

[245] Shou Wen Chieh Tzu, Vol. i, p.2b.

[246] Kuo Mo-jo cites 'Po Ts'u' (卜辞). The oral boric inscriptions of the Shang dynasty. c. 16th-11th century B. C. on tortoise shells or animal bones.

[247] Karlgren, B., 'Some Fecundity Symbolism in Ancient China', Bulletin of the Museum of Far Eastern Antiquities, No. 2, 1930, p. 1.

[248] Torii Ryuzo (鸟居龙藏), 'The Study of Chinese Dolmens', Yen Ching Hsue Pao (The journal of Yen Ching University), Vol. 31, 1946, pp. 135-136.

[249] Kia Ku Tzu (甲骨字), Shang Oracle Inscriptions. Vol. 1, pp. 4-5.

[250] Karlgren, Loc. cit. p.2.

[251] Li Chi (礼记), Vol. 4, ' Chu Li', p. 12b in Ssu pu pei yao ed.

[252] The Menhir and Dolmen megaliths which were discovered in the north and northneast of China in the Stone Age (3,500 B.C.) stand for male and female organs.

[253] Ho Ping-ti, The Cradle of the East, Chinese University of Hong Kong, 1975, p. 248; 'mu' (牡) and 'pin' (牝); Kuo Mo-jo, Kia Ku Tru (甲骨字), Shang Oracle Inscriptions, Vol. 1, p.6.

[254] Under the rule of emperor Yu (禹), 2100-1600 B. C., the sacrificial system of 'she' (社) began to be established. The character 'she' is composed of two parts: the radical '礻,示' symbolizes spirit, whereas the character 't'u' (土,米 soil) implies the sourse of life, i.e., from the earth all things are produced. T'u (土) stands for phallus: '𐄷' in the inscription on ancient bronze objects; '𐄷' appears in oracle inscription on the Shang dynasty (c. 16th-11th century B.C.) The I Ching (the Book of Changes 易经) runs: the sun and moon have their place in the sky; but the grains, grass and trees have their place on the earth. Vol. 3, p. 21b in Ssu pu pei yao ed.

[255] The tree is regarded symbolically as a source of life by means of which there seems to be expressed one of religious man's most profound longings for a life ever renewed. Thus the tree is conceived as the personification of the deity. Reno, S.J., 'Religious Symbolism: a plea for a comparative approach', Folklore, Vol. I, 197, pp.78-79; Chien Han Shu (206 B.C. - A.D. 24) by Pan Ku (班固), Vol. 5 'Chiao Ssu Chi'(郊祀志) p. 1210. Taipei: Chung Hua Press. Han Kao emperor (汉高祖, 206-195 B.C.) prayed to the tree Fan yü - the god of soil (she 社) at the village Fan Yü of Fan district.

[256] Shou Wen Chieh Tzu (说文解字), Vol. 11, p.4a 'she' (社)

[257] Chou Li (周礼), Vol. 19, 'Hsiao Tsung Po' (小宗伯), p. 3b in Ssu pu pei yao ed.

[258] Karlgren, Loc. cit., p. 18.

[259] Karlgren, Loc. cit. , p. 7.

[260] Hsin Chung Kuo ti Kao-ku Shou-huo (新中国的考古收获),
Peking, 1962, pp.14-15; Kuo Mo-jo, Chung Kuo Shih-kang (中国史
纲), Peking, 1962, pp. 52-53.

[261] Po Hu Tung (白虎通), Comprehensive discussions at the
White Tiger Lodge. Later Han dynasty, Pan Ku, Vol. 7, 'San
Kang Liu Chi' (三纲六纪) Three cardinal Guides and six Laws,
p.58 in Ssu pu pei yao ed.

[262] Fortes, M. African Systems of Thought:'ancestor worship', prefaced
by Fortes and G. Dieterlen. International African Seminar, 3rd, 1960.
Salisbury, December 1960, pp. 16-20.

[263] Tso Chuan, Master Tao chiu's Enlargement of Ch'un Ch'iu (Spring
and Autumn Annals 春秋左传), 722 to 453 B.C. , Vol.13, p.8b.

[264] On basis of the ancient religion and the constitution of the Greek
and Roman family the dead ancestor accepted no offerings save from
his own family and desired no worship save from his own descendants.
De Coulanges, Fustel, The Ancient City, New York, 1956, p.34.

[265] Maspero, G. La Chine. Paris. 1952, pp .53-54.

[266] Chao, Paul, 'The Chinese Natural Religion; Confucianism and
Taoism', Asian Studies, Vol. XX, April, August and December
1982, p.54.

[267] Tylor, Edward R., Religion in Primitive Culture, Vol. II, New
York 1958, P,205.

[268] Hsun Tzŭ (荀子) vol. XIII, p.60, 12b in Ssu pu pei yao ed.

[269] Radcliffe-Brown, A. R., Structure and Function in Primitive
Society. Free Press, Illinois, 1952, p. 159.

[270] Mencius (孟子) , Vol. IV, Le Low (离妻) , pp. 12a-12b. Ssu pu
pei yao ed.

[271] Conway, M. D., The Life of Thomas Paine. London, 1909,
p.244.

[272] Aron, R., Main Currents of Sociological Thought L New Yorkı
Doubleday 1968, p. 122.

[273] Comte. A., Systeme de Politique Positive. Vol. IV, p.63.

[274] Lun Yü (论语), II 'Pa Yih' (八佾), p.4a, Sppy edition.

[275] Ibid.

[276] Lun Yü (论语) the Analects, Vol. IV Shu Erh (述而), p. 4a in
Ssu pu pei yao ed.

[277] Lun Yü (论语) the Analects, Vol. XI Hsien Tsin (先进), p. 2b in
Sppy.

[278] Lun Yü (论语) the Analects Vol. I Wei Cheng (为政), p. 8a Sppy.

[279] Lun Yü (论语) Vol. VI Hsien Tsin (先进), p. 2b Confucius was concerned with man; man is the proper means of study, not only of man, but also of the universe; universe, according to Fung Yu-lan, is a spiritual whole in which there is only one world, the concrete actual world that we ourselves experience. Fung Yu-lan, A Short History of Chinese Philosophy. New York 1948 p.309.

[280] Moore, Charles, Philosophy: East and West. Princeton University Press, 1946, p.147.

[281] Ibid- , p.147.

[282] As the Confucians do not believe in God, immortality conceived in the Confucian doctrine and the eternal life Christianity has preached are poles apart. Most Chinese people crave for something which is immortality in this natural world, but not beyond this present life. Both Lao's and Confucius' work and ideas have continued to be imbibed. However, Dubs refuses to believe in earth immortality put forward by Lao Tzu. Chao, Paul. The Chinese Natural Religion: Confucianism and Taoism. Asian Studies, Vol. XX, April, August and December 1982, p.47; Dubs, H. H. , Ssu Erh Pu Wan (思而不问), Asia Minor, 1954, pp.149-161.

[283] The word "Egypt" descends from the Greek Aiguptos, which is in turn comes from the Egyptian expression "Hi-ku-path" meaning literally "mansion of the soul of Ptah" (the god). Ptah was the local god of Memphis. The word "gipsy" is shortened or an earlier "gipsyan" and is simply Egyptian. Harris. J. R. The Legacy of Egypt Oxford: at the Clarendon Press, 1971. p. 204.

[284] Morenz, S., Egyptian Religion, trans. by E. Keep. New York: Cornell University Press, 1978, p. 251.

[285] The ancient Egyptians had their folk myths which explain the origin of the world; they believed that in the beginning only the ocean existed and in this ocean appeared an egg (a flower) from which was born the Sun God. He had four children: Geb, Shu, Tefnut. and Nut. Cottrell, L. Life Under the Pharaohs. N. Y. Pan Books Ltd. London 1962. p. 21.

[286] Leach, Edmund, "Why did Moses have a sister?" in Structuralist Interpretation of Biblical Myth. Ed. E. Leach and D. Alan Aycock. Cambridge University Press 1983. p. 35. History is to refer to what seems to be more or less probable, while myth is to refer to what seems to be improbable, and is not concerned so much with a

succession of events as history is with moral significance of situation', myth is timeless and is placed in though beyond or above historical time. Evans-Pritchard. Anthropology and History a lecture delivered in the University of Manchester. Manchester University Press. 1961, p. 8.

[287] Leach, Edmund, "The Mother's Brother in Ancient Egypt" Royal Anthripological Institute News. ISSN. 0307-6776. August 1976, No. 15, p. 20.

[288] Leach, E. "Why did Moses have a sister?" Loc. cit., p. 43.

[289] Exodus, 11, 10,

[290] Massey, Gerald. Ancient Egypt. 2 vols. Vol. I, new York:

[291] Leach, F_.. Loc. cit., p. 43.

[292] Ibid.

[293] Matthew, 2. 16: Exodus 1, 16.

[294] Leach. E. Loc. cit.

[295] Budge. E. A. Wallis, Osiris and the Egyptian Resurrection. Vol I, p. 606.

[296] Budge, Osiris and the Egyptian Resurrection. pp. 60-61.

[297] Kamic, the word "kamitic" stands for the ancient Egypt country and means the Black Land. Kamitic specifically refers to one cultural products of Egypt and her cognate Nile valley civilization. Kamitic is a synonym of Egyptians.

[298] Osiris, Lord of Eternity appears in the form of a mummy with the head of the Ben-nue-bird-phonix. This name proves the idea of an existence renewed and prolonged indefinitely: we discover the god's bennu bird, the phoenix emblematic of his immortality whose head is crowned with the Isia symbols of the Uraeus, the solar disk and the lunal crescent. See Tran Tan Tinh, Le culte d'Isis a Pompei. Paris 1964, p. 142. Pl. 8. figure 2. The phoenix is commonly associated with Christ because it is supposed to rise eternally from the ashes of the fire in which it perished. Watts. Alan W., Myth and Ritual in Christianity. Boston: Beacon Press, 1968, p. 160: according to Harris. The phoenix, a fabulous eastern bird of excellence, comes surely from the Egyptian species of heron and is sacred to the Egyptians. Harris, The Legacy of Egypt. p. 203.

[299] Hart. George, A Dictionary of Egyptian Gods and Goddesses. London: Routledge & Kegan Paul. 1986. p. 157; James E. O, Tree of Life. Leiden, 1966.

[300] Budge. An Egyptian Hieroglyphic Dictionary. Vol, 1. pp. 78-81.

[301] Newman Erichm, The Origin and History of Consciousness. trans. by R. P. Hull, Princeton University Press 1970. Fl. 29, after page 240.

[302] Witt, R. E.. Isis and the Graeco-Raman World. N. Y. Cornell University Press.

[303] Massey. G., Ancient Egypt. N. Y. Samuel Weiser, Inc. 1970, p. 69.

[304] Leach E. "Why did Moses have a sister?" Loc. cit. p. 20.

[305] Budge. An Egyptian Hieroglyphic Dictionary. Vol. I p. 56. The evil one Sat-an is destructive power "an" in the Egyptian language is a "mark" of emphasis.

[306] Budge, The Gods of the Egyptians. p. 220.

[307] Higgins, Godfey, The Celtic Druits. Los Angeles: Philosophical Research Library, 1977. p. 173.

[308] Macquitty, William. Island of Isis. N. Y. Charles Scribner's Sons. 1976. He assures us of the influence of Isis throughout the world and he says that it was from Alexandria that Horus and Isis entered the legend that surrounds Buddha in Gandhara in northern India and then travelled to China where the goddess Isis bears a resemblance to the Chinese Queen Kuan-Yin who like Isis was also Queen of the Sea. The Chinese goddess of Mercy - Kuan-Yin was worshipped by those who desire offspring and corresponds to the Lucina of the Romans. She is also called the Goddess of the Southern Sea and has been compared to the Virgin Mary. Giles G. Glossary of Reference: Kuan Yin.

[309] Horus was the heir of Set) who is the god of earth and the foster father in the life of earth. Masey. G. Ancient Egypt. Vol. II. pp. 825, 853.

[310] Thoth is the moon god and creator god who is the patron of writing and the exact science. David, A., Rosalie, The Ancient Egyptians. London: Routledge & Kegan Paul. 1973. p. 27.

[311] The dove which represents the Holy Spirit at the conception of Christ is evidently a phallic symbol. Budcock, C R., The Psycho-analysis of Culture. Oxford: Basil Blackwell. 1980, pp. 171-72; Medieval arts present the conception of Christ by the Spirit in the figure of the dove with its back in a tube which passed under the skirts of the virgin. Watts. Myth and Ritual in Christianity. Boston: Beacon Press, 1970, 179-180 rote.
The Dove is often pictured and perched in the world tree as the symbol of the Great Mother's all-giving love; the dove continued through. Roman times to be the companion of the love Goddess Venus as well as a Biblical symbol of peace. Preston. James J. (ed.) Mother Worship. University of North Carolina Press, 1982, p. 101.

[312] Another scene is one of the salient contrast of Egyptian beliefs that the gods gather around the infant (Horus) to adore him: in the New

Testament the heavenly hosts gather above the infant Jesus to praise and adore him; the three Wise or Magi and Melchior, Balthasar and Gaspar who are connected with Persian religious tales: the Magi were watching a Mount of the Lord from generation to generation until a great star appeared that would signal the coming of a savior. See Robert Wm. Smith. in 'The World Book. Encyclopedia' Magi.

[313] Revelation. VIII. 8.

[314] Ibid..XXI. XXII.

[315] Massey, Gerald. Ancient Egypt. Vol. II, 753.

[316] Massey, Gerald. Natural Genesis. Vol I, p. 127.

[317] Budge, An Egyptian Hieroglyphic Dictionary. Vol. II, p. 367.

[318] Ankh holds the position in the sepulchres of the Great Osiris. This ankh-sign proves the Christians to have belonged to the Osirian religion, the Christ of which was Horus. the Christ who was continued by the Gnostics Massey, G. Natural Genesis, p. 435.

[319] Harris, J. R. The Legacy of Egypt. p. 4.

[320] Massey. Gerald. Natural Genesis, Vol I, p. 448.

[321] Mount Calvary is mount of crucifixion- the proper name of the place where Christ was crucified. In the Book of Acts it is clearly related that Jesus was hanged from a gibbet. rather than being nailed to a cross, Book of Acts, ch. 5, 30-31.

[322] Budge, Osiris and the Egyptian Religion of Resurrection. Vol. I. pp. 79-80.

[323] St. John, Ch. I, 1,2.

[324] Massey, Gerald, Ancient Egypt. Vol. I, p. 521.

[325] Watts, Myth and Ritual in Christianity. p. 30: To God the Son (hypostasis) as the divine Wisdom. the Church has been applied the famous passage: "the Lord possessed me . . . from the beginning, ere ever the earth was."

[326] Massey, Loc. cit., p. 525.

[327] Mes-ia is the Great Prince of Great Man, and retains the connotation of rebirth and sonship. This is at par with the sense inherent in the term 'messiah' as used by Christians and Jews.

[328] Mathew, Ch. 26, 12.

[329] St. John. Ch. XI, 1-44.

[330] Lazarus; its root is 'czar' which is 'asar - the name of Osiris. 'L' is in the Semitic definite article 'the'. The terminal 'us' is the Egyptian 'as' meaning 'to call' or 'to hail'. Literally, 'Lazarus' means the Osiris called forth. See Budge, Art Egyptian Hieroglyphic Dictionary. p. 79.

[331] Massey. G. Ancient Egypt, p. 844.

[332] St. John. Ch. 11, 29, 33.

[333] Massey, G. Ancient Egypt, Vol. 11. p. 844.

[334] William R. Smith, The Religion of the Semites. London, 1889, p. 230.

[335] Budge, Osiris and Egyptian of Resurrection, p. 39:. Osiris was greatly devoted to agriculture; he was brought up in Nysa, a town of Arabia Felix, when he discovered the use of the vine and was first to drink wine and taught people how to make and preserve wine.

[336] Mass. The blood sacrifice of the Spanish 'misa' stands for 'mass'; the blood wafer, raw flesh and unleavened bread were the types of this sacrifice, and the German 'miza' is the name of the unleavened bread. R. Briffault. The Mothers, 2 vols. Vol. i, p. 175. New York 1931.

[337] Budge, Hieroglyphic Dictionary. Vol 1, p. 79.

[338] Lichteim, Miriam, Ancient Egyptian literature. Berkely. University of California Press, 1973, pp. 36-38.

[339] Massey. G, Ancient Egypt, vol. II, pp. 869-70.

[340] Ibid. p. 871.

[341] Budge, Hieroglyphic Dictionary, p. 310.

[342] St. John, ch. 1, 32.

[343] Massey, G., Natural Genesis, Vol 2, p. 417.

[344] Trede. Th., Das Heidentum in der Romischen Kerche. (the Heathendom or paganism of Romanic Church) Gotha, 1889-1981, iii, 144 sq.

[345] Budge. Osiris and the Egyptian Resurrection, vol. 11, p. 60.

[346] David, A. Rosalie, The Ancient Egyptians. London, Routledge & Kegan Paul 1972, p.175.

[347] In the liturgy of St. John Chrysostornn it is easy to find the expressions which are reminders of the religion supplanted by Christianity. The canonical Gospels can be shown to be a collection of Sayings from the Egyptian myths and eschatology. See Massey, G. Ancient Egypt, Vol. II, p. 897.

[348] The breath of life returned to Osiris and in consequence occurred his resurrection from the dead; his son Horus became a king and rules on earth: later he became the third person of the great Egyptian trinity of Osiris, Isis and Horus. See Jackson, John G.. Introduction to African Civilization. A Citadel Press Book. 1993, p. 129.

[349] Massey, G. Ancient Egypt, p. 184. For Egyptians neither Jews nor Christians would have had a god at all; either the one, or three or three-in-one; there is no beginning anywhere with the concept of a 'one god'. Ibid p. 184;
We should note that the death-resurrection theme is associated with Isis, Horus and Osiris. Jung, Carl G., observed that this Egyptian triad is an

anticipation of the Christian virgin-Jesus complex. Jung, Psychology and Religion. New Haven : Yale University Press, p. 85.

[350] Leach, Edmund, 'The Mother's Brother in Ancient Egyot', Royal Anthroplogical Institute News. August 1976, Number 15, p. 20.

[351] Ibid. p. 19.

[352] Watts, Myth and Ritual in Christianity, p. 188.

[353] Morey, C. R., Early Christian Art. Princeton University Press, 1942, p. 89.

[354] Shafer (ed.) Byron E., Religion in Ancient Egypt. N. Y. Carnell University Press. 199 1, p. 43.

[355] Cooper. W. R. The Horus Myth in its Relation to Christianity. London, 1877. p. 49.

[356] Witt. R. E., Isis in the Graeco-Roman World. N. Y. Carnell University Press. 1971. p. 280.

[357] Renan, E., Marc-Aurele et la fin du monde antique. Paris, 1884, p. 570; Lafaye. G., Histories du culte des divinites d'Alexandrie. Paris, 1884; Dill, S., Roman Society in the Last Century of Western Europe. London 1899, pp. 79-84, 85 sq.

[358] "Nimbus of rays upon an Egyptian monument of the Imperial Period" Annales du Service des Antiquites de L'Egypt. Cairo. Shortly after the birth of Christ, a god was worshipped who was portrayed with a nimbus of rays about his head, and holding his arms in a pasture characteristic of Mithra. that is, Helios-Mithra. This is evidence that Meroitic civilization (Approx. 300 B. C.-A. D. 350) belonged to the world of Hellenism and Roman imperial rule. See Morenz, Siegfried Egyptian Religion. Cornell University Press, 1992, p. 243. Mithras states that the cult answered the need of salvation which Christianity was to satisfy.

[359] Harris, The Legacy of Egypt, p. 164.

[360] The Coptic and Ethiopian rites obviously offer close parallels to Isaianism, for example. howling, dancing, liturgical fans and rattles. See Fortescue. A. K. Ceremonies of the Roman Rite. London 1941. Passim.

[361] Ibid. p. 308: A wooden clapper or rattle may be used instead of the bell; this practice existed in the Ethiopian church.

[362] Bruno thinks of the same instrument as used by women worshipers of Isis; that is, timbrel or sistrum. Fortescue. A. K. Loc. cit., p. 29.

[363] Marenz, Egyptian Religion, trans. by Ann Keep, pp. 4-5.

[364] Morenz S., Thiologische Literaturzeitung. Leipzig from 1950. Berlin-Leipzig, 75, 1950, cols. 709ff. chp. 7.

[365] Morenz, Loc. cit., p. 4.

[366] Hadas. M. The Homeric Gods -- the Spiritual Significance of Greek Religion. London, 1955. p. 164

[367] St. Paul, Philippines. 1, 21-23.

[368] Luke. XVI, 19ff.

[369] Ratschow, C. I I., Magic and Religion (Magic and Religion). Gutersloh. 1955. 130: 'Egyptian religion in fact never found the way to religion'. Thus whoever reads Ratschow's book will doubtless be convinced that once the Egyptians had reached the stage of historical consciousness, the realization of God, with all characteristics laid down by Ratschow, is considered to all intents and purposes essential for existence of true religion, i.e., outgrowing the hounds of a magical level.

[370] Book of Acts. 11, 19.

[371] Briffault. R 'The Mothers', London: George Allen and Unwin Ltd. 1952, 3 vols,

[372] Witt. R. E.. Isis is the Graeco-Roman World. Cornell University Press, 1971. p. 186.

[373] Harris. J. K.. The Legacy of Egypt. Oxford: At Clarendon Press, 1971, p. 392.

[374] Scott. W., Hermetics. Oxford, 1824, p. 34.

[375] Mullena. A. W.. 'Isis mit dem Horusskindes Munchner Jahrbuch der bildeden Kunst, XIV (1963. 7-38

[376] Harris, Op. cit. p. 170.

[377] Harris, Op. cit, p. 171.

[378] See Leipzig thesis still unpublished by R. Unger. 'Die Mutter mit dem Kinde in Agypten, 1957: for reference to the figure on the Virgin Mary, pp. 111ff. Cited by S. Morenz. Egyptian Religion. Cornell University Press, 1992. Note 129, p. 350.